Teach Yourself VISUALLY™

HTML CSS

2nd Edition

by Guy Hart-Davis

Visual
A Wiley Brand

Teach Yourself VISUALLY™ HTML and CSS

2nd Edition

Published by John Wiley & Sons, Inc., Hoboken, New Jersey. Published simultaneously in Canada and the United Kingdom.

ISBNs: 9781394160686 (paperback), 9781394160693 (ePDF), 9781394160709 (ePub)

For general information on our other products and services or for technical support, please contact our Customer Care Department within the United States at (800) 762-2974, outside the United States at (317) 572-3993 or fax (317) 572-4002.

For technical support please visit https://hub.wiley.com/community/support.

If you believe you've found a mistake in this book, please bring it to our attention by emailing our reader support team at wileysupport@wiley.com with the subject line "Possible Book Errata Submission."

Wiley also publishes its books in a variety of electronic formats. Some content that appears in print may not be available in electronic formats. For more information about Wiley products, visit our web site at www.wiley.com.

Library of Congress Control Number: 2023938158

Cover images: © Svetlana Ivanova/Getty Images

Cover design: Wiley

SKY10050664_071023

About the Author

Guy Hart-Davis is the author of more than 175 computer books, including *Teach Yourself VISUALLY iPhone 14*, *Teach Yourself VISUALLY MacBook Pro and MacBook Air*, *Teach Yourself VISUALLY Google Workspace*, *Teach Yourself VISUALLY Chromebook*, *Teach Yourself VISUALLY Word 2019*, *Teach Yourself VISUALLY iPad*, and *Teach Yourself VISUALLY Android Phones and Tablets*, 2nd Edition.

Author's Acknowledgments

My thanks go to the many people who turned my manuscript into the highly graphical book you are holding. In particular, I thank Jim Minatel for asking me to write the book; Lynn Northrup for managing the book's writing and technical review and improving the text; Kim Wimpsett for skillfully editing the text; Doug Holland for reviewing the book for technical accuracy and contributing helpful suggestions; Susan Hobbs for proofreading the book minutely; and Straive for laying out the book.

How to Use This Book

Who This Book Is For

This book is for the reader who has never used this particular technology or software application. It is also for readers who want to expand their knowledge.

The Conventions in This Book

① Steps

This book uses a step-by-step format to guide you easily through each task. **Numbered steps** are actions you must do; **bulleted steps** clarify a point, step, or optional feature; and **indented steps** give you the result.

② Notes

Notes give additional information — special conditions that may occur during an operation, a situation that you want to avoid, or a cross reference to a related area of the book.

③ Icons and Buttons

Icons and buttons show you exactly what you need to click to perform a step.

④ Tips

Tips offer additional information, including warnings and shortcuts.

⑤ Bold

Bold type shows command names, options, and text or numbers you must type.

⑥ Italics

Italic type introduces and defines a new term.

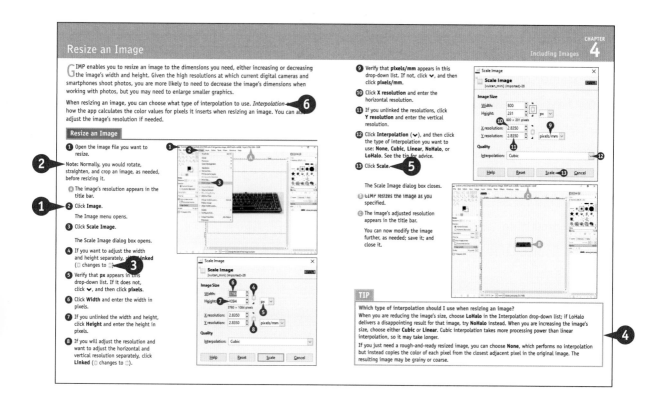

Table of Contents

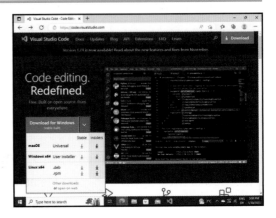

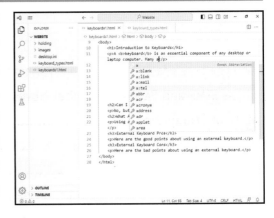

Chapter 3   Structuring a Web Page

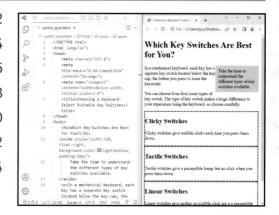

Chapter 4   Including Images

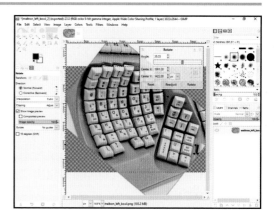

Table of Contents

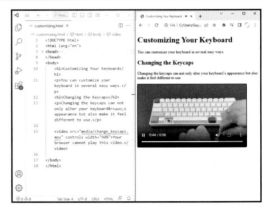

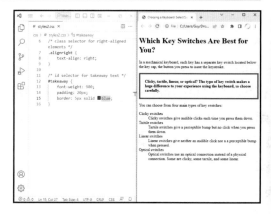

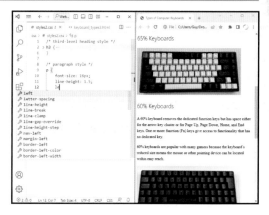

Table of Contents

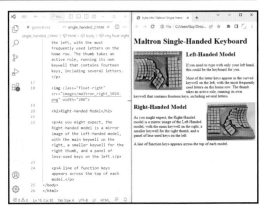

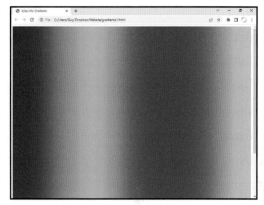

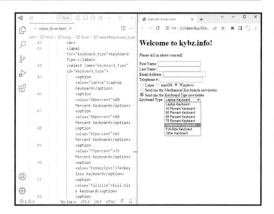

Table of Contents

Chapter 12   Taking Your Website to the Next Level

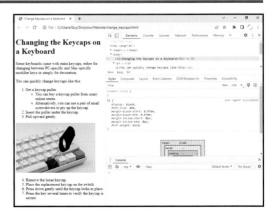

CHAPTER 1

Getting Ready to Create Websites

In this chapter, you get ready to create your website or websites. You learn the essentials of how the Web works and the technologies that power it, plan your website, and install the apps you will need to create the website. You also get a domain name and web hosting if you do not already have them.

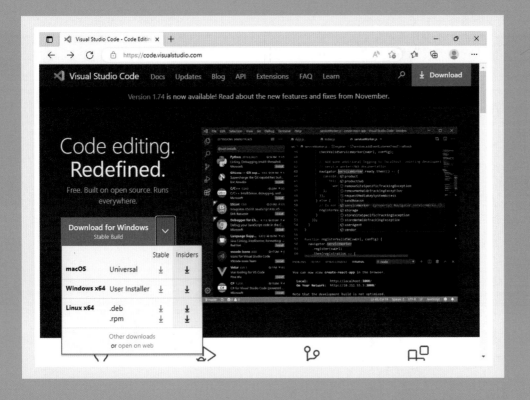

Grasp How the Web Works

The World Wide Web, nowadays usually just called the Web, consists of a vast number of websites accessible through the Internet using a web browser. Each website contains one or more web pages — usually, many more. Each web page is identified by a unique address called a *Uniform Resource Locator*, or URL. To request a web page, the user enters its URL in a web browser app, either by typing the URL or by clicking a link. The web server hosting the website transmits the requested page to the browser, which displays the contents for the user to view.

What Is a Web Page?

A *web page* is a digital document that is accessed through the Web using a web browser app. Web pages are components of websites, discussed next, which are hosted on web servers, discussed later.

Web pages can contain text, images, audio or video files, and other digital resources, such as documents that visitors can download. Web pages are arranged and formatted using Hypertext Markup Language, HTML or short, and Cascading Style Sheets, CSS. Web pages contain contents that can be static or dynamic; they may also contain interactive features, such as forms, that enable visitors to input data or interact with the content.

What Is a Website?

A *website* is a collection of web pages hosted on a web server and made accessible to web browsers via the Web. A website typically contains multiple pages that are connected to each other by hyperlinks, forming a coherent structure that lets visitors navigate quickly between the various areas of the website.

A website typically aims to serve a specific purpose. For example, a personal website might showcase the owner's interests and talents; an organization's website might explain that organization's purpose and aims and encourage visitors to join; or a company's website might present the company in the best possible light and provide ways to buy its products.

What Is a Web Server?

A *web server* is software that responds to requests from web clients, such as web browsers, and returns content if it is available and permitted. A web server stores web pages, images, videos, and other content so that it can serve them to clients.

A web server can run on almost any computer hardware, from diminutive computers such as the Raspberry Pi series up to dedicated server machines deployed in full-scale facilities called *server farms*. As of this writing, many web servers are deployed on cloud-based infrastructure, such as Amazon Web Services, AWS, or Microsoft Azure.

A web server can run on just about any computer operating system, including Windows, macOS, Linux, and the mobile operating systems iOS, iPadOS, and Android.

Web servers are a critical part of Internet infrastructure and deliver web content to users throughout the world.

What Is a Web Browser?

A *web browser* is an app used to access and display web pages and other content on the Web. Using a web browser, you can go to a web page either by typing or pasting its address or by clicking a link. Web browsers use Hypertext Transport Protocol, HTTP, or its secure variant, Hypertext Transport Protocol Secure, HTTPS, to request web pages from web servers and then display the content in the browser window.

Popular web browsers include Google Chrome, Mozilla Firefox, Microsoft Edge, and Apple's Safari. These browsers have many features to make browsing easier and faster, such as bookmarks and tabbed browsing.

How Does a Web Browser Find the Web Server Hosting a Website?

When you enter a website's URL into the browser's address box, the browser uses the Domain Name System, DNS, to discover the Internet Protocol address, or IP address, for the web server hosting the website. DNS uses a hierarchical system of servers to organize, store, and return the IP address associated with each domain name.

A *domain name* is a text-based identifier that represents a unique location on the Internet. For example, `www.wiley.com` is the domain name of the website for John Wiley & Sons, Inc., publisher of this book and many others. A domain name consists of multiple parts. The rightmost part is the top-level domain, or TLD — in this case, `.com`. Moving toward the left, the next part — in this case, `wiley` — is the second-level domain. The next part, `www`, is the subdomain.

Understanding HTML, CSS, and Responsive Web Design

Before you start creating pages for your website, you will likely find it helpful to understand the essentials of HTML and CSS, the two languages with which you will be working throughout this book. This section introduces you to HTML and CSS. It also gives you an executive overview of responsive web design, an approach intended to make websites equally accessible by different types of devices with different screen sizes and resolutions.

HTML standards and CSS standards are developed and maintained by the World Wide Web Consortium, W3C, with contributions from many companies and organizations, including the makers of the major browsers.

What Is HTML?

HTML is the abbreviation for Hypertext Markup Language, a language used to create web pages. *Hypertext* means text that includes hyperlinks to other locations on the same page or to other pages, so when you click the linked text, the browser displays the linked location or page.

HTML enables you to "mark up" text and other elements with codes that specify how the elements appear. For example, you can mark up a paragraph as a first-level heading by enclosing it in the appropriate HTML codes, which are `<h1>` at the beginning and `</h1>` at the end:

`<h1>This Is a Heading 1 Paragraph</h1>`

Similarly, you can mark up a paragraph as being regular "paragraph" text by enclosing it in `<p>` and `</p>` codes:

`<p>This is a paragraph of regular text.</p>`

The nearby illustration shows how this heading and paragraph look using the Google Chrome browser's default styles for the `h1` element (A) and the `p` element (B). You can control the formatting by defining and applying styles of your own.

HTML is currently at version 5, which is generally referred to as HTML5. But rather than being a fixed version, HTML5 is what is called a *living standard*, with development continuing and new features being released. So although HTML5 was first released in January 2008 and went through a major update in October 2014, it is still the current version as of this writing in April 2023 — and it looks likely to remain the current version for at least several years to come.

This Is a Heading 1 Paragraph

This is a paragraph of regular text. B

What Is CSS?

CSS is the abbreviation for Cascading Style Sheets, a language used to format web pages written in HTML. CSS enables you to control the visual layout and appearance of web pages, including the fonts, colors, spacing, and positioning used for text and other elements.

CSS consists of text-based instructions that specify the formatting to apply to particular elements. For example, you could create an `h1` style to format the `h1` element mentioned in the previous section.

You can implement CSS in three ways: as an external file, as styles embedded in the HTML document, or as styles applied inline within a particular HTML tag. Using an external file is usually best, because it enables you to format multiple HTML documents using a single style sheet. When you need to make changes, you can change the external CSS rather than having to change the individual documents.

How Do You Create HTML and CSS?

Both HTML and CSS consist of text-only files, so you can create them using even the most basic text editor, such as the Notepad text editor included with Windows. However, to create HTML and CSS quickly and accurately, you will usually do better to use a text editor or integrated development environment that provides features for entering and checking code. Such text editors are often referred to as code editors.

This book recommends Microsoft's Visual Studio Code, a free code editor that runs on Windows, macOS, and Linux and that includes some integrated development environment features. See the section "Install Visual Studio Code," later in this chapter, for instructions on getting Visual Studio Code.

What Is Responsive Web Design?

In the early days of the Web, most people browsing it would use a desktop computer or laptop computer with a screen capable of displaying at least a moderate amount of information — say, 1024 × 768 resolution or higher. Most web pages were designed and coded to be easily readable on such screens. If you accessed such a web page using a much smaller or lower-resolution screen, you would likely see only part of the page's width at a readable size and would need to scroll horizontally to see the rest.

Nowadays, visitors use many different types of devices, from desktop computers with huge screens all the way down to tablets and smartphones with comparatively tiny screens. This variety of browsing devices means that one-size-fits-all web design is no longer satisfactory for most websites.

To cater to different devices, website builders use an approach called *responsive web design*. Responsive web design creates pages that can adapt to different device types, different screen sizes, and changes in orientation between portrait and landscape.

In responsive web design, a web page's layout and content automatically adjust to suit the screen size of the browsing device. Responsive web design uses flexible grid systems, images, and typography to change a web page's layout. It uses media queries to apply different styles suited to the device's screen size.

Responsive web design has several clear advantages over static web design. First, a responsive web page delivers a consistent user experience across different types of devices rather than favoring some devices over others. Second, a responsive web page is easier for visitors to read, navigate, and use. Third, a responsive web page improves accessibility, enabling people with disabilities to access it satisfactorily. Fourth, a responsive web page can improve search engine optimization, or SEO for short.

Understanding Static and Dynamic Web Pages

For your website, you can create either static web pages or dynamic web pages. A *static* web page is one whose content is fixed and does not change unless the page is edited. By contrast, a *dynamic* web page is one whose content changes as needed.

Static web pages are well suited to some purposes, and you will likely want to create some static pages for your website. However, it is likely that many of your web pages will benefit from displaying up-to-date information or from responding to a visitor's needs, so you will need to create dynamic pages, too.

Comparing Static Web Pages with Dynamic Web Pages

Static web pages are straightforward to create using HTML and CSS, the technologies on which this book focuses. Some static web pages may also benefit from functionality using the JavaScript scripting language.

Static web pages are suitable for websites that do not need frequent updates or content changes, such as company websites, landing pages, and personal blogs. Static web pages are also more secure than dynamic web pages, because they do not have a database connection that hackers might be able to exploit. Static pages may have a fixed format, but they can also be responsive, using media queries — discussed in Chapter 10 — to adapt to the screen of the device requesting them.

Given a fast Internet connection, static web pages should load quickly for visitors, because the server needs only to provide the existing file. By contrast, dynamic web pages typically require the server to perform some processing before it can send the web page to the browser.

Dynamic web pages are more complex than static web pages and take more work to create. Dynamic web pages require the use of server-side scripting languages such as PHP, ASP.NET, and Java.

Dynamic web pages enable you to create more interactive and feature-rich websites that can be updated frequently. Dynamic web pages are great for websites that benefit from frequent updating, such as news sites, social media sites, or e-commerce sites. Dynamic web pages give you greater flexibility than static web pages, because you can customize them to meet the needs of your company or organization.

As an example of the difference between static web pages and dynamic web pages, consider a web page that displays the menu for a restaurant. If you create a static page, the menu remains the same unless you edit the file. That is doable, but you might need to change the menu every day, updating the dishes and the prices. Instead, you could create a dynamic web page that pulls in the details of the day's special dishes from a database, together with the current price for each menu item. This way, the menu remains current without you needing to edit it.

What Is a Responsive Website?

A *responsive* website is one built to adapt automatically to different screen sizes and resolutions so as to provide a good viewing experience on all devices. Your website is likely to attract visitors using desktop computers, laptop computers, tablets, and smartphones, so you should make sure that your website appears in a satisfactory way on different screen sizes, resolutions, and aspect ratios.

A responsive website uses a CSS feature called *media queries* to determine the screen size and resolution of visiting devices and to adjust the layout, font sizes, and image sizes to suit the devices.

Comparing Responsive Websites and Nonresponsive Websites

A responsive website is a website that checks what type of device is accessing the site and displays its contents in a suitable way for that device. For example, if you visit a responsive website using your desktop computer, which has a large screen, the website serves your computer versions of the pages formatted for the large screen.

By contrast, if you go back to the same responsive website using your mobile phone, the web server serves up versions of the pages formatted to suit the smaller screen.

A nonresponsive website simply gives each visitor the same type of page, regardless of whether it fits the visiting device or not. The nonresponsive website does not check to see what type of device is visiting.

Normally, you would want to create a responsive website rather than a nonresponsive website. Building a responsive website has several key advantages:

- The website's content is consistently usable across different devices using a single codebase. You do not need to create separate websites for different types of devices.

- Having a single codebase simplifies developing and updating the website and reduces maintenance costs.

- Having the website viewable and usable on different devices can increase brand recognition and increases the likelihood of visitors sharing your website on social media, which may drive extra traffic to the website. Such success naturally also depends on the quality of your website's content; responsiveness helps, but it is no panacea.

See Chapter 10 for information on making your website responsive.

Understanding Tools for Creating Web Pages

Many different types of tools are available for creating web pages and websites. This section summarizes the various types of tools available and then points you toward the tools this book uses to illustrate creating HTML and CSS files.

Both HTML files and CSS files contain only text, so you can create these files by using a text editor. However, you will likely prefer to use a code editor, an app that helps you enter code correctly and quickly. You will probably also need a graphics-manipulation app for creating images suitable for use on web pages.

Text Editors

A *text editor* is an app for creating and editing text. Both HTML files and CSS files consist only of text, so you can use even the most rudimentary text editor to create and edit them. For example, Windows includes the venerable but still serviceable text editor Notepad, shown editing an HTML file in the nearby illustration.

Notepad and other text editors offer no specific features for creating HTML and CSS. Some purists prefer this type of minimalist approach, but most people benefit from having help in completing and checking code.

```
🗋 form3 - Notepad                                         —   □   ×
File  Edit  Format  View  Help
<!DOCTYPE html>
<html lang="en">
<head>
        <meta charset="UTF-8">
        <meta http-equiv="X-UA-Compatible" content="IE=edge">
        <meta name="viewport" content="width=device-width, initial-
scale=1.0">
        <title>kybz.info: Visitor Form</title>
</head>
<body>
        <h1>Welcome to kybz.info!</h1>
        <p>Please tell us about yourself and your interests.</p>

        <form action="">
    <fieldset width="400">
        <legend>Your Details</legend>
            <label for="first_name">First Name:</label>
            <input type="text" name="first_name" id="first_name">
            <label for="last_name">Last Name:</label>
            <input type="text" name="last_name" id="last_name">
            <br>
        <br>
            <label for="email">Email Address:</label>
            <input type="email" name="email" id="email">
            <label for="telephone">Telephone #:</label>
            <input type="tel" name="telephone" id="telephone"
pattern="[0-9]{3}-[0-9]{3}-[0-9]{4}">
                                    Ln 16, Col 38    100%   Unix (LF)      UTF-8
```

Word Processors

A *word processor* is an app for creating documents consisting of text, graphics, and other objects, laid out and formatted as needed. While you *can* use a word processor to create HTML files and CSS files, it is not usually a good choice, as it brings a plethora of features that you must avoid using, such as formatting, layout, graphical objects, and revision marking.

Where a word processor may be helpful is for creating web pages from your existing word processing documents. For example, Microsoft Word enables you to save documents to three web formats: the Single File Web Page format; the Web Page format; or the Web Page, Filtered format. Normally, you would choose the Web Page, Filtered format, because it gives the most compact result, retaining only the information needed to display the web page and discarding information relevant only to the document in Word format. The Web Page format saves all the Word formatting information as well, effectively saving the entire Word document in HTML format. The Single File Web Page format creates a large file containing all the objects required to make up the Word document.

Code Editors

A *code editor* is a text editor enhanced with extra features for creating code — anything from HTML code to programming code. Normally, a code editor is your best choice for creating HTML files and CSS files from scratch and editing them thereafter.

The nearby illustration shows automatic code completion (A) in Microsoft's Visual Studio Code, the free code editor that this book recommends for working with HTML and CSS. See the section "Install Visual Studio Code," later in this chapter, for instructions on putting Visual Studio Code on your computer.

Other widely used code editors include Sublime Text, www.sublimetext.com, which costs $99 after a free

evaluation without a time limit but with reminders to buy; UltraEdit, www.ultraedit.com, which offers a free 30-day trial and then costs $79.95 per year for a subscription or $149.95 for a "perpetual" license; and Notepad++, www.notepad-plus-plus.org, which is free but runs only on Windows.

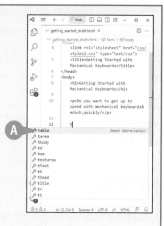

Website Builders

Website builders are simplified tools that enable you to build a website by dragging and dropping predesigned elements onto a customizable template. Website builders are good for people or small businesses that want to create a straightforward website quickly and without coding.

Widely used website builders include Weebly, www.weebly.com; Wix, www.wix.com; and Squarespace, www.squarespace.com. Most website builders offer web hosting, so you need not find a separate web host.

Many web hosts provide access to one or more website builders. So if you already have a web host, see whether it offers a website builder.

Content-Management Systems

A *content-management system*, abbreviated CMS, is a web-based app for creating, managing, and publishing web pages, blog posts, and images. CMSs provide a wide range of templates for websites, giving you many choices of design and functionality. They also provide tools for

managing and publishing content, including scheduling posts, integrating social media, and SEO optimization.

Widely used CMS platforms include WordPress, www.wordpress.com; Joomla, www.joomla.org; and Drupal, www.drupal.org.

Graphics Tools

To create image files suitable for your website, you will need a graphics-manipulation tool. This book recommends GIMP, the GNU Image Manipulation Program, which is free and runs on Windows, macOS, and Linux. It is available from www.gimp.org; see the section "Install GIMP," later in this chapter.

If you work with graphics professionally, you may already have a suitable graphics-manipulation tool, such as Adobe Photoshop or Adobe Illustrator. Such tools are more than adequate for creating image files for your website. Adobe,

www.adobe.com, offers Photoshop and Illustrator as either single-app subscriptions or as part of a subscription to its Creative Cloud suite of more than 20 apps. Special pricing is available for students, teachers, schools, and universities.

If you have Windows, you might also want to try the built-in Paint app; if it proves inadequate, try the free version of Paint.net from www.getpaint.net. If you have macOS, you might also experiment with the capabilities of the built-in Preview app and the Photos app. For Linux, go straight to GIMP.

Prepare to Create Your Website

Before creating your website, you may need to choose a web host on which to host the website, register a domain name under which the website will appear on the Web, and get and apply a Secure Sockets Layer, SSL, certificate to secure the traffic between your website and its visitors.

Which steps you will need to take depends on your situation. If you or your company already have web hosting, skip that step; likewise, skip the domain name and SSL certificate steps if you already have those. When ready, move on to the next section, "Install Visual Studio Code."

Choose a Web Host

If you or your company do not have a web host, start by identifying a suitable one and signing up for a hosting plan appropriate to your needs.

Many web hosts are available, as you can find in seconds by searching on the Web. When evaluating web hosts, you will normally want to consider the following features:

- **Price.** Use price to select a range of web hosts and plans that you can afford, and then apply the other factors in this list to grade the hosts and plans. Do not judge on price alone in isolation.

- **Uptime and reliability.** Your website needs to be up, running, and available 24/7 to serve visitors. Choose a web host that offers a high percentage of uptime — 99.9 percent uptime is considered the minimum uptime percentage for dedicated hosts — and high reliability.

- **Customer support.** Make sure the web host offers strong customer support via all the channels you will want to use — email support, phone support, and live chat support.

- **Performance and speed.** Web users easily become frustrated with sites that are slow to load, so make sure your web host delivers fast loading speeds. Look for a web host that uses a content delivery network, CDN for short. A CDN is a geographically distributed server system that delivers web content to visitors based on their geographical location rather than delivering all content from a central point that may be geographically distant from some visitors.

- **Scalability.** Make sure the web host enables you to upgrade your hosting plan as your website and its traffic grow. Such scalability helps you avoid outgrowing your web host and having to move to another host, which is a major and expensive upheaval.

- **Security, backup, and recovery.** The web host should provide SSL certificates, malware detection, and firewalls to keep websites secure. The host should also offer set-and-forget backup features to keep your website's data protected in case of corruption or hardware failure, plus easy-to-use tools for recovering your website from the latest viable backup.

Register a Domain Name

If you do not have a domain name for your website, now is the time to get one. Open a browser window to a domain registrar, search to identify an available domain name that suits you, and register it. The nearby illustration shows the registration interface at Pair Domains.

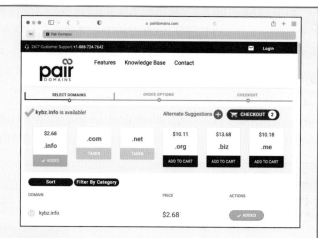

As of this writing, these are five of the leading domain registrars:

- GoDaddy, www.godaddy.com

- Domain.com, www.domain.com

- Namecheap, www.namecheap.com

- Google Domains, https://domains.google

- Porkbun, www.porkbun.com

All these domain registrars offer a wide range of top-level domains, or TLDs. These TLDs range from .com, .org, and .net — three of the original six TLDs created in the 1980s — to newer TLDs such as .art, .biz, and .shop. Prices vary wildly, with the most popular TLDs being far more expensive.

Various TLDs are restricted to bodies that meet qualification criteria. For example, the .gov TLD is reserved for U.S. government agencies and entities, the .mil TLD is reserved for the U.S. military, and the .edu TLD is reserved for accredited post-secondary education institutions in the United States. Disappointingly, the .cat TLD is restricted to the Catalan linguistic and cultural community, but the .dog TLD, the .pet TLD, and the .animal TLD are open to all.

Choose a Type of SSL Certificate

SSL is the abbreviation for Secure Sockets Layer, a networking security protocol used to establish an encrypted link between a web browser and a web server, ensuring that all data passed between them remains private and secure even if it is intercepted in transit. To make sure that browsers can access your website safely, you will need to get an SSL certificate and apply it to the website's domain.

You have two main options for getting an SSL certificate. First, you can get an SSL certificate from your domain registrar when you register the website's name. Second, many web hosts offer SSL certificates for the domains you host on their servers. A third option is to get an SSL certificate from a different domain registrar, but this circuitous approach is seldom beneficial.

Usually, you would want to find out what SSL certificates your web host offers before paying for an SSL certificate from your domain registrar.

Various types of SSL certificates are available, such as the following:

- A *trial certificate* is a time-limited certificate that enables you to test whether the certificate meets your needs; if it does, you can buy another certificate to replace it.

- A *positive certificate* enables encryption for your website's data and has a relatively small relying party warranty, $10,000.

- A *basic certificate* also enables encryption but has a much higher relying party warranty, $250,000.

- A *positive wildcard certificate* enables encryption for multiple subdomains within your domain, so you do not need to buy a separate certificate for each subdomain.

Install Visual Studio Code

As explained in the section "Understanding Tools for Creating Web Pages," earlier in this chapter, a code editor is your workaday tool for creating and editing HTML documents and CSS files. Many different code editors are available, but this book recommends Visual Studio Code, a powerful but free code editor from Microsoft. Visual Studio Code runs on Windows, macOS, and Linux, with a similar interface on each platform.

Microsoft offers two separate builds of Visual Studio Code. The Stable build is what you will normally want to install. The Insiders build contains new features and fixes and may not be entirely stable.

Install Visual Studio Code

1 In a web browser, go to code.visualstudio.com.

The Visual Studio Code website's home page appears.

2 Click **Download Stable Build**. This button shows your computer's operating system, which the page automatically detects.

A If you want to download Visual Studio Code to use on a computer with a different operating system or if you want to download an Insiders build rather than a Stable build, click the drop-down arrow (∨), and then click **Download** (⤓) for the operating system and build you want.

The download begins.

3 Open the browser's Downloads pane or window. For example, in Microsoft Edge, click **Downloads** (⤓) if the Downloads pane does not open automatically.

4 Open the downloaded file. For example, in Microsoft Edge, click **Open file** under the downloaded file's name.

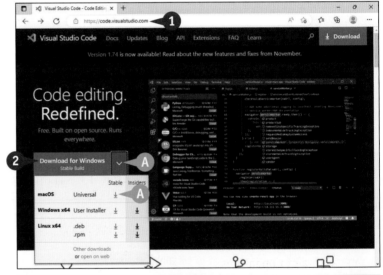

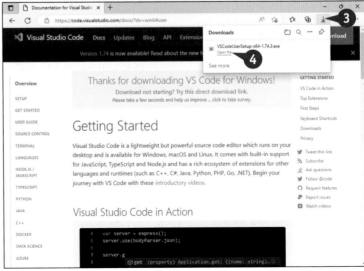

On Windows, the installer runs automatically.

5 On the License Agreement screen, click **I accept the agreement** (○ changes to ◉) if you want to proceed with the installation.

6 Click **Next**.

7 On the Select Destination Location screen, click **Next** (not shown).

8 On the Select Start Menu Folder screen, click **Next** (not shown).

The Select Additional Tasks screen appears.

9 Select **Create a desktop icon** (☑) if you want to create a desktop icon for Visual Studio Code.

10 Select the two **Add "Open with Code" action** check boxes (☑) to give yourself an easy way to open files and folders in Visual Studio Code from File Explorer. See the second tip for details.

11 Select **Register Code as an editor for supported file types** (☑) to register Visual Studio Code with Windows as an app that can open file types such as HTML and CSS.

12 Select **Add to PATH (requires shell restart)** (☑) to add Visual Studio Code to the Windows path. This tells Windows where to find Visual Studio Code.

13 Click **Next**, and then click **Next** again on the Ready to Install screen.

The installation runs.

The Completing the Visual Studio Code Setup Wizard screen appears.

14 Click **Launch Visual Studio Code** (☑ changes to ☐) if you do not want to launch Visual Studio Code.

15 Click **Finish**.

The Setup Wizard closes.

Visual Studio Code opens, and you can configure it as explained in the next section.

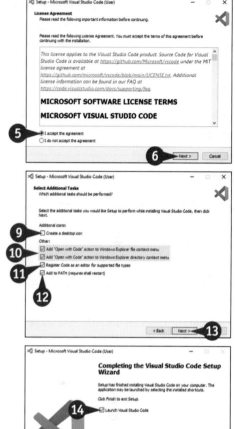

How do I install Visual Studio Code on macOS?
Double-click the downloaded Zip file to decompress it, and then drag the Visual Studio Code app file to the Applications folder.

What do the "Open with Code" options do?
Selecting **Add "Open with Code" action to Windows Explorer file context menu** (☑) enables you to open file types that Visual Studio Code supports by right-clicking them in File Explorer and then clicking **Open with Code** on the contextual menu. Similarly, selecting **Add "Open with Code" action to Windows Explorer directory context menu** (☑) enables you to open folders in Visual Studio Code.

Meet and Configure Visual Studio Code

The first time you run Visual Studio Code, the app usually displays the Get Started with Visual Studio Code screen, which walks you through some initial configuration steps. You can return to the Get Started with Visual Studio Code screen later if you like; alternatively, you can use the app's other means of accessing its settings to configure the app to work the way you prefer.

The first change you will likely want to make is to the theme, which controls the overall look of Visual Studio Code. The app includes various dark themes and various light themes; third-party themes are also available.

Launch Visual Studio Code and Meet the Welcome Screen

Start by launching Visual Studio Code in the usual way for your computer's operating system. For example, on Windows, click **Start** (⊞) to display the Start menu, and then click **Visual Studio Code** (✕).

The first time you launch Visual Studio Code, the app automatically displays the Welcome screen, which encourages you to choose several key configuration settings. For example, you can click **Get Started with VS Code** to display the Get Started with VS Code screen, shown here, which provides links to several key settings. You can also configure these settings later, as explained in the following subsections.

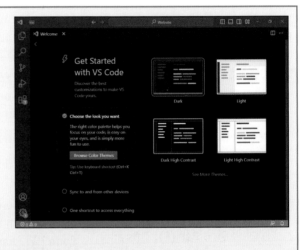

Choose the Theme for Visual Studio Code

By default, Visual Studio Code uses its Dark+ theme, which is easy on the eyes in low-light conditions but tends to get over-inked in books. To change the theme, click **Manage** (A, ⚙) in the lower-left corner to display the Manage pop-up menu, click **Themes** (B) to display the Themes continuation menu, and then click **Color Theme** (C), as shown here.

In the Color Theme picker, press ⬆ and ⬇ to move the selection highlight up and down the list of themes. Visual Studio Code displays a preview of the selected theme. When you settle on the theme you want, press Enter to apply it. From here on, this book uses the Light+ V2 (Experimental) theme for readability.

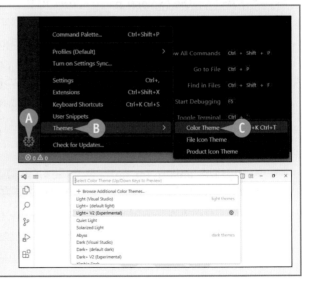

Identify the Key Elements of the Visual Studio Code Window

The Visual Studio Code window includes the following key elements:

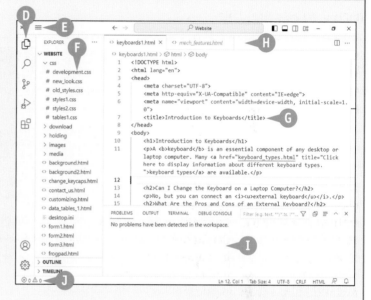

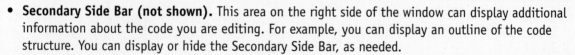

- **Activity Bar (D).** This vertical bar on the left side of the window provides quick access to several different panels that you can display one at a time in the Primary Side Bar.

- **Menu icon (E).** When the menu bar is not displayed, click **Menu** (≡) to show the menu list, and then click the menu you want to open.

- **Primary Side Bar (F).** This area, which appears on the left side of the window by default, displays any of several panels, such as the Explorer panel shown in the nearby illustration. You switch from one panel to another by clicking the buttons in the Activity Bar. You can display or hide the Primary Side Bar as needed.

- **Secondary Side Bar (not shown).** This area on the right side of the window can display additional information about the code you are editing. For example, you can display an outline of the code structure. You can display or hide the Secondary Side Bar, as needed.

- **Editor (G).** This main area is where you edit your files.

- **Tab bar (H).** The Tab Bar displays a tab for each open document. You can click the tab for the document you want to display.

- **Panel (I).** This area to the bottom of the window has tabs that enable you to display different items: Problems, Output, Terminal, and Debug Console. You can display or hide the Panel, as needed.

- **Status Bar (J).** This narrow horizontal bar across the bottom of the window shows information about the current state of the Editor, including the language mode, the line and column numbers, and the number of problems detected.

continued ▶

V isual Studio Code has a highly configurable interface that enables you to display only the elements you want to see at any particular time. The Activity Bar lets you display the panel you want to use in the Primary Side Bar, but you can hide the Primary Side Bar when you want to concentrate on your code in the Editor.

Visual Studio Code offers many preferences that you can set to control the way the app works. This section shows you how to set two of the most important preferences, Auto Save and Font Size.

Change the Layout of the Visual Studio Code Window

The four buttons in the upper-right corner of the Visual Studio Code window enable you to adjust the app's layout:

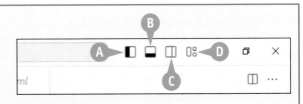

- **Toggle Primary Side Bar (A, ▯).** Click this button to toggle the display of the Primary Side Bar. Alternatively, press `Control`+`B` on Windows or Linux or `⌘`+`B` on the Mac.

- **Toggle Panel (B, ▭).** Click this button to toggle the display of the Panel. Alternatively, press `Control`+`J` on Windows or Linux or `⌘`+`J` on the Mac.

- **Toggle Secondary Side Bar (C, ▯).** Click this button to toggle the display of the Secondary Side Bar. Alternatively, press `Control`+`Alt`+`B` on Windows or Linux or `⌘`+`Option`+`B` on the Mac.

- **Customize Layout (D, ▯▯).** Click this button to display the Customize Layout pane, shown nearby.

The Customize Layout pane contains four sections: the Visibility section, the Primary Side Bar Position section, the Panel Alignment section, and the Modes section.

In the Visibility section (E), you can choose which elements to display and which to hide. Move the pointer over the element you want to display or hide. The Displayed icon (F, ◉) or the Hidden icon (G, ⊘) appears to the right of the element. Click this icon to toggle the element between displayed and hidden.

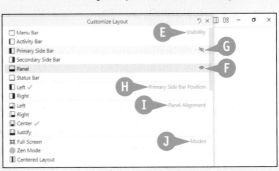

In the Primary Side Bar Position section (H), click **Left** (▯) or **Right** (▯) to control which side the Primary Side Bar appears. The default is Left.

In the Panel Alignment section (I), click **Left** (▭), **Right** (▭), **Center** (▭), or **Justify** (▭), as needed.

In the Modes section (J), click **Full Screen** (⛶) to switch to Full Screen Mode; click **Zen** (◎) to switch to Zen Mode, which strips down the Visual Studio Code interface to a minimum; or click **Centered Layout** (▯) to switch to Centered Layout Mode. You can apply any or all of these three modes.

When you finish choosing options in the Customize Layout pane, click **Close** (✕) to close the pane.

Configure Auto Save and Font Size

In Visual Studio Code, click **Menu** (K, ≡) to display the menu list, and then click **File** to open the File menu. Click **Preferences** to open the Preferences submenu, and then click **Settings**. The Settings screen appears.

The Commonly Used settings category normally appears at first. If another category appears, click **Commonly Used** (L).

Click **Files: Auto Save** (M, ✔), and then click **afterDelay**. This setting makes Visual Studio Code save you changes automatically after a short delay. This book's instructions assume that you are using the afterDelay setting. The other available settings are off; onFocusChange, which saves changes when you move the focus to a different part of Visual Studio Code; and onWindowChange, which saves changes when you move the focus to a different window.

Click **Editor: Font Size** (N) and type the font size you want to use in the editor.

Optionally, click **Editor: Font Family** (O) and type the font family you want to use in the editor. Visual Studio Code uses the first font — in the example, Consolas — if it is available, falling back to subsequent named fonts if necessary; if none of the named fonts is available, it falls back to the generic font family — in this case, monospace. If the font name includes a space, enter the font in quotes, as in 'Courier New' in the example.

As you can see, Visual Studio Code has a huge number of features. You can browse through them by clicking the categories in the left pane or search for specific settings by clicking **Search settings** (P) and typing your search term.

When you finish configuring settings, click **Close** (✕) to close the Settings screen.

Install GIMP

To create suitable image files for your website, you will need an image editor app. Many apps are available, some free and some not, so you have plenty of choices. The best cross-platform solution is GIMP, the GNU Image Manipulation Program. GIMP is a free and open-source image editor that runs on Windows, macOS, Linux, and other operating systems.

Install GIMP on Windows 10 or Windows 11

To install GIMP on Windows 10 or Windows 11, click **Start** (⊞) to display the Start menu, and then click **Microsoft Store** (▦) to open the Microsoft Store app. Click **Search apps, games, movies, and more** at the top of the app window, type **gimp** (A), and then press Enter. In the search results, click **GIMP**, and then click **Install** (B).

Once GIMP is installed, you can launch it by clicking **Start** (⊞) and then clicking **GIMP** (🐺).

Install GIMP on macOS

As of this writing, GIMP is not available on Apple's Mac App Store.

To install GIMP on macOS, open a browser window or tab to the GIMP website, www.gimp.org (C). Click the **Download** tab (D) at the top of the window to display the Downloads page, locate the current stable version for macOS, and then click either **Download GIMP via BitTorrent** (E) to download GIMP via the BitTorrent file-sharing service or **Download GIMP Directly** (F) to download GIMP from the GIMP website. The buttons offer you the choice of downloading for Apple Silicon, Apple's home-grown M-series processors, or for Intel, the processors used by older Macs; choose appropriately.

If the Do You Want to Allow Downloads on www. gimp.org? dialog box opens, click **Allow**.

When the download finishes, click **Show Downloads** (Ⓓ), and then click the GIMP disk image file in the Downloads list. A Finder window opens showing the contents of the GIMP Install package. Drag the GIMP icon (G) to the Applications folder shortcut.

After installation finishes, click **View** to open the View menu, and then click **Show Toolbar** to display the toolbar and the sidebar. Go to the Locations section of the sidebar and click **Eject** (⏏) to eject the GIMP disk image file. You can then delete the file from the Downloads folder if you do not want to keep it.

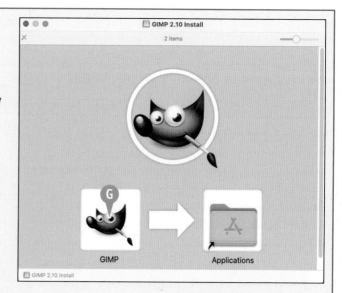

With the app installed, you can run GIMP by clicking **Launchpad** (⠿) to display the Launchpad screen and then clicking **GIMP** (🐾).

Install GIMP on Linux

You have several options for installing GIMP on Linux, including installing it via your distribution's software-management app.

If your computer is running Ubuntu, the easiest approach is to open a terminal window and update the package list by issuing the following command:

```
sudo apt-get update
```

Once the package list is up to date, install GIMP and all necessary dependencies by issuing the following command:

```
sudo apt-get install gimp
```

When installation finishes, you can launch GIMP either by opening the application menu and clicking **GIMP** (🐾) or by issuing the gimp command in a terminal window:

```
gimp
```

Install the Major Browsers

Most operating systems come with a single browser app — for example, Windows comes with the Microsoft Edge browser, macOS includes Apple's Safari browser, and ChromeOS features Google's Chrome browser. But while each of these browsers works fine for web browsing, you will likely want to install a full deck of major browsers so that you can test your web pages with all of them and work through any compatibility problems that arise.

As of this writing, the four leading browsers are Chrome, Mozilla Firefox, Safari, and Microsoft Edge.

Which Browsers Are Most Widely Used?

A wide range of web browsers are available, but as of this writing in spring 2023, Google's Chrome dominates the market. Breakdowns of web browser usage (see the nearby pie chart) tend to be illustrative rather than exact, but most figures agree that Chrome has between two-thirds and three-quarters of traffic. Next comes Apple's Safari with approximately one-fifth of traffic, mostly thanks to its inclusion on every iPhone, every iPad, and every Mac.

After Safari is Microsoft Edge, included with Windows 10 and Windows 11, with a little less than 5 percent of traffic. Mozilla Firefox has around 3 percent; Samsung Internet has around 2.5 percent, as does Opera. Other browsers, such as Vivaldi and the now-terminated Internet Explorer, make up the remaining 3 percent of traffic.

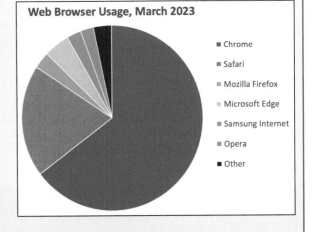

Web Browser Usage, March 2023

- Chrome
- Safari
- Mozilla Firefox
- Microsoft Edge
- Samsung Internet
- Opera
- Other

How Do Chrome, Safari, Mozilla Firefox, and Microsoft Edge Compare to Each Other?

All four browsers support a wide range of features that let users browse the web efficiently and enjoy web content. Each browser supports HTML5, CSS3, and JavaScript. Each offers the following seven key features:

- **Tabbed browsing.** You can open multiple web pages on separate tabs within a single window.

- **Bookmarks.** You can mark web pages so that you can quickly visit them again.

- **History.** The browser automatically keeps a list of pages you visit, enabling you to return to them easily.

- **Private or "Incognito" browsing.** This mode lets you turn off history when you do not want the browser to track it.

- **Autofill.** The browser stores data you enter in form fields — for example, address data — so that it can fill in those fields automatically in future forms.

- **Password storage.** The browser enables you to store passwords securely so that you can enter them in web pages without typing.

- **Extensions.** You can extend the browser's functionality by installing extensions, third-party add-ons.

  Beyond these features, which are arguably essential for browsing the web nowadays, each browser offers features of its own. For example:

- Chrome is tightly integrated with Google services such as Gmail and Google Drive, and it offers Chrome apps, web apps that run by using the Chrome browser.

- Microsoft Edge offers tight integration with Office 365 and other Microsoft services.

- Mozilla Firefox offers a highly customizable interface and strong privacy features.

- Safari integrates tightly with Apple device features such as Continuity, which lets you start browsing on one device and continue on another, and Apple's Keychain password manager. Safari also offers a Reader Mode to reduce ads and interruptions on web pages.

Which Browsers Should You Install?

Unless you have strong reasons to do otherwise, you should probably install all four of the leading browsers — Chrome, Safari, Mozilla Firefox, and Microsoft Edge — on your development computer. Having all four browsers available will enable you to make sure that your web pages display correctly on the vast majority of computers.

Install the Browsers and Choosing Configuration Options

You can download the browsers from the following sites:

- Chrome: `www.google.com/chrome`

- Safari: `https://support.apple.com/downloads/safari`

- Firefox: `www.mozilla.org/en-US`

- Edge: `www.microsoft.com/edge/download`

Installing the browsers is straightforward enough, but you will typically need to make the following three choices:

- **Whether to make the new browser the default browser for your computer.** For example, in the Make Firefox Your Go-To Browser dialog box, you would click **Skip this step** to turn down the offer to make Firefox the default browser.

- **Whether to import bookmarks from your current browser.** Importing bookmarks is handy when you are switching permanently or semipermanently from one browser to another, but when installing multiple browsers for use in parallel, you may want to keep separate bookmarks.

- **Whether to sync your browser data across your devices.** Syncing bookmarks, passwords, and settings data across all the devices on which you use a particular browser can be a great boon for consumers. But when you are installing the browsers on your computer for testing, you may prefer to keep the data unsynced.

Create a Folder Structure for Your Website

Part of the planning for your website should be choosing and implementing a folder structure for the website. Normally, you would set up this folder structure both on your development computer — or development server — and on the live web server so that you can copy files from your development environment to your live environment without having to change the relative paths to the folders.

There is no official "approved" folder structure for websites, so you can arrange folders as best suits you and your colleagues. This section suggests approaches to get you started.

List the File Types Your Website Will Use

Start by making a list of the different types of files your website will use. The following types are widely used, but your website may well have others:

- HTML documents and CSS files
- Images
- Fonts
- Audio files and video files
- JavaScript script files
- Documentation files about the website
- Reusable code and templates

```
∨   Website
        css
        docs
        download
        fonts
        images
        includes
        js
        vendor
```

Identify the Directories Your Website Will Need

Next, decide where you will store these items. Table 1-1 and the nearby illustration show a fairly typical list of directories, but you will likely want to create your own custom version.

Table 1-1:   Typical Directories in a Website's Structure

Folder	Explanation
/	The root directory, the top level of the website. You will put the main `index.html` file, your web pages, and other essential files, such as a `robots.txt` file, in this directory. The other directories are children of the root directory.
/css	The directory for storing the CSS files you use to style your web pages. If you have many CSS files, consider creating subdirectories to organize them more tightly.
/docs	The directory for storing documentation files.
/download	The directory for storing files your website makes available for download.
/fonts	The directory for storing font files the website uses.
/images	The directory for storing image files.
/includes	The directory for storing templates or reusable code.
/js	The directory for storing JavaScript script files.
/vendor	The directory for storing third-party frameworks or libraries your website uses. See Chapter 12.

Adapt the List to Suit Your Needs

Looking at this list, you might ask where the audio files and video files go in the directory structure. As the directory structure makes no provision for these file types, you will need to decide on a suitable place.

You could simply create an `/audio` directory for audio files and a `/videos` directory for video files. But to keep the directory structure compact, you might prefer to create a directory such as `/media` or `/assets` to contain subdirectories for audio, video, and perhaps images. For example:

```
/media
        /audio
        /images
        /videos
```

Or:

```
/assets
        /audio
        /images
        /videos
```

When deciding on a location for your video files, keep in mind that video's hefty file sizes will increase the load on your web server. If your website serves many videos to visitors, consider offloading the burden by storing the video files on a CDN.

Create the Directory Structure

Once you have made the design decisions, you can create the directory structure using standard commands for your computer's operating system. For example:

- **Windows.** Open a File Explorer window showing the folder in which you will place the root directory. Right-click open space in the folder, click or highlight **New** on the contextual menu, and then click **Folder** on the continuation menu. Type the directory name and press `Enter` to apply the name. Press `Enter` again to open the directory. You can then create subdirectories inside it.

- **macOS.** Open a Finder window to the folder in which you will place the root directory. Press `Control`+click or right-click to display the contextual menu, and then click **New Folder**. Type the directory name and press `Return` to apply it. Double-click the directory to open it so that you can create subdirectories inside it.

- **Linux.** Open a Terminal window, use the `cd` command to navigate to the appropriate directory, and then use the `mkdir` command to create the root directory. Use the `chdir` command to change directory to the root directory, and then create subdirectories inside it.

CHAPTER 2

Creating Your First Web Pages

In this chapter, you briefly study the anatomy of a web page before launching Visual Studio Code, configuring it, and using it to create your first web pages. You learn to add headings, text, and comments to web pages; view a page's source code and validate HTML; and create hyperlinks between web pages.

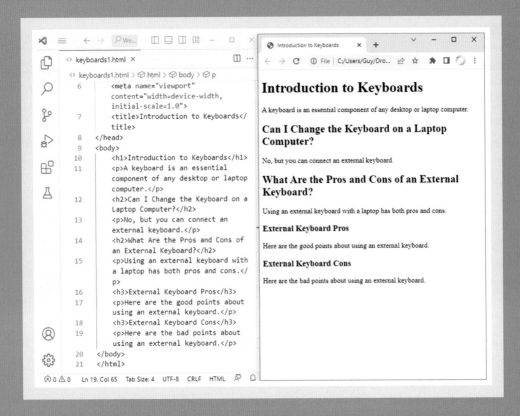

Study the Anatomy of a Web Page

I n HTML, each web page has the same basic structure, no matter how simple or complex the page is.

An HTML web page starts with a DOCTYPE definition that specifies the document's encoding type. Next comes a statement of the language used, such as lang="en" to indicate English. After that, the web page consists of a head element and a body element. The head element contains information about the document, such as the page title and the base URL for links. The body element holds the remaining content of the web page, such as headings, text, and linked media files.

Identify the Four Key Elements of a Web Page

Each valid HTML page must contain four key elements, as illustrated in the nearby code:

- **DOCTYPE declaration.** This declaration tells the browser the document type of the HTML page. The browser needs this information to interpret the document's codes correctly.

- **<html> tags.** The whole of the web page appears between the opening <html> tag and the closing </html> tag. These tags show you the standard format for two-part tags: The closing tag consists of a forward slash, /, and the same text as the opening tag. For example, you use the <p> opening tag to tell HTML to start a paragraph and the </p> closing tag to end the paragraph.

- **head element.** This element contains the metadata for the document, including the character set used for encoding and the title, which most web browsers display in the title bar.

- **body element.** This element contains the content of the web page, such as the text of headings, paragraphs, and lists, and links to external content, such as images.

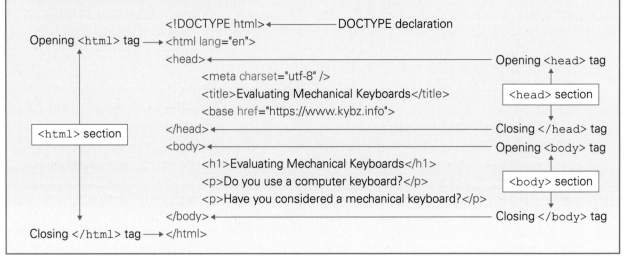

```
                            <!DOCTYPE html>  ———————————  DOCTYPE declaration
Opening <html> tag  ———→   <html lang="en">
                            <head>  ←———————————————————————  Opening <head> tag
                               <meta charset="utf-8" />
                               <title>Evaluating Mechanical Keyboards</title>      <head> section
                               <base href="https://www.kybz.info">
                            </head>  ←——————————————————————  Closing </head> tag
                            <body>  ←———————————————————————  Opening <body> tag
                               <h1>Evaluating Mechanical Keyboards</h1>
                               <p>Do you use a computer keyboard?</p>             <body> section
                               <p>Have you considered a mechanical keyboard?</p>
                            </body>  ←——————————————————————  Closing </body> tag
Closing </html> tag  ———→   </html>
```

Understanding the DOCTYPE Declaration

Each HTML page begins with a declaration of the document type using the DOCTYPE keyword. The DOCTYPE declaration for an HTML5 document is straightforward and short:

```
<!DOCTYPE html>
```

Given that HTML5 has been in use for 15 years now, this is the DOCTYPE declaration you are likely to see most often. But if you work with legacy web pages, you are likely to see other DOCTYPE declarations, so it is helpful to be able to recognize them.

HTML version 4 and Extensible Hypertext Markup Language, XHTML, use more complex DOCTYPE declarations that include the details of the document type definition, DTD, the page uses. For example, the HTML 4 Strict standard uses the following DOCTYPE declaration:

```
<!DOCTYPE HTML PUBLIC "-//W3C//DTD HTML 4.01//EN"
"http://www.w3.org/TR/html4/strict.dtd">
```

Similarly, the XHTML 1.1 standard uses the following DOCTYPE declaration:

```
<!DOCTYPE html PUBLIC "-//W3C//DTD XHTML 1.1//EN"
"http://www.w3.org/TR/xhtml11/DTD/xhtml11.dtd">
```

The opening <html> tag for an XHTML doctype includes the xmlns attribute, which provides details of the XHTML namespace the document uses:

```
<html xmlns="http://www.w3.org/1999/xhtml">
```

A *namespace* is a particular class of elements in which each element has a unique name. For example, XHTML uses a different namespace than HTML 4, but some names in the separate namespaces are the same.

Understanding HTML Validity and Validation

An HTML document must be valid in order to display properly and consistently in all browsers. *Valid* means the document contains all the essential elements in an acceptable order and that all the formatting tags are correct, complete, and in the right places.

You can perform an informal validity check by opening an HTML document in several browsers and seeing if it displays correctly. But because browsers encounter many pages that contain errors, the browsers are built to tolerate errors and display pages as well as they can, so opening an HTML document in a browser is not a strict test of the HTML's validity. For a strict check, you can use validity checkers built into many web development tools or online checkers such as the W3C Markup Validation Service checker at https://validator.w3.org.

Tell Visual Studio Code Which Folder to Use

Before creating HTML files, tell Visual Studio Code which folder to store them in. This can be either an existing folder or a folder you create now from within Visual Studio Code. After identifying the folder, you instruct Visual Studio Code whether to trust the folder's parent folder — the folder that contains the folder.

Visual Studio Code's primary sidebar includes an Explorer pane that enables you to create, manage, and open folders and files. Working in the Explorer pane in Visual Studio Code is easier and quicker than working in a File Explorer window.

Create a Folder for Your Website

1 In Visual Studio Code on Windows, click **Menu** (☰), and then click **File**.

On macOS and Linux, click **File**.

The File menu opens.

2 Click **Open Folder**.

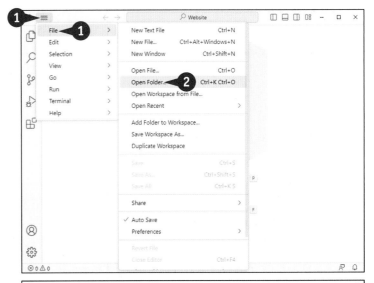

The Open Folder dialog box appears.

3 Navigate to the folder in which you want to store the folder containing your website.

Note: If you want to use an existing folder, navigate to that folder and select it.
Go to step **6**.

4 Click **New Folder**.

Visual Studio Code creates a new folder in the folder, gives it the default name *New folder*, and selects the name.

5 Type the name for the folder, and then press Enter to apply it.

6 Click **Select Folder**.

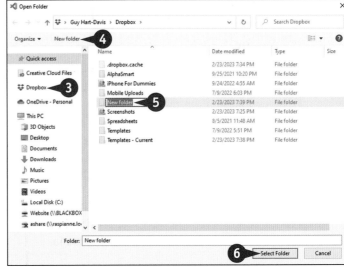

30

The Open Folder dialog box closes.

The Do You Trust the Authors of the Files in This Folder? dialog box opens.

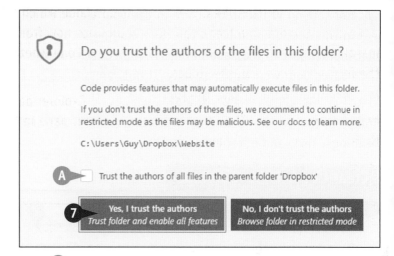

Ⓐ If you want to trust the folder that contains this folder, select **Trust the authors of all files in the parent folder** (☑).

❼ Click **Yes, I trust the authors**.

Note: If you do not trust the authors of the files, click **No, I don't trust the authors**.

The Do You Trust the Authors of the Files in This Folder? dialog box closes.

Ⓑ Visual Studio Code opens the primary sidebar with the Explorer pane displayed.

Ⓒ The folder you selected appears.

Ⓓ You can click **Collapse** (⌄) to collapse a section of the Explorer pane.

Ⓔ You can click **Expand** (>) to expand a section of the Explorer pane.

Note: Move the pointer over the folder section of the Explorer bar to display the New File button and New Folder button.

Ⓕ You can click **New File** (🗋) to create a new file in the folder.

Ⓖ You can click **New Folder** (🗀) to create a new folder in the folder.

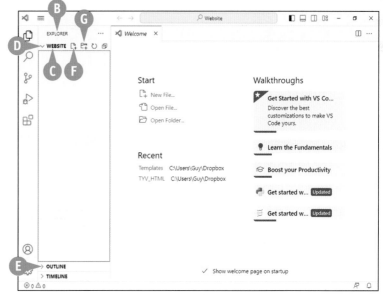

TIP

How do I stop the folder name from appearing in the Search box in the Visual Studio Code title bar?
After you open a folder, its name appears in the Search box in the title bar of the Visual Studio Code app. To remove the name, close the folder by clicking **File** — on Windows, click **Menu** (≡) and then click **File** — and then clicking **Close Folder** on the menu.

Create Your First Web Page

After setting Visual Studio Code to use your website's folder, you can create your first web page. In this section, you begin the page, adding a title to the page header and inserting some placeholder text in the page's body. If you configured the AutoSave feature in Settings, Visual Studio Code saves your work automatically. If not, press `Control`+`S` on Windows or Linux or `⌘`+`S` on the Mac when you want to save the file.

Complete this section before the following several sections, in which you view the page and then add headings, text, and other elements.

Create Your First Web Page

1 In Visual Studio Code, click **Explorer** (⬚).

The primary sidebar opens, showing the Explorer pane.

Note: If Visual Studio Code does not automatically expand the folder section of the Explorer pane, click **Expand** (>) to expand it.

2 Click **New File** (🗋).

An edit box appears.

3 Type the filename, including the `.html` file extension, and then press `Enter`.

The example uses the filename `keyboards1.html`.

Visual Studio Code creates the file and displays it in the main pane.

The insertion point appears in the first line of the file, which is numbered 1.

4 Type `!`.

The AutoComplete list opens, showing available AutoComplete entries that start with the character !.

5 Click the first item, which is identified as an Emmet abbreviation.

Note: You can also expand the Emmet abbreviation by pressing `Tab` with the abbreviation highlighted.

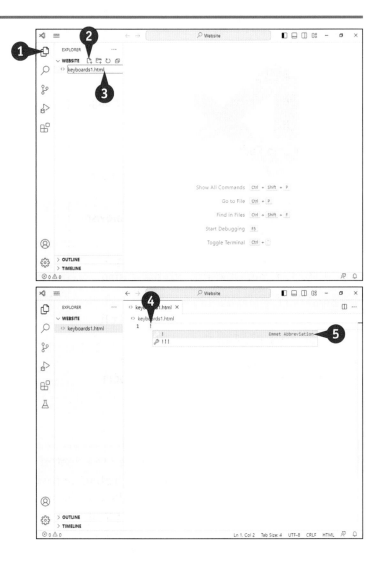

Visual Studio Code expands the abbreviation, entering the skeleton code of a web page in place of the exclamation point.

Ⓐ The DOCTYPE declaration specifies html, making this an HTML5 document.

Ⓑ The opening <html> tag specifies lang="en", setting the language to English.

Ⓒ The opening <head> tag and closing </head> tag delimit the head section, which contains meta information and the page's title.

Ⓓ The opening <body> tag and closing </body> tag delimit the body section, which is empty.

Ⓔ The closing </html> tag ends the web page.

❻ Double-click **Document** on line 7.

Visual Studio Code selects the word.

❼ Type the title you want to give the web page.

Note: The web page's title appears in the browser's title bar. If the web page is on a browser tab, the title appears on the tab.

❽ Click in line 10 and type the opening <p> tag, text of your choosing, and the closing </p> tag — for example:

<p>Do you use a keyboard with your computer?</p>

Ⓕ You can click **Explorer** (🗗) to close the primary sidebar, giving yourself more room to work on the web page.

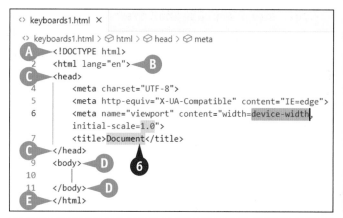

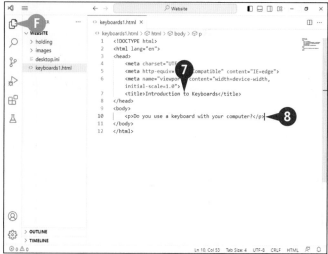

TIP

What is the tiny pane of illegible text on the right of the Visual Studio Code window?
This pane contains the Minimap, a visual feature for navigating quickly through your code. The Minimap provides essentially a thumbnail view of the code in the main pane. Move the pointer over the Minimap to display a gray highlight showing you one screen's worth of the code, scroll up and down to the code you want to view, and then click the display that screen's worth of code in the main pane. If you do not find the Minimap useful, click **View** on the menu bar and then click **Minimap** to turn the Minimap off.

Open the Web Page in a Browser

Visual Studio Code does not have a built-in browser for viewing web pages, but you can quickly open a web page in a browser to view the page. Displaying the page makes it easy for you to see the effects of the changes you make in the HTML code. You can use whichever browser you prefer; this section uses Google Chrome for the example.

This section assumes that you have created a web page in Visual Studio Code, as explained in the previous section, "Create Your First Web Page."

Open the Web Page in a Browser

① In Visual Studio Code, with your web page open, right-click the web page's tab.

The contextual menu opens.

② Click **Reveal in File Explorer**.

Note: If the primary sidebar is displayed and showing the Explorer pane, you can also right-click the web page file and then click **Reveal in File Explorer** on the contextual menu.

A File Explorer window opens to the web page's folder.

Note: If you want to open the web page in your default web browser, simply double-click the file.

③ Right-click the web page file, click or highlight **Open with** on the contextual menu, and then click the appropriate browser — for example, **Google Chrome**.

Note: If your computer has a large monitor, splitting the screen between your Visual Studio Code window and a browser window can help you work efficiently. If you have two monitors, you may want to place Visual Studio Code on one monitor and the browser on the other.

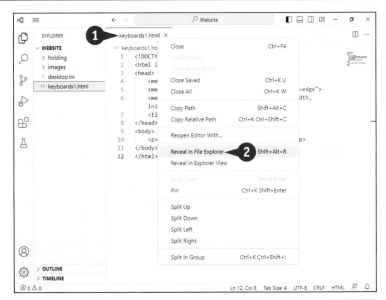

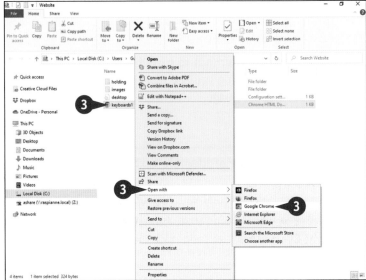

A browser window or tab opens showing the web page.

You can now arrange the browser window and the Visual Studio Code window so that you can see both. The following steps show one easy way to do this using the Windows Snap feature.

④ Click the title bar of the browser window and drag left or right until the pointer hits the edge of the window.

Ⓐ Windows Snap resizes and positions the window to fit that half of the screen.

Ⓑ Windows Snap displays a thumbnail for each other open window you can place in the other half of the screen.

⑤ Click the Visual Studio Code window.

Ⓒ Windows Snap positions that window in the other half of the screen.

You can now make changes in the Visual Studio Code window.

Ⓓ Click **Refresh** (such as C in Google Chrome) to refresh the web page to make it show your latest changes.

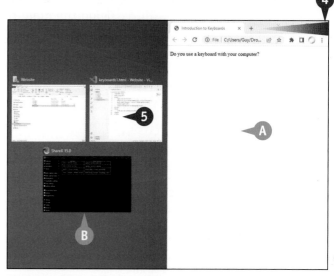

TIP

Which is the best browser to use for viewing pages as I work?
Any of the major browsers — Google Chrome, Microsoft Edge, Mozilla Firefox, Apple's Safari — will work fine. To ensure that your pages work consistently, rotate through a variety of browsers to view the pages. The easiest way to switch among browsers is to right-click the file in a File Explorer window, click or highlight **Open With**, and then click the browser you want to use this time.

Add Headings and Text

Most web pages benefit from having a structure that uses different heading levels. HTML provides six levels of headings, with `h1` being the highest level of heading and `h6` being the lowest level. Two or three levels of headings are often enough.

In this section, you add three levels of headings to your web page, with paragraphs of regular text separating the headings. The screens in this section show the Visual Studio Code window and the Google Chrome browser window tiled vertically using Windows Snap. You can either follow this arrangement or arrange the windows however best suits you.

Add Headings and Text

1 In Visual Studio Code, with your web page open, select the whole of line 10, the one paragraph in the `body` element.

2 Type **h1** to start creating an opening `<h1>` tag using an Emmet abbreviation:

`h1`

The pop-up menu opens, with the h1 Emmet abbreviation item selected by default.

3 Click **h1**, or simply press `Tab`.

Visual Studio Code expands the abbreviation to the full tag pair, the opening `<h1>` tag and the `</h1>` tag, placing the insertion point between the two.

4 Type the text of the top-level heading.

5 Click after the closing `</h1>` tag, and then press `Enter` to create a new line.

6 Type **p** to start creating an opening `<p>` tag using an Emmet abbreviation.

The pop-up menu opens, with the p Emmet abbreviation item selected by default.

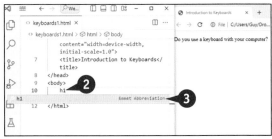

7 Click **p** or press `Tab`.

Visual Studio Code expands the abbreviation to the full tag pair.

8 Type a paragraph of body text.

9 Click **Refresh** (⟳).

Google Chrome displays the changes made to the web page.

A The first-level heading stands out clearly.

10 Click in the beginning of line 12.

11 Type some text that includes second-level headings, between `<h2>` and `</h2>` tags, and body paragraphs, between `<p>` and `</p>` tags — for example:

```
<h2>Can I Change the Keyboard
on a Laptop Computer?</h2>
<p>No, but you can connect an
external keyboard.</p>
<h2>What Are the Pros and Cons
of an External Keyboard?</h2>
<p>Using an external keyboard
with a laptop has both pros and
cons.</p>
```

12 Click **Refresh** (⟳) to refresh the browser.

13 Continue the page by typing some text that includes third-level headings, between `<h3>` and `</h3>` tags, and further body paragraphs — for example:

```
<h3>External Keyboard Pros</h3>
<p>Here are the good points
about using an external
keyboard.</p>
<h3>External Keyboard Cons</h3>
<p>Here are the bad points about
using an external keyboard.</p>
```

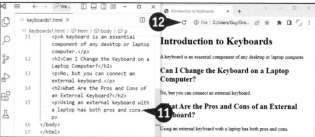

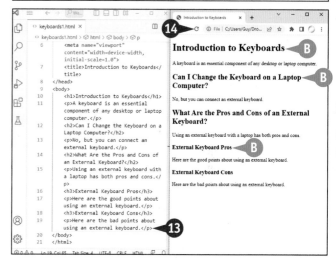

14 Click **Refresh** (⟳) to refresh the browser.

B You can clearly see the three levels of headings.

TIP

How do I select text in Visual Studio Code?

Visual Studio Code enables you to use most standard means of selection. For example, you can hold down ⇧Shift and press ⬅, ➡, ⬆, or ⬇ to select text with the keyboard. You can click and drag with the pointer; or you can click at the beginning of what you want to select and then press ⇧Shift+click at the end. You can double-click to select a word or triple-click to select a whole paragraph.

Nest One Element Within Another Element

As you have seen already in this book, HTML enables you to place an element within another element. For example, apart from the DOCTYPE declaration at the beginning, the html element contains the whole of a web page: Within the html element are the head element and the body element, each of which contains other elements.

Placing one element inside another element is called *nesting* an element. When you nest an element inside another element, it is important that you close the nested element before closing the element in which it is nested.

Grasp How Nesting Works

To nest one element within another element, first enter the opening tag and closing tag for the containing element. For example, the body element of a web page uses the opening `<body>` tag and the closing `</body>` tag:

```
<body></body>
```

You can then nest an element between the opening and closing tags. For example, you might nest a paragraph, as shown here.

```
<body><p>Here is a paragraph.</p>
</body>
```

If you are going to nest many elements, you will probably want to place the outer element's tags on separate lines so that you can easily see where the element starts and ends. Indenting the nested elements helps distinguish them visually without changing the semantic meaning of the HTML, because browsers ignore the indentation. For example:

```
<body>
    <h1>Here Is a First-Level Heading</h1>
    <p>Here is a paragraph.</p>
</body>
```

The key to nesting elements is that you must close a nested element before you close the element that contains it. If you close the containing element before the nested element, errors occur, and the HTML is not valid. The following example closes the body element before closing the paragraph:

```
<body>
    <h1>Here Is a First-Level Heading</h1>
    <p>Here is a paragraph.
</body>
</p>
```

This example causes an error such as *Saw an end tag after* body *had been closed*.

Add Comments

HTML enables you to include comments. A *comment* is text that appears in the HTML source code but that a browser does not display as part of the web page. Adding comments can be helpful, both as reminders while creating a web page and when you want to document it for others or yourself.

You can also use comments to hide existing elements of a web page, preventing them from being displayed — for example, if something isn't working. This is typically a temporary fix. You would normally remove comments before making a web page available online.

Add Comments

1. Open your web page in Visual Studio Code and in your browser.

2. Click where you want to insert the comment.

3. Type **<!--** to begin a comment tag.

   `<!--`

A. Visual Studio Code automatically inserts `-->` to close the tag:

   `<!-- -->`

4. Type the comment text — for example:

   `<!-- Here is a comment. -->`

B. The comment appears in a different color in Visual Studio Code.

5. Click **Refresh** (↻).

   The comment does not appear in the browser.

6. Click before the first element you want to hide.

7. Type **<!--** to begin a comment tag.

8. Click at the end of the last element you want to hide.

9. Type **-->** to close the comment tag.

Note: A comment can span multiple lines.

10. Click **Refresh** (↻).

C. The elements enclosed by the comment no longer appear.

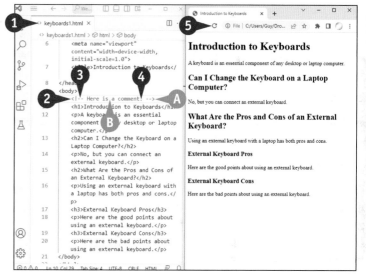

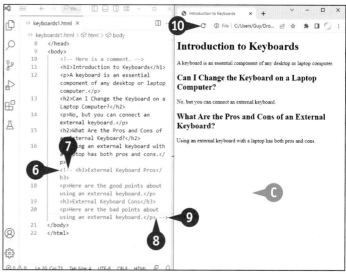

Apply Direct Formatting

HTML gives you various ways to format the text and objects in your web pages. Direct formatting is the most straightforward way of changing the appearance of text or an object. For example, you can apply attributes such as boldface, italic, or underline to specific parts of your text by putting the appropriate tags around them.

Direct formatting is easy and effective, but it is not efficient. Formatting via CSS is much more efficient and allows easier updating. However, you should recognize and understand direct formatting, because you will likely encounter it on many web pages.

Apply Direct Formatting

1 Open your web page in Visual Studio Code and in your browser.

2 Click before a word to which you want to apply boldface.

3 Type the opening `<b>` tag:

`<b>`

4 Click after the word and type the closing `</b>` tag, so the tags enclose the word like this:

`<b>keyboard</b>`

5 Click **Refresh** (↻).

Ⓐ The word appears in boldface in the browser.

6 Click before some text to which you want to apply italic and underline.

7 Type the opening `<i>` tag and the opening `<u>` tag:

`<i><u>`

8 Click after the text and type the closing `</u>` tag and the closing `</i>` tag.

Note: Close the nested `<u>` tag before closing the `<i>` tag that contains it.

9 Click **Refresh** (↻).

Ⓑ The text appears in underlined italics in the browser.

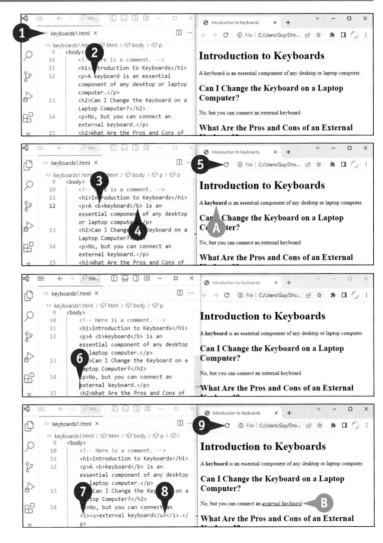

40

View a Page's Source Code

Normally, when you open a web page in a browser, the app displays the results of the HTML — for example, a bright, graphical web page. But sometimes you may want to view a page's source code instead. Viewing the source code can help you understand how a particular element is implemented in HTML or let you identify a problem that prevents a page from rendering correctly.

The techniques for viewing a page's source code vary from browser to browser. This section shows you how to view source code in Google Chrome, Firefox, Microsoft Edge, and Safari.

Display a Page's Source Code in a Browser

In Google Chrome, Mozilla Firefox, and Microsoft Edge, you can display a page's source code by right-clicking the page and then clicking **View page source** on the contextual menu.

On macOS, Safari makes life more difficult. First, you must add the Develop menu to the menu bar. To do so, click **Safari** and **Preferences** to open the Safari Preferences window; click **Advanced** to display the Advanced tab; and then select **Show Develop menu in menu bar** (☑). You can then click **Develop** on the menu bar and click **Show Page Source**; alternatively, Control-click or right-click the page and click **Show Page Source** on the contextual menu.

The source code for a complex page may seem overwhelming, but if you look at the beginning, you can recognize standard elements such as the DOCTYPE declaration (A), the opening `<html>` tag (B), the opening `<head>` tag (C), assorted `<meta>` tags (D), the opening `<title>` tag (E), and the closing `</title>` tag (F).

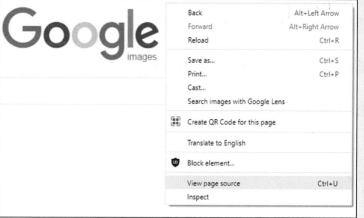

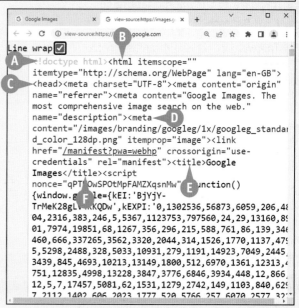

Validate a Web Page

To make sure HTML is correct, you can validate it. Various methods of validating HTML are available. For example, some code editors, integrated development environments, and web-authoring tools have built-in validation features.

This section shows you how to validate HTML using the W3C Markup Validation Service, an online resource provided by the World Wide Web Consortium, W3C, the main international standards organization for the World Wide Web. You can validate by uploading a file, as shown here; by providing the URI of the web page to check; or by simply pasting or typing code into a box.

Validate a Web Page

1. Open a browser window to `https:// validator.w3.org`.

2. Click **Validate by File Upload** to follow this example.

Ⓐ You can click **Validate by URI** to validate a web page that is already online.

Ⓑ You can click **Validate by Direct Input** to validate code you paste — or type — into a box.

3. Click **Choose File**.

The Open dialog box appears.

4. Navigate to the appropriate folder.

5. Click the file.

6. Click **Open**.

7. Click **Expand** (▶ changes to ▼) next to More Options.

The More Options section expands.

Ⓒ The filename appears in the File box.

Ⓓ You can click **Character Encoding** (✔) and specify a particular character encoding instead of "(detect automatically)."

Ⓔ You can click **Document Type** (✔) and specify a particular document type instead of "(detect automatically)."

Ⓕ You can click **Group Error Messages by Type** (◯ changes to ◉) to group error messages. The List Messages Sequentially setting is the default.

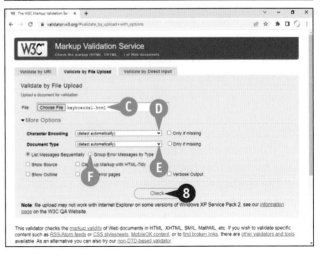

8. Click **Check**.

The Markup Validation Service checks the HTML in the file.

G The error list identifies errors found in the HTML.

H The file contains the tag `<bdy>`, a misspelling of the `<body>` tag that encloses the `body` element of an HTML document.

I Because the `<body>` tag is missing, the closing `</body>` tag also causes an error.

J Another error occurs because there is no `</bdy>` closing tag to close the `<bdy>` tag.

9 Looking at the errors, correct the HTML, click **Choose File**, and upload the corrected file.

10 Click **Check**.

The Markup Validation Service checks the HTML in the file.

K The *Document checking completed. No errors or warnings to show.* message indicates that the file has been validated.

L You can click **Close** (⊠) to close the browser window.

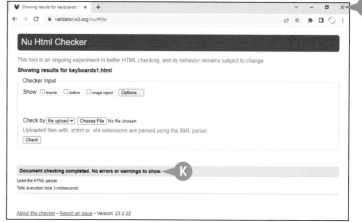

TIP

Why does the Markup Validation Service show errors for an HTML file that displays correctly in a browser?

The Web contains massive amounts of faulty HTML, so browsers are built to be tolerant of errors and to display web pages as well as they can. This means that viewing a web page in a browser is not an effective check of whether the page's HTML is valid. To ensure that your web pages display correctly in all browsers, be sure to validate every page's HTML and remove any errors.

Create Another Web Page

In this section, you create a second web page in Visual Studio Code, using the same techniques as for the first page you created earlier in this chapter. You create this page to provide a destination for a hyperlink you create later in the chapter. The page does not need to be complex; it just needs to be present so that you can establish the link to it from the previous page.

Create Another Web Page

1 In Visual Studio Code, click **Explorer** (⎙).

The primary sidebar opens, showing the Explorer pane.

2 Move the pointer over the folder's heading and click **New File** (⊞).

An edit box appears.

3 Type the filename, including the `.html` file extension, and then press Enter.

The example uses the filename `keyboard_types.html`.

Visual Studio Code creates the file and displays it in the main pane.

4 Type `!`.

The AutoComplete list opens, showing available AutoComplete entries that start with the character `!`.

5 Click the Emmet abbreviation item.

Visual Studio Code expands the abbreviation, entering the skeleton code of a web page in place of the exclamation point.

6 With the default title text, *Document*, selected, type the web page's title.

7 Click before the `</body>` tag and enter some straightforward HTML. Here is an example:

```html
<h1>Types of Computer Keyboards</h1>
<p>Many types of computer
keyboards are available.</p>
<p>With a little research, you
can find just the right type of
keyboard for you!</p>
```

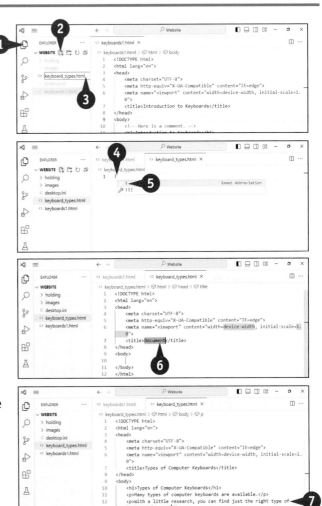

Understanding the Essentials of Hyperlinks

The Web uses *hyperlinks*, often called simply *links*, to create connections between different web pages or parts of pages. Clicking a link on one page causes the browser to display the linked page, either in the same browser window or tab or in a new browser window or tab.

In this section, you learn the essentials of hyperlinks and identify the HTML elements that make up a hyperlink. In the following sections, you create first straightforward hyperlinks and then hyperlinks that redirect the browser to a different destination.

Identify the Components of a Hyperlink

In HTML, a hyperlink uses an `<a>` tag, where the letter *a* stands for *anchor*. The `<a>` tag for a hyperlink uses the following format:

`<a href="address">link text</a>`

Here, the `href` — hyperlink reference — attribute specifies that the anchor tag contains a hyperlink. The link's address, entered in double quotation marks, specifies the destination for the hyperlink. The link text,

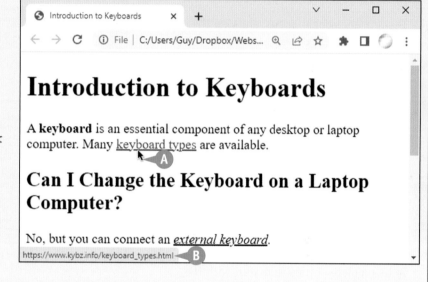

which appears between the opening `<a>` tag and the closing `</a>` tag, provides the text to display on the web page to indicate the link.

For example, the following hyperlink displays the text *keyboard types* and links to the page named `keyboard_types.html` at the site `www.kybz.info`.

`<a href="https://www.kybz.info/keyboard_types.html">keyboard types</a>`

The nearby illustration shows the linked word in context. When you hold the pointer over a link (A), most browsers display the link destination. In this example, Google Chrome displays the link destination in the lower-left corner (B) of the window.

Create a Hyperlink Between Your Web Pages

Now that you have created two web pages, you can create hyperlinks between them. To create a hyperlink, you insert an anchor tag at the appropriate place in the web page, specify the destination for the link, and enter the text to display on the page to represent the link.

The example in this section creates a hyperlink between files stored on your computer rather than files stored on a web server.

Create a Hyperlink Between Your Web Pages

1 In Visual Studio Code, click **Explorer** (□).

The primary sidebar opens, showing the Explorer pane.

Note: If the folder for your website is collapsed, click **Expand** (>) to expand it.

2 Click the web page in which you want to create the hyperlink.

The web page appears in the main part of the Visual Studio Code window.

3 Click to place the insertion point where you want the link.

4 Type **a**.

The AutoComplete list opens, showing available AutoComplete entries that start with the character *a*.

5 Click the first item, which is identified as an Emmet abbreviation.

Visual Studio Code expands the abbreviation to the anchor tags for a hyperlink, as shown next.

`<a href=""></a>`

A Visual Studio Code places the insertion point between the double quotation marks.

6 Start typing the destination for the link between the double quotation marks. The example uses the page `keyboard_types.html`, so you would start typing **keyb**.

The AutoComplete list opens, showing possible matches from your folders.

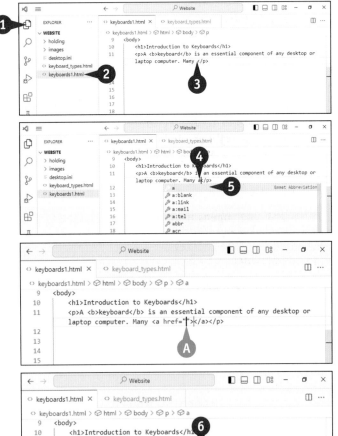

7 If a match is correct, click it.

Otherwise, finish typing the destination.

B The destination appears in your code as blue underlined text to indicate it is a link.

8 Click between the > that closes the <a> tag and the < that opens the </a> tag.

9 Type the text you want the page to display for the link. This example uses the words *keyboard types*.

10 Type any text needed to complete the sentence.

11 Right-click the page name in the Explorer pane and click **Reveal in File Explorer** to display the file in a File Explorer window. Then right-click the file, click or highlight **Open With**, and click the browser.

The web page opens in your chosen browser.

12 Click the link.

The linked page appears.

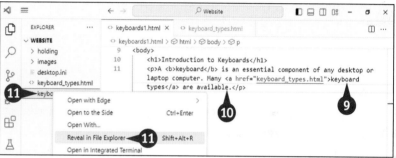

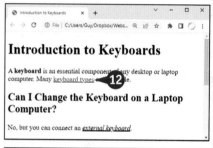

TIP

What other types of hyperlinks can I create using HTML?
Apart from the straightforward type of link shown in this section, you can create links that open new browser tabs or windows, links that redirect the browser to a different destination, and links that start email messages. See Chapter 5 for in-depth information on working with links.

Interpret HTTP Status Codes

HTTP uses five categories of status codes for tracking the interactions between web servers and clients. First, an *information response* occurs when the server receives the request and is working on fulfilling it. Second, a *successful response* indicates the server can fulfil the client's request. Third, a *redirection message* means that the server's response involves redirecting the client's request. Fourth, a *client error response* occurs when the server detects a problem with the client's request. Fifth, a *server error response* happens when the server encounters a problem fulfilling the request. You can use these codes for identifying and troubleshooting problems.

HTTP Status Codes and Their Meanings

Table 2-1 shows the HTTP status code responses you are most likely to encounter in your web browsing and development.

HTTP Code	Code Status	Explanation
Table 2-1: HTTP Status Codes and Their Meanings		
Information Responses		
100	Continue	The client should continue the request if it has not been completed; if the request has been completed, the client should ignore this code.
101	Switching Protocols	The server is switching to the specified protocol following an Upgrade request from the client.
102	Processing	The server is processing a WebDAV request but has no response yet.
Successful Responses		
200	OK	The file request completed successfully.
201	Created	A POST request or PUT request succeeded, creating a new resource, such as a web page.
202	Accepted	The server has received the request but not yet acted on it.
204	No Content	The server has no content to send for the request but is returning the headers in case they are useful.
205	Reset Content	The server instructs the user agent to reset the document that sent the request.
206	Partial Content	The server is returning a response to a Range header that requests only part of a resource.
Redirection Messages		
300	Multiple Choices	The server has multiple resources for the request, and the client needs to pick one.
301	Moved Permanently	The requested URL has been permanently changed to the new URL the server is returning.

HTTP Code	Code Status	Explanation
302	Found	The server has found the requested resource at a different URL, but the client should continue to use the original URL because the change is supposedly temporary.
303	See Other	The server is directing the client to send a GET request to a different URL.
307	Temporary Redirect	Same as for 302, but the client must use the same HTTP method, such as POST, for the new request.
308	Permanent Redirect	Same as for 301, but the client must use the same HTTP method, such as POST, for the new request.
	Client Error Responses	
400	Bad request	The client request is incorrectly formatted or contains deceptive routing.
401	Unauthorized	The client must authenticate itself to access the page.
403	Forbidden	The client does not have permission to access the page.
404	Not Found	The server cannot find the page the client requested. Some servers send a 404 error instead of a 403 error to obscure the fact that the page exists but the client is forbidden to access it.
426	Upgrade Required	The server refuses the request with the protocol the client used but may fulfil the request if the client upgrades to the specified protocol.
429	Too Many Requests	The server is limiting the client because the client has sent too many requests in a given time period.
451	Unavailable for Legal Reasons	The server refuses the request because it cannot legally provide the content; for example, because the content is *geofenced* — restricted — to a specific area that the client is outside.
	Server Error Responses	
500	Internal Server Error	The server has suffered an error it cannot resolve.
501	Not Implemented	The server does not accept the request method used. Servers must accept GET requests and READ requests.
502	Bad Gateway	The server attempted to relay the request to another server but received an invalid response.
503	Service Unavailable	The server cannot fulfil the request because it is overloaded or the server from which it would get the information is down.
504	Gateway Timeout	The server is acting as a gateway, relaying the client's request to another server, but has not received a response from that server in the specified period.

CHAPTER 3

Structuring a Web Page

In this chapter, you learn to structure a web page by using semantic elements, which are elements whose names explain their purpose, such as the `header` element and the `article` element. You also learn how to use the nonsemantic `span` and `div` elements to select parts of a page.

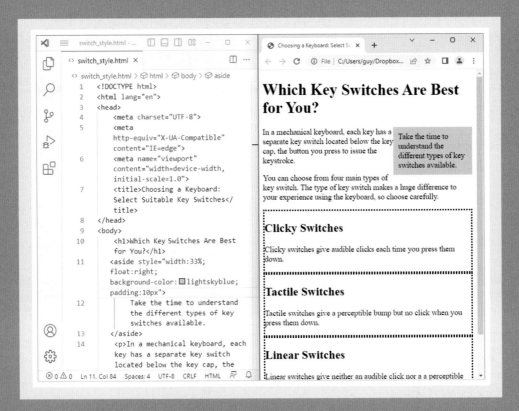

Meet the Elements for Structuring Web Pages

HTML enables you to use a wide variety of elements to structure your web pages. Some elements, such as the header element and the footer element, are *semantic*, which means their names clearly express their roles: The header element goes at the top of a web page or of another element, and the footer element goes at the bottom. Other elements are *nonsemantic*, meaning that their names do not clearly express their roles; for example, the span element specifies a short section of text, and the div element specifies a longer section, without expressing what part of the page those sections represent.

Grasp Semantic and Nonsemantic Elements

To structure your web pages, you will use semantic elements, such as the header element, the figure element, and the section element. To format your web pages, you will use both semantic elements and nonsemantic elements, such as the span element and the div element.

Table 3-1 explains the most useful nonsemantic elements and semantic elements.

Table 3-1: Nonsemantic Elements and Semantic Elements	
Element	**Explanation**
Nonsemantic Elements	
span	Selects part of a paragraph or other short element.
div	Selects one or more paragraphs or other elements.
Semantic Elements	
article	Contains an "article," a self-standing part of the web page. For example, a web page may contain multiple article elements, each containing a separate topic.
aside	Contains a usually small amount of content that is indirectly related to the nearby content or page.
details	Contains extra information that the reader can expand to read or collapse to hide. For example, a details element can act as a widget that can show or hide the information it contains.
figcaption	Contains the caption for a figure element. This element can be nested as either the first child element or the last child element in the figure element.
figure	Contains an illustration, such as a photo, a diagram, or a code listing.
footer	Contains information to be displayed at the bottom of a web page or a particular element, such as copyright information, contact information, or when the page was last updated.
header	Contains information to be displayed at the top of a web page or a particular element, such as a heading and introduction or navigational links.

	Semantic Elements
main	Contains the main content of the page. An HTML file can contain only one main element. The main element can contain elements such as article, aside, footer, header, and nav, but it cannot be placed inside any of these elements.
mark	Contains marked or highlighted text. By default, browsers display the mark element as black text on a yellow background.
nav	Contains a set of navigation links. The link destinations can be either within the page or outside it.
section	Contains a section of a web page. For example, if a page covers several topics at the h2 level, you might create a section element for each topic.
summary	Contains a visible heading within the details element. The viewer can click the heading to display the details.
time	Contains a time or a date and a time. The time element has a datetime attribute that supplies a machine-readable time that search engines and browsers can use.

Header	header element	`<header>`
		. . .
		`</header>`			

Navigation	nav element	`<nav>`
		. . .
		`</nav>`			

Article	article element	`<article>`
		. . .
		`</article>`
			Aside	aside element	`<aside>`
					. . .
					`</aside>`

Section	section element	`<section>`
		. . .
		`</section>`			

Footer	footer element	`<footer>`
		. . .
		`</footer>`			

The above illustration shows a breakdown of a web page structured with semantic elements.

Select Items with `span` and `div` Elements

HTML's `span` and `div` elements enable you to specify just the amount of text you need so that you can format it. You typically use a `span` element to identify text within a paragraph or another short element. For example, you might use a `span` element to identify text to which you want to apply particular font formatting. Similarly, you use a `div` element to specify a "division" or particular section of text, usually consisting of one or more paragraphs. You could then apply formatting, such as a border, to the entire division.

Select Items with `span` and `div` Elements

Select Text with the `span` Element

Note: To work through this section, you may want to turn off Visual Studio Code's HTML Auto Closing Tags feature temporarily. See the first tip.

1. In Visual Studio Code, open the file you want to use.

2. Open the file in a browser window.

3. In Visual Studio Code, click to place the insertion point where you want to start the span.

4. Type the opening `<span>` tag, including the `style` attribute and formatting to apply the `red` color to the text:

   `<span style="color:red">`

5. Type the text contents of the span.

Note: To use existing text in the `span` element, click to place the insertion point at the end of that text.

6. Type the closing `</span>` tag:

   `</span>`

7. Type any text that should appear after the `span` element — for example, the rest of the paragraph.

8. Click **Refresh** (⟳).

   The browser displays the updated web page.

Ⓐ The text in the `span` element appears in red.

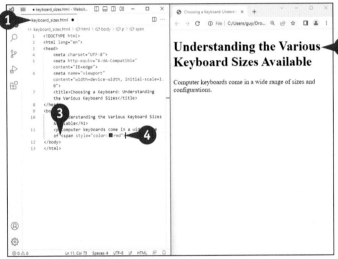

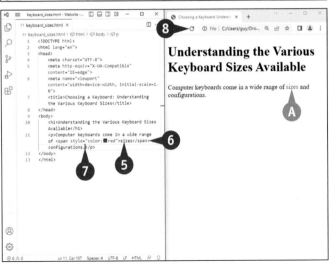

Select Text with the `div` Element

1 Click where you want the `div` element to begin.

2 Type the opening `<div>` tag, including the `style` attribute and formatting to apply right alignment to the text:

`<div style="text-align:right">`

3 Press Enter twice, and then type the ending `</div>` tag:

`</div>`

4 Click to place the insertion point on the blank line.

5 Type an h2 element and one or more p elements — for example:

`<h2>Full-Size Keyboards</h2>`

`<p>Full-size keyboards are usually about 17 inches wide.</p>`

6 Click after the closing `</div>` code, press Enter, and then type another p element — for example:

`<p>Full-size keyboards typically contain between 104 and 108 keys.</p>`

7 Click **Refresh** (↻).

The browser displays the updated web page.

B The text in the `div` element is aligned right.

C The text after the `div` element returns to left alignment, the default.

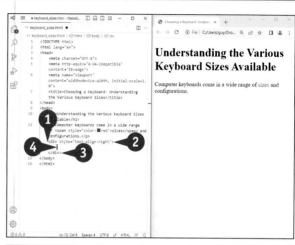

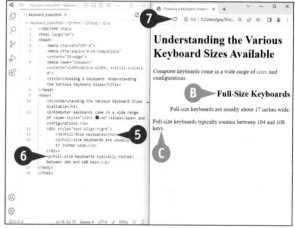

TIPS

How do I stop Visual Studio Code from inserting closing tags automatically?

Disable the Auto Closing Tags feature. Press Control+, on Windows or Linux, or press ⌘+, on the Mac, to display the Settings screen. Click **Search settings** and type **html closing**, and then deselect **Enable/disable autoclosing of HTML tags** (☐).

How else can I format my `span` elements and `div` elements?

Instead of applying style formatting inline, you can use external CSS to format your `span` elements and `div` elements, as explained in Chapter 8. This section formats the elements inline to help keep the example easy to follow. Using external CSS is faster, more efficient, and more flexible than using direct formatting.

Create `header` Elements and `footer` Elements

You can create a header for a web page by using the `header` element. A `header` element starts with the opening `<header>` tag and ends with the closing `</header>` tag; between them, you usually put one or more headings plus any introductory information the page needs. You might also use a header element to provide navigational links to different parts of a long web page.

Similarly, you can create a footer in HTML by using the `footer` element, which starts with the opening `<footer>` tag and ends with the closing `</footer>` tag.

Create `header` Elements and `footer` Elements

1 In Visual Studio Code, either create and save a new file, or open the existing file you want to use.

2 Open the file in a browser window so you can see the results of the changes you make.

3 In Visual Studio Code, click to place the insertion point where you want to start the header.

4 Type the opening `<header>` tag, including the `style` attribute to apply a dotted border:

```
<header style="border-style:
dotted">
```

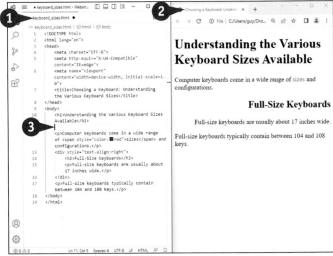

5 Press Enter twice, and then type the closing `</header>` tag:

```
</header>
```

6 Click to place the insertion point on the blank line.

7 Type some content to display in the `header` element — for example:

```
<h2>Keyboard Sizes Explained</h2>

<p>Learn the essentials about
the different sizes of computer
keyboards.</p>
```

8 Click **Refresh** (⟳).

The browser displays the updated page.

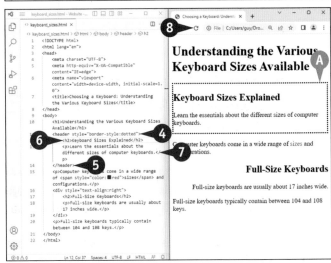

Ⓐ The header appears with a dotted border.

9 Click where you want to start the footer.

Note: Normally, you would place the footer at the bottom of the web page.

10 Type the opening `<footer>` tag, including the `style` attribute to assign first the `background-color` property with the color `aqua` and then the `border-style` property with the type `solid`:

```
<footer style="background-
color:aqua; border-style:
solid">
```

Note: Separate the two properties with a semicolon.

11 Type some text for the `footer` element — for example:

```
<p>Copyright &copy; 2023 M.
Jones Productions</p>
```

Note: `&copy;` is the HTML code for the copyright symbol, ©. See the section "Understanding HTML Entity Codes" in Chapter 8 for more information.

12 Type the closing `</footer>` tag:

```
</footer>
```

13 Click **Refresh** (⟳).

The browser displays the updated page.

Ⓑ The footer appears with a solid border and an aqua background.

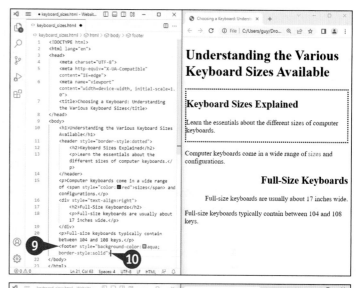

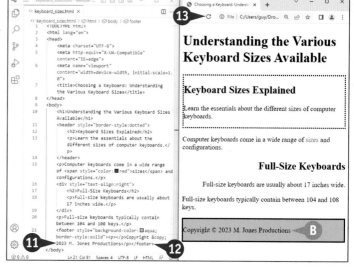

TIP

Can I create multiple `header` elements in a web page?

Yes — you can create as many `header` elements as you need. Each `header` element must be separate: You cannot nest one `header` element within another `header` element. You also cannot place a `header` element inside a `footer` element — as you would probably expect — or within an `address` element.

Similarly, you can create multiple `footer` elements, but you cannot place a `footer` element within a `footer` element, within a `header` element, or within an `address` element.

Add `article` Elements to a Page

When a page includes stand-alone content topics, you can use the `article` element to present those topics as logically separate articles.

An article can be whatever length and complexity the subject and coverage requires. The example articles in this section are very short because of the constraints of the book page.

Add `article` Elements to a Page

1 In Visual Studio Code, either create and save a new file, or open the existing file you want to use.

2 Open the file in a browser window so you can see the results of the changes you make.

3 In Visual Studio Code, click to place the insertion point where you want to start the first `article` element.

4 Type the opening `<article>` tag, including the `style` attribute with the value `border-style:dotted` to make the element's extent easy to see.

```
<article style="border-
style:dotted">
```

5 Type the content for the article — for example:

```
<h2>Clicky Switches</h2>

<p>Clicky switches give
audible clicks each time
you press them down.</p>
```

6 Type the closing `</article>` tag:

```
</article>
```

7 Click **Refresh** (C).

The browser displays the updated page.

A The article appears with a dotted border.

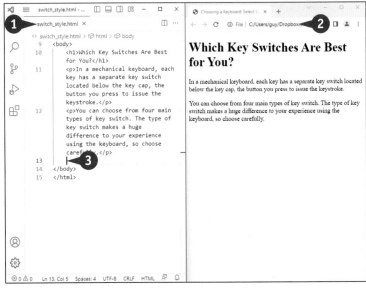

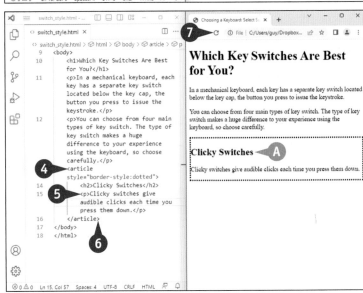

8 Press `Enter` and type the opening `<article>` tag for another article, again specifying a dotted border:

```
<article style="border-style:
dotted">
```

9 Type the contents of the article — for example:

```
<h2>Tactile Switches</h2>
```

```
<p>Tactile switches give a
perceptible bump but no click when
you press them down.</p>
```

10 Type the closing `</article>` tag:

```
</article>
```

11 Click **Refresh** (⟳).

B The second article appears.

12 Repeat steps **8** to **10** to add a third article — for example:

```
<article
style="border-style:dotted">
```

```
<h2>Linear Switches</h2>
```

```
<p>Linear switches give neither an
audible click nor a perceptible
bump when pressed.</p>
```

```
</article>
```

13 Type a comment noting you need to add another article:

```
<!-- add optical switches -->
```

14 Type a body paragraph — for example:

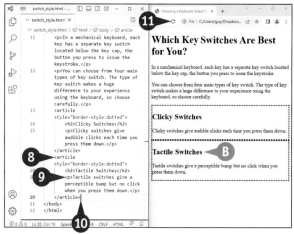

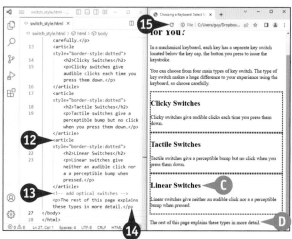

```
<p>The rest of this page explains
these types in more detail.</p>
```

15 Click **Refresh** (⟳).

C The third article appears.

D The body paragraph follows the third article.

TIP

How do I stop the border from touching the text in my `article` elements?
You can apply padding to the `article` element to put some space between the border and the element's contents. For this section, try changing `<article style="border-style:dotted">` to `<article style="border-style:dotted;padding:10px">`, which puts 10 pixels of padding top, bottom, left, and right. You can also apply different padding on the various sides. See the section "Specify Padding and Borders for an Element" in Chapter 9 for more details.

Create Pull Quotes with the `aside` Element

HTML's semantic elements include the `aside` element, which you use to separate some content from the content that surrounds it. An `aside` element can be a useful way to emphasize part of your web page or to draw the reader's attention to the element in which the aside is positioned.

The `aside` element has no specific positioning, but you can use the `style` attribute to position and format the `aside` element as needed to complement your web page.

Create Pull Quotes with the `aside` Element

1 In Visual Studio Code, either create and save a new file or open the existing file you want to use.

2 Open the file in a browser window so you can see the results of the changes you make.

3 In Visual Studio Code, click to place the insertion point where you want to position the `aside` element.

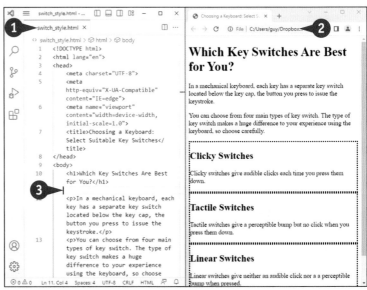

4 Type the opening `<aside>` tag:

`<aside>`

5 Type the contents you want to display in the `aside` element — for example:

```
Take the time to
understand the different
types of key switches
available.
```

6 Type the closing `</aside>` tag:

`</aside>`

7 Click **Refresh** (⟳).

A The `aside` element appears in the page.

Because you have not specified any style formatting, the `aside` element appears like the other paragraphs.

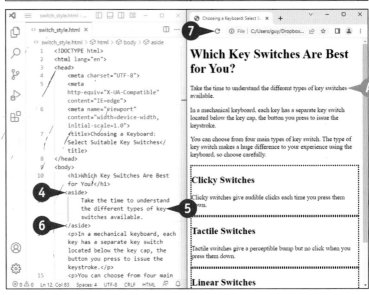

8 Click before the closing > of the opening <aside> tag and type the style attribute, specifying width:33% and float:right, so the tag looks like this:

```
<aside style="width:33%;
float:right">
```

9 Click **Refresh** (C).

B The aside element appears at one-third the page width and floating right.

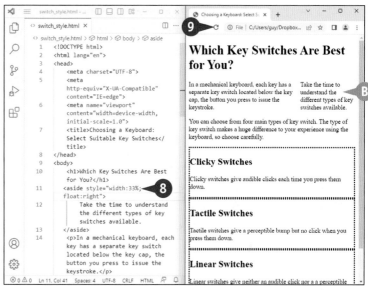

10 Click after float:right and before the double quotes and continue the style attribute formatting, adding background-color:lightskyblue and padding:10px. The complete tag looks like this:

```
<aside style="width:33%;
float:right;background-
color:lightskyblue;
padding:10px">
```

11 Click **Refresh** (C).

C The aside element takes on a light blue background and 10 pixels of padding on each side.

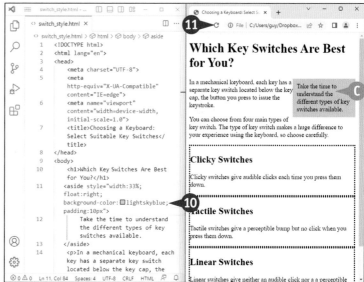

TIP

What are other uses of the `aside` element?
Apart from creating pull quotes, as shown in this section, the aside element is widely used to create sidebars, to implement navigational elements, and for advertising.

Divide a Page Using `section` Elements

HTML's `section` element enables you to divide a web page into separate sections. Because `section` is a semantic element, the page's division into sections should be logical, but you can also use it for practical purposes. For example, you can apply formatting to all the child elements in a `section` element simultaneously by specifying the formatting for the `section` element.

Divide a Page Using `section` Elements

1 In Visual Studio Code, either create and save a new file or open the existing file you want to use.

2 Open the file in a browser window so you can see the results of the changes you make.

3 In Visual Studio Code, click to place the insertion point where you want to begin the first `section` element.

4 Type the opening `<section>` tag:

`<section>`

5 Type the contents for the first section. The example includes an h2 element and a p element:

`<h2>Introduction</h2>`

`<p>The Anne Pro 2 from Obinslab is a 60%-size mechanical keyboard with built-in wireless connectivity.</p>`

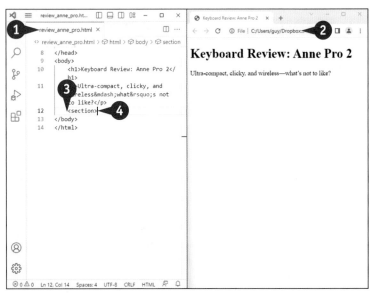

6 Type the closing `</section>` tag:

`</section>`

7 Click **Refresh** (↻).

Ⓐ The section's contents appear in the web page.

There is no visible indication that the section exists.

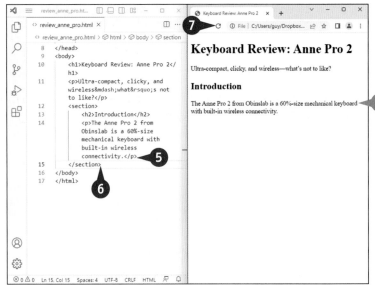

8 Click in the Visual Studio Code window and type the opening `<section>` tag, this time including the `style` attribute and specifying `border-style:dashed`:

```
<section style="border-style:
dashed">
```

9 Type the contents for the second section. The example includes an `h2` element and a `p` element:

```
<h2>Review Considerations</h2>

<p>This review is intended for
general users, not for gamers
specifically.</p>
```

10 Type the closing `</section>` tag:

```
</section>
```

11 Click **Refresh** (⟳).

B The section's contents appear with a dashed outline.

12 Click before the closing `</section>` tag and type the opening `<section>` tag for a subsection, including the `style` attribute and specifying `background-color:lightyellow`:

```
<section style="background-color:
lightyellow">
```

13 Enter an `h3` element and a `p` element. For example:

```
<h3>Switch Type</h3>

<p>The review keyboard uses blue
(clicky) key switches.</p>
```

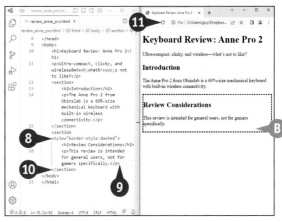

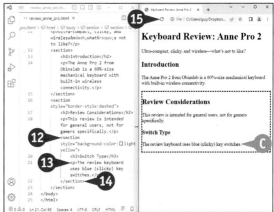

14 Type the closing `</section>` tag for the subsection:

```
</section>
```

15 Click **Refresh** (⟳).

C The subsection appears in the page.

TIP

What is the difference between the `section` element and the `div` element?

Both the `section` element and the `div` element enable you to group child elements and optionally apply formatting to them all at once; you will often see `section` and `div` used more or less interchangeably. However, `section` is a semantic element intended to suggest that all its contents relate to the same theme, whereas `div` is a nonsemantic element that carries no such implication.

Best practice is to use semantic elements, such as the `section` element and the `article` element, to identify particular sections of a web page logically and to use the `div` element only when no semantic element is suitable.

Create Collapsible Sections

The `details` element enables you to create content sections that the user can expand and collapse as needed. For example, you might create a Frequently Asked Questions page for your website that appears at first as a list of questions whose answers are not visible. By clicking a question, the user can expand the content section to display its answer; after reading the answer, the user can click the question again to hide the answer once more. To create this effect, you use the `details` element for the expanding and collapsing and the `summary` element to display the text that is initially visible.

Create Collapsible Sections

1 In Visual Studio Code, either create and save a new file, or open the existing file you want to use.

2 Open the file in a browser window so you can see the results of the changes you make.

3 In Visual Studio Code, click to place the insertion point where you want to begin the first `details` element.

4 Type the opening `<details>` tag, press Enter twice, and then type the closing `</details>` tag:

`<details>`

`</details>`

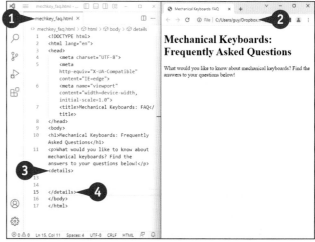

5 Click between the `<details>` tag and the `</details>` tag and type the opening `<summary>` tag, its contents, and the closing `</summary>` tag — for example:

`<summary>What is a mechanical keyboard?</summary>`

6 Type the contents that the `details` element will display when clicked — for example:

`<p>A mechanical keyboard is a keyboard that uses key switches rather than a membrane to register keystrokes.</p>`

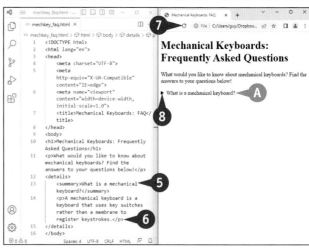

7 Click **Refresh** (⟳).

A The `details` element appears but is collapsed, so you see only the `summary` element.

8 Click **Expand** (▶ changes to ▼).

B The `details` element expands, revealing its contents.

C You can click **Collapse** (▼ changes to ▶) to collapse the `details` element again.

9 Click after the `details` element in Visual Studio Code and type another `details` element, including the `summary` element — for example:

```
<details>

    <summary>What advantages
do mechanical keyboards offer?
</summary>

    <p>Mechanical keyboards feel
better to type on and enable some
people to type faster.</p>

</details>
```

10 Click before the closing `</details>` tag of the second `details` element (not shown).

11 Type a nested `details` element. Specify the `style` attribute with the value `margin-left:20px`, as in this example:

```
<details style="margin-left:20px">

    <summary>Keyboard Feedback
</summary>

        <p>Keyboard feedback can
contribute to both typing enjoyment
and speed.</p>

</details>
```

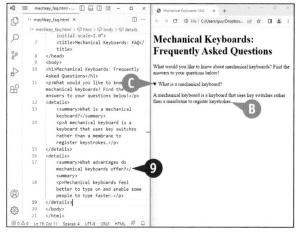

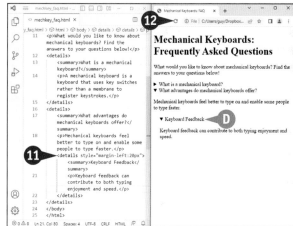

12 Click **Refresh** (↻).

The updated page appears.

D You can expand both the outer `details` element and the nested `details` element.

TIP

Must I include the `summary` element in each `details` element?

Normally, including the `summary` element is helpful, because it enables you to display suitable text to the right of the Expand arrow (▶) for the `details` element. However, you can omit the `summary` element without causing an error. If you do so, HTML displays the default text `Details` to the right of the Expand arrow (▶).

CHAPTER 4

Including Images

To make your web pages richer and more appealing, you can include images in them. This chapter shows you how to create suitable image files using GIMP, the GNU Image Manipulation Program; insert images in your web pages and control how they appear; and display alternate text for browsers that cannot display an image file.

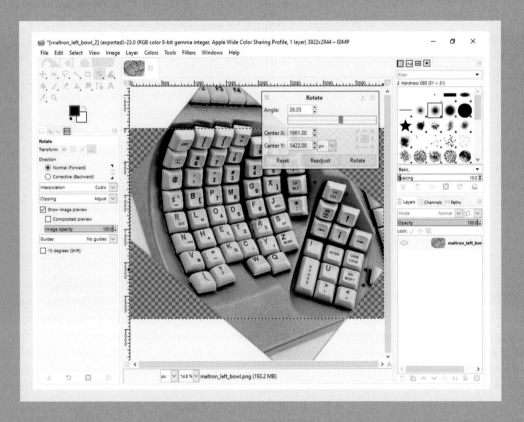

Grasp the Essentials of Web Image Formats

Computers use many different image formats, from the JPEG format most digital cameras capture to the RAW format preferred by photography professionals, and from the animated GIF format to the business-oriented TIFF format. Most web browsers can display an impressive range of image formats, but to make your website generally accessible and fast to load, you must choose suitable formats for the images you include in your web pages. This section gives you an overview of key image formats. The following sections explain how to use the GIMP app to create suitable image files.

Understanding Why Image File Size Is Important

If you are creating web pages you will post on the Web, you will likely want to keep file sizes down to a sensible minimum so that your web pages load quickly even when the web server hosting the site is busy and when visitors are using slower Internet connections. If you are developing pages for an internal website that all visitors will access across fast connections, file size may be less of a concern; but even so, most companies and organizations prefer to conserve bandwidth than to squander it.

HTML files and CSS files contain only text, so they have small file sizes and transfer quickly. Image files, audio files, and video files tend to be much larger and can greatly increase the amount of data a browser needs to transfer to load a web page. So you will normally want to choose compact file formats for such media files. You will also want to create files that have suitable quality for the website rather than posting the highest-quality files possible, which will have larger file sizes.

Identify the Factors Affecting Image File Size

The following factors affect image file size:

- **Resolution.** The larger an image's dimensions, the more pixels the image contains, and the larger the file size. For example, an image 512 pixels wide by 384 pixels high contains 196,608 pixels; an image 1024 pixels wide by 768 pixels high contains 786,432 pixels — four times as many — because it is twice as wide and twice as high. Each pixel contains data that contributes to the file size.

- **File format.** Different file formats use different compression algorithms, which affect the file size. The key difference is between *lossy compression*, which reduces file size but also reduces image quality, and *lossless compression*, which preserves image quality and typically reduces file size less than lossy compression. The JPEG file format uses lossy compression, whereas the PNG file format uses lossless compression. The result is that JPEG files are typically smaller than PNG files but have lower image quality.

- **Color depth.** Each color requires data to represent it in the file, so the more colors an image has, the larger its file size will be.

- **Compression level.** Some file formats, such as JPEG, allow you to adjust the level of compression used. Greater compression delivers smaller file sizes but also usually reduces image quality.

- **Image content.** The more complex the image's content, the more data is needed to represent it in the file. For example, a colorful photo of a landscape contains many colors and requires a lot of data, whereas a simple line drawing — say, a red arrow on a black background — requires relatively little data.

- **Image metadata.** Metadata is data describing the image, such as its GPS location, the camera's shutter speed and aperture, and the number of colors. Metadata typically takes up only a modest amount of space.

Understanding the Most Widely Used Web Image Formats

Most images on the Web use one of the following four formats:

- **JPEG.** JPEG, Joint Photographic Experts Group, uses lossy compression and can deliver a massive reduction in file size. You can control the level of compression. JPEG is a good choice for photos in web pages.

- **PNG.** PNG, Portable Network Graphics, uses lossless compression to deliver full-quality images with a modest reduction in file size. PNG files are a reasonable choice for photos in web pages but are typically substantially larger than JPEG files of the same content.

- **GIF.** GIF, Graphics Interchange Format, is an older file format that has a maximum of 256 different colors. This limitation keeps down the file size, and GIF uses lossless compression to reduce it further. The color restriction makes GIF unsuitable for photos, but it is good for logos and other graphics that need only a restricted color set. GIF also enables you to create simple moving images.

- **SVG.** SVG, Scalable Vector Graphics, uses text in the Extensible Markup Language, XML, to describe two-dimensional images. SVG is suitable for creating images that use shapes and lines.

Most photo and graphics editors can create JPEG, PNG, and GIF files, along with various other formats. Most illustration apps can export drawings as SVG files.

Launch GIMP and Perform Essential Moves

GIMP — the GNU Image Manipulation Program — is a powerful tool for editing image files. In this section, you get started with GIMP by launching the app and opening an image file in it. With the image file open, you zoom in or out, as needed. When you finish making changes to the image file, as discussed in the following sections, you use the Overwrite command to save the changes back to the original image file, overwriting it. You then close the image file — and close GIMP if you have finished working with it. See the section "Install GIMP" in Chapter 1 for instructions on installing GIMP.

Launch GIMP and Perform Essential Moves

Launch GIMP and Open an Image File

① Launch GIMP using the standard technique for your computer's operating system.

For example, on Windows, click **Start** to open the Start menu, and then click **GIMP** (🖌).

Note: On the Mac, click **Launchpad** (⠿) to display the Launchpad screen, and then click **GIMP** (🖌).

On Linux, display the list of apps and click **GIMP** (🖌).

GIMP opens.

② Click **File**.

The File menu opens.

③ Click **Open**.

Note: On Windows and Linux, you can press Control + O to display the Open dialog box. On macOS, press ⌘ + O.

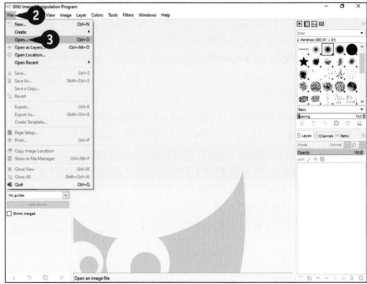

The Open Image dialog box appears.

4 Navigate to the folder that contains the image file you want to open.

Ⓐ The breadcrumb bar shows the trail of folders to the current folder.

5 Click the image file.

Ⓑ The Preview box shows a preview of the image.

Note: If the message *Click to create preview* appears in the Preview box, click it to create a preview of the current image.

6 Click **Open**.

Note: If the Convert to RGB Working Space? dialog box opens, offering to convert the image's embedded color profile to GIMP's built-in sRGB color profile, click **Keep**.

The image file opens.

Note: You can open multiple image files at once.

Ⓒ The image appears in the center part of the window.

Ⓓ The Toolbox appears in the upper-left corner.

Ⓔ The image's thumbnail appears on the image's tab on the tab bar, which enables you to navigate from one open image to another.

TIP

Why does GIMP have a dark interface on my computer, unlike in the book?
GIMP enables you to choose from different color themes for the user interface. To change themes, click **Edit** and **Preferences** to open the Preferences dialog box, and then click **Theme** in the left pane. In the Theme pane, go to the Select Them box and click the theme you want, and then click **OK**. The default theme is Dark; this book uses the System theme, which is more readable on the printed page than Dark is.

continued ▶

GIMP enables you to zoom in or out on an image to see the area with which you want to work. GIMP provides two easy means of zooming: first, the Zoom continuation menu on the View menu on the menu bar; and second, the Zoom pop-up menu on the status bar. The Zoom pop-up menu provides a variety of preset zoom percentages, such as 800%, 400%, 200%, 100%, 50%, 25%, and 12.5%. The Zoom continuation menu offers greater flexibility, including the Fit Image in Window command and the Zoom to Selection command, so it is typically more helpful.

Launch GIMP and Perform Essential Moves (continued)

Zoom In or Out on the Image File

Ⓐ To zoom quickly to a preset percentage, you can click **Zoom**, and then click the percentage on the Zoom pop-up menu.

❶ Click **View**.

The View menu opens.

❷ Click **Zoom**.

The Zoom continuation menu opens.

Ⓑ To zoom to a different percentage, click **Other**; specify the zoom ratio, such as 1:6, or the zoom percentage, such as 18%, in the Zoom Ratio dialog box; and then click **OK**.

Ⓒ You can click **Revert Zoom** to revert to the previous zoom level.

❸ Click **Fit Image in Window**.

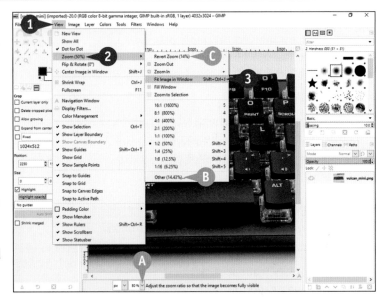

The image appears at the zoom you specified.

Following the example, the full image appears in the window.

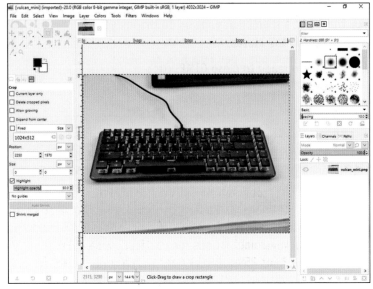

Save Changes to an Image File and Close It

Note: After making changes to an image file, you use GIMP's Overwrite command to save those changes to the original file. You then close the file. This procedure may seem peculiar, but it is effective. The alternative is to save the changes to a file in GIMP's XCF format and then export that file in the image format you want.

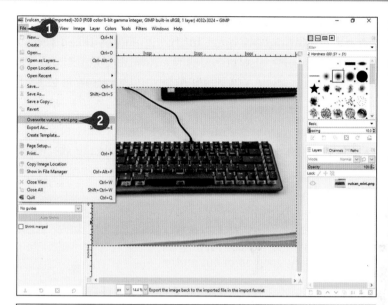

1 After making changes to an image file, click **File**.

The File menu opens.

2 Click **Overwrite**. This command shows the name of the file you will overwrite — for example, *Overwrite vulcan_mini.png*.

GIMP exports the file, including the changes you have made, overwriting the existing file.

Ⓓ The status bar readout shows that the file has been exported.

3 Click **Close** (☒).

The image file closes.

4 If you are ready to close GIMP, click **Close** (☒).

GIMP closes.

TIPS

Can I zoom in and out using keyboard shortcuts?
Yes. Press ⊟ to zoom out or ⊞ to zoom in. Press Control + Shift + J to give the Fit Image in Window command. Press 5 to zoom to 1600%, 4 for 800%, 3 for 400%, 2 for 200%, or 1 for 100%. Add Shift to the key combinations for fractional values: Press Shift + 2 for 50%, Shift +3 for 25%, Shift +4 for 12.5%, or Shift +5 for 6.25%.

What is XCF?
XCF is GIMP's native image format, the format in which GIMP stores image data by default. The abbreviation stands for eXperimental Computing Facility.

Rotate or Straighten an Image

GIMP enables you to rotate an image 90° clockwise, 90° counterclockwise, or 180°. These quick rotations are great for fixing photos taken with the camera upside down or in the wrong orientation. GIMP also provides the Arbitrary Rotation command, which lets you rotate an image by exactly the angle you need. Arbitrary Rotation is especially useful for straightening an image shot askew.

GIMP also allows you to flip an image horizontally or vertically. Flipping an image horizontally switches left and right, whereas flipping an image vertically switches the top and bottom.

Rotate or Straighten an Image

1 Open the image file you want to rotate or straighten.

2 If necessary, zoom in or out on the image.

Note: If you need to straighten the image but not rotate it, go to step **6**.

3 Click **Image**.

The Image menu opens.

4 Click **Transform**.

The Transform continuation menu opens.

A You can click **Flip Horizontally** to flip the image horizontally.

B You can click **Flip Vertically** to flip the image vertically.

5 Click the appropriate Rotate command. In this example, you would click **Rotate 180°**.

C The image rotates the way you specified.

6 If you need to straighten the image, click **Image**.

The Image menu opens.

7 Click **Transform**.

The Transform continuation menu opens.

8 Click **Arbitrary Rotation**.

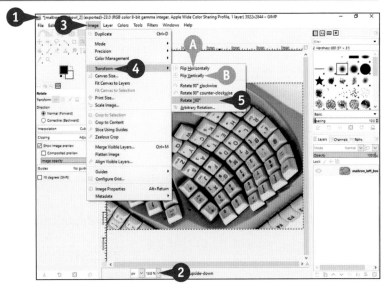

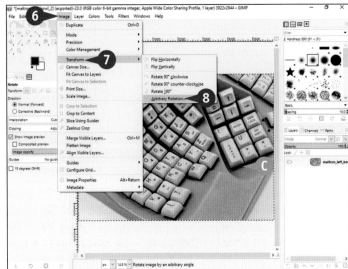

The Rotate dialog box opens.

D The crosshair (⊕) indicates the center of rotation. See the tip.

9 Drag the slider to adjust the angle.

E If you know the precise angle of rotation needed, you can enter it in the Angle box.

F The image rotates, enabling you to preview the effect of the rotation before applying it.

10 Click **Rotate**.

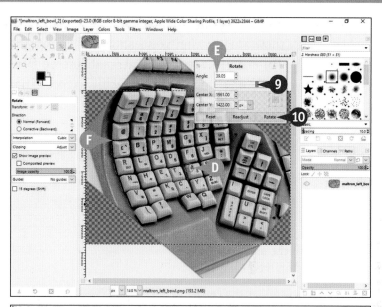

The Rotate dialog box closes.

G The image rotates the way you specified.

You can now modify the image further, as needed; save it; and close it.

Crop an Image

Unless you compose your photos with uncanny accuracy, you will likely need to crop them so that they show exactly what you want, with no extraneous content. GIMP enables you to crop images easily. For many images, you will want to crop freely to the precise dimensions you want. For others, you may want to crop to a specific aspect ratio, such as 3:2 — three units wide for every two units high.

Crop an Image

1 Open the image file you want to crop.

2 If necessary, zoom in or out on the image so that you can see more than the area to which you want to crop the image.

You can use either the Zoom pop-up menu or the Zoom continuation menu on the View menu.

3 Click **Crop Tool** ( ).

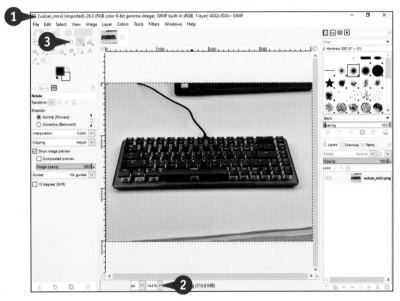

The Crop Tool becomes active.

The crop pointer ( ) appears.

4 Drag diagonally to select the area you want to keep.

Note: You can drag diagonally in any direction.

A frame appears around the area you selected.

5 If necessary, drag a corner or a side of the frame to adjust the area.

Note: You can move the selection area by clicking inside it and dragging.

6 When you have selected the area you want, double-click inside the frame to execute the crop.

Note: You can also press Enter to execute the crop.

A The cropped image appears.

You can now modify the image further, as needed; save it; and close it.

How do I crop an image to a specific aspect ratio?
Click **Crop Tool** ( ) to activate the Crop Tool. In the Crop pane, on the left side of the GIMP window below the Toolbox, select the check box (☑) to the left of the first, unnamed drop-down list. Click that list's drop-down button (⌄), and then click **Aspect ratio**. In the text box below the drop-down list, select the existing aspect ratio and type your aspect ratio, such as **3:2**, over it. GIMP then constrains the crop area as you drag.

Resize an Image

GIMP enables you to resize an image to the dimensions you need, either increasing or decreasing the image's width and height. Given the high resolutions at which current digital cameras and smartphones shoot photos, you are more likely to need to decrease the image's dimensions when working with photos, but you may need to enlarge smaller graphics.

When resizing an image, you can choose what type of interpolation to use. *Interpolation* controls how the app calculates the color values for pixels it inserts when resizing an image. You can also adjust the image's resolution if needed.

Resize an Image

1 Open the image file you want to resize.

Note: Normally, you would rotate, straighten, and crop an image, as needed, before resizing it.

A The image's resolution appears in the title bar.

2 Click **Image**.

The Image menu opens.

3 Click **Scale Image**.

The Scale Image dialog box opens.

4 If you want to adjust the width and height separately, click **Linked** (⬚ changes to ⬚).

5 Verify that **px** appears in this drop-down list. If it does not, click ⌄, and then click **pixels**.

6 Click **Width** and enter the width in pixels.

7 If you unlinked the width and height, click **Height** and enter the height in pixels.

8 If you will adjust the resolution and want to adjust the horizontal and vertical resolution separately, click **Linked** (⬚ changes to ⬚).

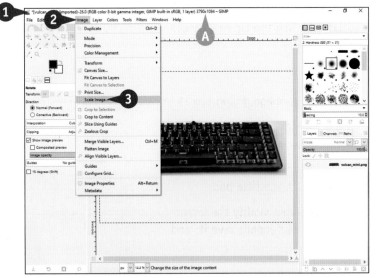

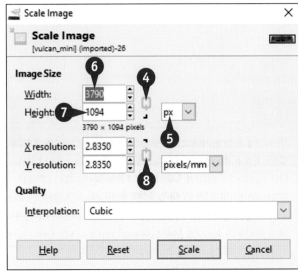

78

9 Verify that **pixels/mm** appears in this drop-down list. If not, click ⌄, and then click **pixels/mm**.

10 Click **X resolution** and enter the horizontal resolution.

11 If you unlinked the resolutions, click **Y resolution** and enter the vertical resolution.

12 Click **Interpolation** (⌄), and then click the type of interpolation you want to use: **None**, **Cubic**, **Linear**, **NoHalo**, or **LoHalo**. See the tip for advice.

13 Click **Scale**.

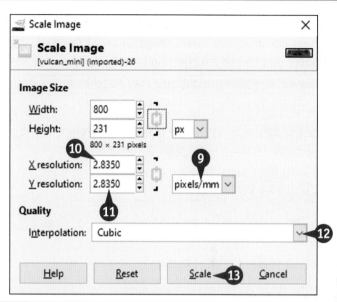

The Scale Image dialog box closes.

B GIMP resizes the image as you specified.

C The image's adjusted resolution appears in the title bar.

You can now modify the image further, as needed; save it; and close it.

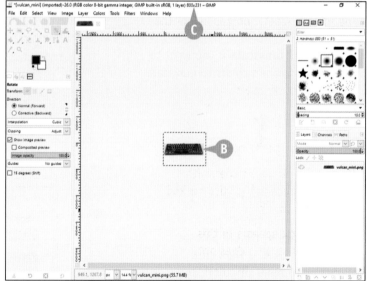

Which type of interpolation should I use when resizing an image?

When you are reducing the image's size, choose **LoHalo** in the Interpolation drop-down list; if LoHalo delivers a disappointing result for that image, try **NoHalo** instead. When you are increasing the image's size, choose either **Cubic** or **Linear**. Cubic interpolation takes more processing power than linear interpolation, so it may take longer.

If you just need a rough-and-ready resized image, you can choose **None**, which performs no interpolation but instead copies the color of each pixel from the closest adjacent pixel in the original image. The resulting image may be grainy or coarse.

Reduce the Number of Colors in an Image

The more colors an image contains, the larger its file size will be, so you may want to reduce the number of colors in an image to bring down its file size. GIMP's Indexed Color Conversion feature enables you to reduce the number of colors either to a maximum you specify, such as 256 colors, or to a palette optimized for use on the web. Generally, the web-optimized palette is the best choice for images you will use in your web pages.

Reduce the Number of Colors in an Image

1 Open the image file in which you want to reduce the number of colors.

2 Click **Image**.

The Image menu opens.

3 Click **Mode**.

The Mode continuation menu opens.

A The dot (●) indicates the current color mode — in this case, RGB.

B You can click **Grayscale** if you want to convert the image's colors to grayscale tones.

4 Click **Indexed**.

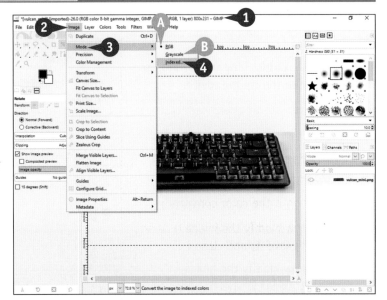

The Indexed Color Conversion dialog box opens.

C If you want to reduce the image to a specific number of colors, click **Generate optimum palette** (○ changes to ◉). Then click **Maximum number of colors** and enter the number.

5 Click **Use web-optimized palette** (○ changes to ◉).

6 Select (☑) **Remove unused and duplicate colors from colormap**.

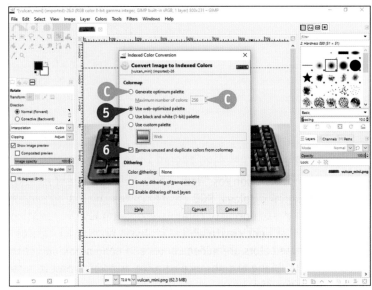

⑦ Click **Color dithering** (∨), and then click **None**.

Note: *Dithering* is a technique used to simulate a larger range of colors using a limited color palette. Dithering places small dots of different colors in close proximity to one another to create the illusion of a new color.

⑧ Click **Convert**.

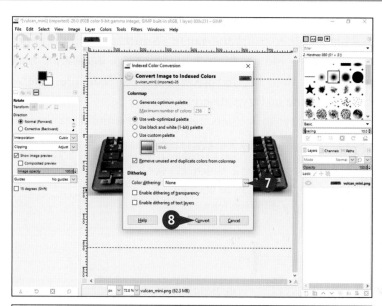

The Indexed Color Conversion dialog box closes.

GIMP performs the color conversion.

You can now modify the image further, as needed; save it; and close it.

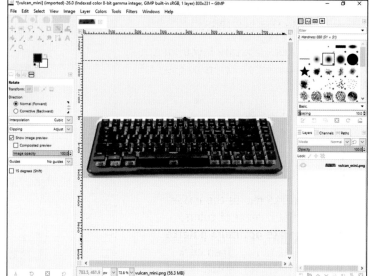

What is RGB?
RGB is the abbreviation for "Red, Green, Blue," a color model used to represent colors on computer screens and other digital displays. RGB creates colors combining varying intensities of red, green, and blue light. The amount of each primary color used determines the resulting color. For example, equal amounts of red, green, and blue light create white, while no light at all creates black. In RGB, the resulting color gets lighter as more colors are added together. Each color channel in RGB is represented by a value in the range 0–255, with 0 being the absence of color and 255 being the maximum intensity. Black is RGB(0,0,0); white is RGB(255,255,255).

Convert an Image to the Format You Need

Gimp enables you to convert an image file from one format to another by opening the image file and then using the Export As command. This capability can be useful for creating the types of image files you need for your web pages. Depending on the export format, you may be able to configure options for the exported file. For example, when exporting a file to the JPEG format, you can adjust the quality setting to strike a balance between image quality and file size. You can also choose whether to include metadata and a thumbnail picture in the exported image.

Convert an Image to the Format You Need

1 Open the image file you want to convert to a different format.

2 Click **File**.

The File menu opens.

3 Click **Export As**.

Note: You can press Control + Shift + E to give the Export As command. On the Mac, press ⌘ + Shift + E.

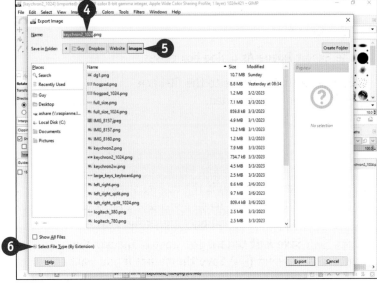

The Export Image dialog box opens.

4 In the Name box, edit the filename, as needed.

5 Specify a different folder, if needed.

6 Click **Expand** (⊞ changes to ⊟) next to **Select File Type (By Extension)**.

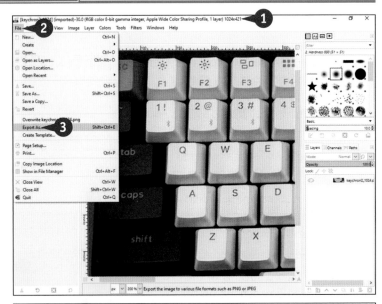

The Select File Type by Extension box expands.

7 Click the file type to which you want to convert the image.

8 Click **Export**.

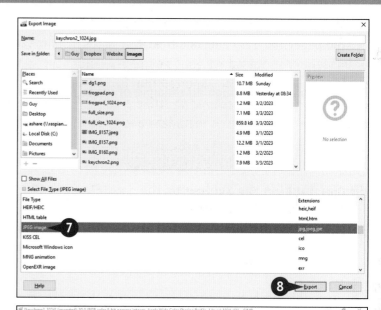

Depending on the file type, an Export Image As dialog box may open. For example, when you export to the JPEG format, the Export Image as JPEG dialog box opens.

9 Choose options for the file format — for example, by dragging the **Quality** slider.

A You can click **Expand** (⊞ changes to ⊟) to expand the Advanced Options section of the Export Image as JPEG dialog box.

Note: The available options in the Export Image As dialog box depend on the file format.

10 Click **Export**.

The Export Image As dialog box closes.

GIMP exports the image to the filename and location you specified.

What are the key options for exporting a JPEG file?

The most important option is the Quality setting. Because the JPEG format uses lossy compression, a high-quality JPEG file contains much more data than a low-quality JPEG file; the disadvantage is that the high-quality file has a correspondingly higher file size.

Select (☑) **Save Exif Data** if you want to include the file's Exchangeable Image Format data in the exported file. Select (☑) **Save thumbnail** if you want to include a thumbnail image in the exported file.

Learn the HTML for Images

To place an image file on a web page, you insert an img element at the appropriate point in the web page. The img element creates a space in which the browser then places the image.

This section introduces you to the syntax for the img element. The following section, "Insert an Image," walks you through an example of using the img element to insert an image in a web page.

Understanding the Syntax for the img Element

The img element uses a self-closing tag, which looks like this in HTML 5: <img>. In earlier versions of HTML, self-closing tags included a space and a forward slash before the closing > — for example, <img />. These older tags still work, but you no longer need to include the space and forward slash.

The img element has two required attributes:

- src. This attribute specifies the address at which the image file is located. For example, the src attribute for the following <img> tag specifies that the image file is called keyboard1.jpg and is located in the images folder:

  <img src="images/keyboard1.jpg">

- alt. This attribute specifies alternate text to display if the image file cannot be shown. For example, the src attribute for the following <img> tag specifies that the image file is called keyboard1.jpg and is located in the images folder. The alt attribute specifies the text A keyboard.

  <img src="images/keyboard1.jpg" alt="A keyboard">

As well as from the two required attributes, the <img> tag has 10 optional attributes:

- height. This attribute specifies the display height of the image in pixels. Setting the image's height by including the height attribute in the tag does work, but it is better to use CSS to control image size.

- width. This attribute specifies the display width of the image, either in pixels or as a percentage of the available width in the browser window. As with the height attribute, including this attribute in the tag does work, but using CSS is preferable. The following example makes the image occupy 90 percent of the available width in the browser window:

  <img src="images/keyboard1.jpg" alt="A keyboard" width="90%">

- **sizes.** This attribute specifies different image sizes to use for different web page layouts.

- **srcset.** This attribute specifies a set of image files to use for different clients — for example, a smaller image for smaller screens.

- **ismap.** This attribute, when included, specifies that the image is an image map. See the section "Create Multiple Links from an Image" in Chapter 5 for information about image maps.

- **usemap.** This attribute provides the name of an image to use as an image map. See the section "Create Multiple Links from an Image" in Chapter 5 for an example of how you use this attribute.

- **loading.** This attribute controls how the browser loads the image. You can set `loading` to `eager` to make the browser load the image immediately, to `lazy` to make the browser load the image only when the part of the page containing the image comes into view on the screen, or to `auto` to have the browser determine whether to act eager or act lazy. Omitting the `loading` attribute from the `<img>` tag also lets the browser use its default behavior; for most browsers, the default behavior is lazy loading.

  `<img src="images/keyboard1.jpg" alt="A keyboard" loading="lazy">`

- **longdesc.** This attribute specifies a URL that provides a detailed description of the image.

- **referrerpolicy.** This attribute tells the browser which referrer information to use when retrieving an image. You can set this attribute to `no-referrer`, `no-referrer-when-downgrade`, `origin`, `origin-when-cross-origin`, or `unsafe-URL`.

- **crossorigin.** This attribute enables the browser to use images from third-party sites that permit cross-origin access.

Insert an Image

In the previous section, "Learn the HTML for Images," you met the `img` element, which enables you to display an image in a web page. In this section, you use the `img` element to add a picture to a page. You use the `img` element's `alt` attribute to specify alternative text to display for accessibility purposes or if the image file is not available; and you use the `width` attribute to control the width at which the image appears relative to the window's width.

Insert an Image

1 In Visual Studio Code, open the file to which you want to add the image.

2 Open the file in a browser window.

3 In Visual Studio Code, click to place the insertion point at the appropriate point in the HTML.

4 Type **im**.

The expansions list appears.

5 Click **img**.

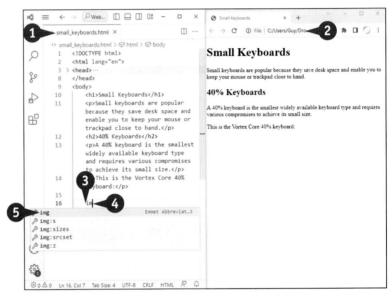

The `<img>` tag appears, including the `src` attribute and the `alt` attribute:

`<img src="" alt="">`

6 With the insertion point between the double quotation marks after `src=`, start typing the path and filename of the image file.

The list of matching items appears.

7 Click the appropriate item.

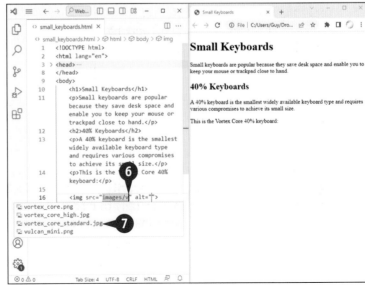

The path and filename appear within the double quotation marks after `src=`.

8 Press `Tab` (not shown).

The insertion point moves to between the double quotation marks after `alt=`.

9 Type the text to display if the browser cannot display the image file.

10 Click **Refresh** (C).

The web page refreshes.

A The image appears, but is too wide for the window.

11 Click just before the closing `>` of the `<img>` tag.

12 Type a space followed by **width="90%"**.

13 Click **Refresh** (C).

The web page refreshes.

B The image changes size so that it is 90 percent of the width of the browser window. The browser automatically adjusts the image's height proportionally.

Note: Leave the HTML file to the browser window open so that you can continue working on the page in the next section, "Create a Figure with a Caption."

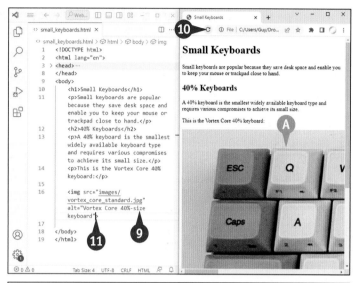

TIP

How can I make a browser display the alt text for an image?
One way is to turn off the display of images in the browser. For example, in Chrome, click **Menu** (⋮), click **Settings**, and then click **Privacy and security** (🛡). Next, click **Site settings** (⇄) to display the Site Settings screen, and then click **Images** (🖾) to display the Images screen. Click **Don't allow sites to show images** (🖾; ○ changes to ◉). Now load the web page, and you will see the alt text.

When working on the web page, it is quicker to temporarily change the filename or path — for example, by deleting a character. You can then refresh the page, and the alt text will appear.

Create a Figure with a Caption

Instead of simply inserting an image in a web page, you can create a figure element, which identifies its contents as being a figure. You place the img element inside the figure element but otherwise specify the image information as usual; you can also use the figure element for other graphical items, such as diagrams or charts. You can add a caption to the figure element by including the figcaption element, which you also place inside the figure element.

Create a Figure with a Caption

1 In Visual Studio Code, resume work in the file you used in the previous section, "Insert an Image."

2 Click to place the insertion point on the line before the start of the <img> tag.

3 Type the opening <figure> tag, including the style attribute to define a simple border that will enable you to see where the figure element is:

```
<figure style=
"border-style:solid;
border-width:thin;
border-color:black">
```

4 Click to place the insertion point after the end of the <img> tag.

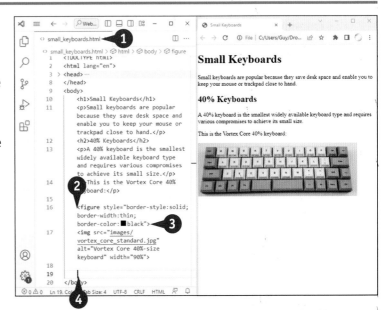

5 Type the closing </figure> tag to end the figure element, enclosing the img element inside the figure element:

```
</figure>
```

6 Click to place the insertion point on the blank line before the </figure> tag.

7 Click **Refresh** (⟳).

The web page refreshes.

Ⓐ The border shows the extent of the `figure` element.

Ⓑ The image appears in the `figure` element.

⑧ In the Visual Studio Code window, type **fig**.

The expansions list appears.

⑨ Click **figcaption**.

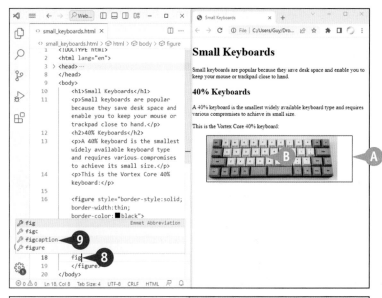

Visual Studio Code inserts the opening `<figcaption>` tag and closing `</figcaption>` tag, placing the insertion point between them.

⑩ Type the text of the caption.

⑪ Click **Refresh** (↻).

The web page refreshes.

Ⓒ The figure caption appears.

TIP

What is the advantage of using the `figure` element?

Using the `figure` element has several benefits. First, the element improves accessibility for those with disabilities, because screen readers and other assistive technologies can identify the element and convey the relationship between the graphical element and its caption. Second, the `figure` element helps search engines determine the page's context and relevance, which can help improve your site's search rankings and visibility. Third, you can format the `figure` element and its contents more easily via CSS, as discussed in Chapter 7 and subsequent chapters. Fourth, your page is easier for yourself and your colleagues to read, understand, and maintain.

CHAPTER 5

Working with Links

Most web pages include links for navigating to other locations on the same site, navigating to pages on other sites, or taking other actions. In this chapter, you learn to create links that enable visitors to navigate among your website's pages, download files and create email messages, and play audio and video files.

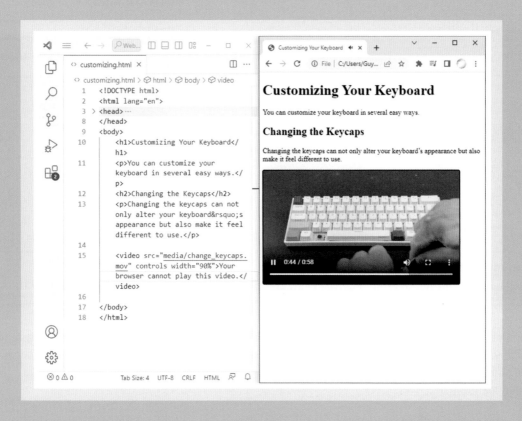

Grasp the Essentials of Links

Links are one of the defining features of the Web. A *link*, or more formally a *hyperlink*, is an element that you can click to go instantly to another web page or another website, or to take an action, such as starting an email message. Many links appear as underlined text, but you can also create links that appear as images or other graphical objects.

In this section, you learn which different types of links exist and identify their components. You also learn how absolute links differ from relative links and discover which type to use when in your web pages.

Understanding the Different Types of Links

HTML supports various kinds of links, enabling you to use links in different ways in your web pages.

The most straightforward type of link is a text-based link. By default, text-based links appear in blue font with an underline (A), but you can format them differently if you so choose. After you click a text hyperlink, its default formatting changes to scarlet font with an underline, enabling you to see which links you have followed before.

Image hyperlinks use an image as the display component for the link. Other object hyperlinks use other objects — for example, a shape — as the display component.

> Here is a text link. A
>
> B

When you move the pointer over a link, it changes from the standard arrow pointer to the link pointer (B), an upward-pointing right hand with the forefinger extended, facing away from you. This change of pointers enables you to recognize links easily no matter what form they take.

Identify the Components of a Link

A text link has the following components, as shown in the nearby illustration.

• The anchor element creates the link. The anchor element uses an opening `<a>` tag and a closing `</a>` tag.

Opening `<a>` tag   Link text

```
Click <a href="https://www.kybz.info/index.html">here</a>.
```

`href` keyword   Equal sign   Link destination   Closing `</a>` tag

- The `<a>` tag marks the start of the anchor. The `href` attribute, discussed next, appears within the `<a>` tag.

- The `href` attribute contains the hyperlink reference information, the destination to which the link points. After `href=`, the link's destination appears inside double quotation marks.

- The link text appears between the `<a>` tag and the `</a>` tag.

- The `</a>` tag ends the anchor.

Distinguish Absolute Links and Relative Links and Choose Between Them

HTML enables you to use either absolute links or relative links.

An *absolute link* includes the full address of the link's destination, including the prefix that tells the browser what protocol to use. For example, the following link is absolute:

```
href="https://www.kybz.info/index.html"
```

The URL specifies the protocol to use, HTTPS, and it gives the full path to the file containing the web page — in this case, the file `index.html`.

A *relative link* includes only the part of the address needed to get to the destination from the page that contains the link. If the destination is a web page in the same folder as the page that contains the link, the relative link can contain only the destination page's filename — for example:

```
href="page2.html"
```

If the destination file is in a different folder, the relative link must provide enough information to reach that folder. For example, the following link goes to a file called `logo14.png` located in the `images` folder on the same website:

```
href="images/logo14.png"
```

You will typically want to use relative links between pages on your own website, because the links will continue to work when you move your website from one location to another. For example, you might develop your website on your local computer and then move it to your web host, uploading the folders so that the relative positions of the pages remain the same.

Use absolute links when linking from your web pages to external websites. Because the addresses are complete, they are unaffected by your moving the website from your local computer to your web host.

Create a Link to a Web Page

M any links go to other web pages, either on the same website or on a different website. Most likely, you will need to link many of the pages on your website to each other so that visitors can navigate quickly and easily from page to page.

In this section, you create a link from text on one web page to another web page on the same website. To follow the example, the destination web page — the page to which the link leads — should already exist; if necessary, create the page before following the example.

Create a Link to a Web Page

1 In Visual Studio Code, either create and save a new file, or open the existing file you want to use.

2 Open the file in a browser window so you can see the results of the changes you make.

3 In Visual Studio Code, either click to place the insertion point or select existing text where you want to insert the link.

Note: The example shows selecting existing text and replacing it with the link.

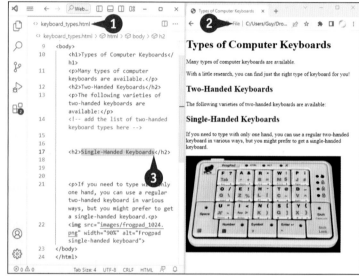

4 Type **a**.

The list of text expansions appears.

5 Click **a**.

A Visual Studio Code enters the `<a>` tag, including the `href` attribute, placing the insertion point between the double quotes:

```
<a href=""></a>
```

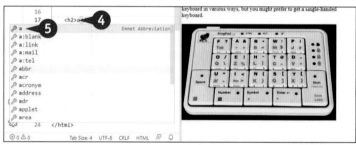

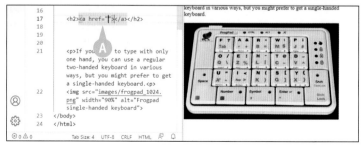

6 Type the first letter of the name of the destination page.

B A list of pages starting with that letter appears.

7 Click the destination page.

C The page's name appears as the destination for the hyperlink reference.

8 Press `Tab` (not shown).

The insertion point moves to between the `<a>` and `</a>` tags.

9 Type the text you want the link to display.

10 Click **Refresh** (⟳).

D The link appears.

In the example, the link has H2 formatting.

You can click the link to display the linked page.

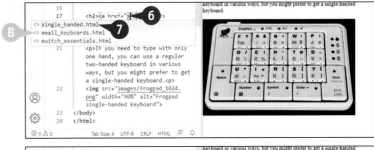

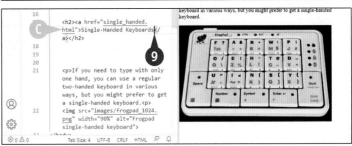

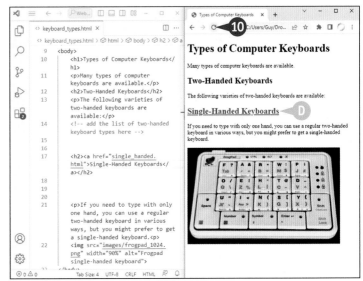

How do I create a link to a page on another website?
Start the `<a>` tag as explained in the main text, but then type or — preferably — paste the page's full URL, such as `www.stochastic.info/introduction.html`. Press `Tab` to move the insertion point to between the `<a>` and `</a>` tags, and then type the text you want the link to display.

How do I create a link that opens in a new tab?
Create the `<a>` tag as explained in the main text, but add the `target` attribute with the value `_blank` — for example,
`<a href="40board.html" target="_blank">`.

Create a Link to Elsewhere on the Same Web Page

HTML enables you to create a link to a different location in the same web page. This type of link is especially useful for longer web pages or pages that contain multiple distinct sections. For example, you might place links at the top of a page to sections further down the page; and in those sections, you might place links back to the top of the page.

To implement this kind of link, you place a named anchor at the appropriate point in the web page. The anchor consists of an anchor tag, `<a></a>`, that includes the `name` attribute.

Create a Link to Elsewhere on the Same Web Page

1 In Visual Studio Code, either create and save a new file, or open the existing file you want to use.

2 Open the file in a browser window so you can see the results of the changes you make.

3 In Visual Studio Code, click to place the insertion point where you want to insert an anchor at the top of the page.

Note: Press <kbd>Enter</kbd> to add blank lines as needed.

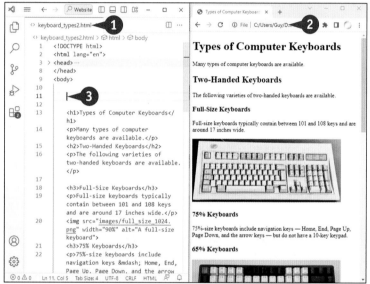

4 Type the opening `<a>` tag. Include the `name` attribute and assign the name **top** to it, like this:

`<a name="top">`

5 Type the closing `</a>` tag:

`</a>`

6 Scroll down to the end of the web page.

Note: You can move the insertion point to the end of the file by pressing <kbd>Control</kbd>+<kbd>End</kbd> on Windows or Linux. On the Mac, press <kbd>⌘</kbd>+<kbd>⬇</kbd>.

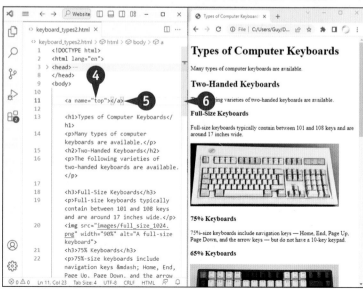

7 If you scrolled, click to place the insertion point where you want to insert the link for returning to the top of the page (not shown).

8 Type **p** to display the expansions list, and then click **p**.

A The opening <p> tag and closing </p> tag appear.

9 Type **a**.

The expansions list appears.

10 Click **a**.

B The opening <a> tag and closing </a> tag appear, together with the href attribute.

11 Type **#top** as the link destination.

12 Press Tab (not shown).

The insertion point moves to after the <a> tag.

13 Type the display text for the link — for example:

Return to top of page

14 Click **Refresh** (C).

The web page refreshes.

15 Scroll to the bottom of the page.

16 Click the link.

The top of the page appears.

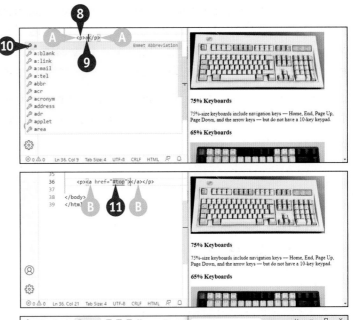

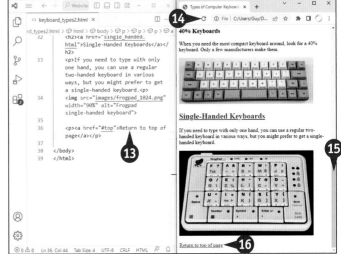

TIP

How do I create a link to a particular anchor on another web page?
To link to a particular place on another web page, place # and the anchor name at the end of the address. For example, to link to the anchor named start in the file named switch_types.html, you would use switch_types.html#start in a relative URL. In an absolute URL, you would include the full address — for example, https://www.kybz.info/switch_types.html#start.

Specify the ScreenTip for a Link

When a visitor holds the pointer over a link on a web page, the browser typically displays the link's destination in some user interface element — for example, on the status bar. This display is often helpful to the visitor if they know to look for it, but some of the displays are too discreet to attract attention.

To make sure a link get the user's notice, you can add further text to display when the pointer is over the link. To do so, you add the `title` attribute to the link's anchor tag and assign the display text to this attribute.

Specify the ScreenTip for a Link

1 In Visual Studio Code, open the existing file you want to use.

2 Open the file in a browser window.

3 Move the pointer over the link.

Ⓐ The link's destination appears.

4 In Visual Studio Code, click to place the insertion point in the link to which you want to add the display text.

Note: Position the insertion point between existing attributes rather than inside an attribute or its value.

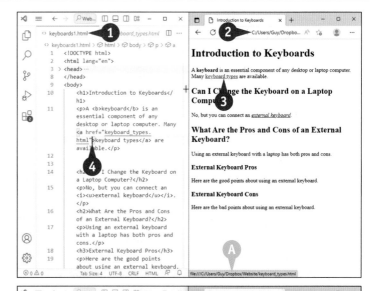

5 Type **title**, an equal sign, and the text you want to display, as in the following brief example:

```
title="Click here to display
information about different
keyboard types."
```

6 Click **Refresh** (⟳).

The browser refreshes the web page.

7 Move the pointer over the link.

Ⓑ The ScreenTip appears.

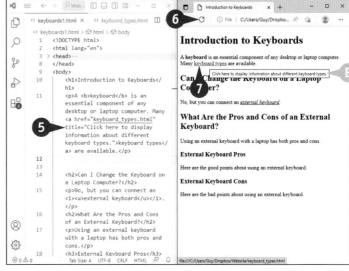

Redirect the Browser to a Different Page

Sometimes you may need to redirect visitors from one web page to another web page. For example, if you have two domains, one primary and one secondary, you may want to redirect visitors from the secondary domain to the primary domain.

Normally, you would perform this redirection at the server level, which is more efficient; consult your web host about how to configure redirection. But if circumstances prevent you redirecting via the server, you can implement redirection by using the `http-equiv` meta tag in the header of the appropriate web page, as explained here.

Redirect the Browser to a Different Page

1 In Visual Studio Code, either create and save a new file, or open the existing file you want to use.

A If you create a new file, enter any text needed to explain that the page will redirect the visitor.

2 Open the file in a browser window.

3 In Visual Studio Code, click to place the insertion point between tags in the header.

4 Type the `<meta />` tag, placing inside it `http-equiv="refresh"` to force a refresh, `content=1` to implement a one-second delay, and the `URL` parameter with the URL to which to redirect the browser — for example:

```
<meta http-equiv="refresh"
content=1; URL="https://www.
kybz.info"/>
```

5 Click **Refresh** (⟳).

The web page refreshes and then automatically redirects to the specified URL after one second.

Note: You can change the value of `content=` to vary the delay. For example, `content=0` specifies no delay.

Create a Link for Downloading a File

HTML enables you to create a link that downloads a file from your website to the visitor's computer. You create a download link by placing an anchor tag at the appropriate place in the web page, assigning the download file's path and name to the `href` attribute, and entering the display text for the link. Consider reminding visitors they can use the Save As command to save the file.

Locating the download files in a separate directory, such as a `download` directory, lets you manage them more easily than does strewing them amid your website's HTML documents.

Create a Link for Downloading a File

1 In Visual Studio Code, either create and save a new file, or open the existing file you want to use.

2 Open the file in a browser window.

3 In Visual Studio Code, click to place the insertion point for inserting the download link.

4 Type **a** and then click **a**.

Visual Studio Code enters the opening `<a>` tag, `href` attribute, and closing `</a>` tag.

5 Start typing the path to the file the link will download.

6 If the pop-up menu displays the file, click it. If not, finish typing the name.

7 Press Tab (not shown).

The insertion point moves to after the `>` of the opening `<a>` tag.

8 Type the display text for the link.

9 Click **Refresh** (C).

Ⓐ The link appears.

10 Right-click the link.

The contextual menu appears.

11 Issue the Save As command. For example, in Chrome, click **Save Link As**.

The Save As dialog box opens, and you can specify where to save the file.

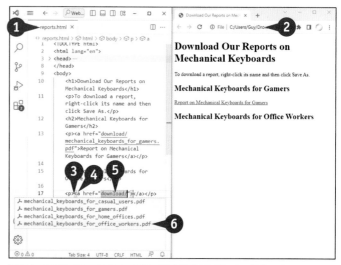

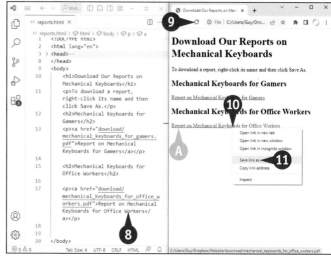

Create a Link That Starts an Email Message

HTML enables you to create a link that starts creating a new email message in the visitor's default email app. This capability is useful for various purposes, such as providing an easy way to let visitors email your company or organization. The link not only can enter the message's email address but also its subject line, which can be especially helpful for uses such as sales queries or customer-service issues.

To create a link that starts an email message, you specify the `mailto` protocol and provide the information you want entered in the message by default.

Create a Link That Starts an Email Message

1 In Visual Studio Code, open the file you want to use.

2 Open the file in a browser window.

3 In Visual Studio Code, click to place the insertion point where the link should go.

4 Type **a** and then click **a**.

Visual Studio Code enters the opening `<a>` tag, `href` attribute, and closing `</a>` tag.

5 Inside the double quotes, type **mailto:** followed by the email address — for example:

`<a href="mailto:help@kybz.info"`

6 If you want to include a subject line, type **?subject=** followed by the text — for example:

`<a href="mailto:help@kybz.info?subject=Customer Query">`

7 Press `Tab` (not shown).

The insertion point moves to after the `>` of the opening `<a>` tag.

8 Type the display text for the link.

9 Click **Refresh** (🔄).

Ⓐ The link appears.

10 Click the link.

Your default email app opens and creates a message with the details specified in the link.

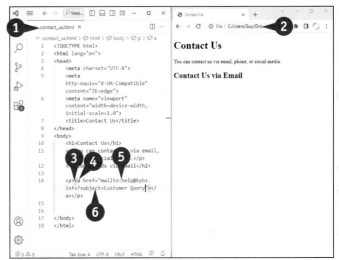

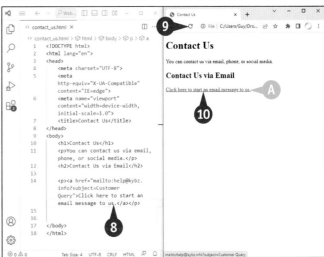

Create a Link from an Image

T ext links are the quintessential type of links on the Web, but HTML also enables you to create links from images and other objects. For example, you might add hyperlinks to thumbnail images that display the full-size images or related information. Because some visitors may not see the images, it is usually a good idea to provide an alternative link, such as a text link, as well as an image link.

In this example, you add a link to an image already placed in a web page. If you prefer, you can also first add the link and then insert the image.

Create a Link from an Image

1 In Visual Studio Code, open the file you want to use.

2 Open the file in a browser window so you can see the results of the changes you make.

3 In Visual Studio Code, click to place the insertion point before the `<img>` tag for the existing image you will turn into the link.

4 Type **a**.

The expansions list appears.

5 Click **a**.

Ⓐ The opening `<a>` tag and closing `</a>` tag appear, together with the `href` attribute.

6 Start typing the filename of the destination page.

Note: To link to an external site, type or paste the full URL.

The completions list appears.

7 Click the appropriate page.

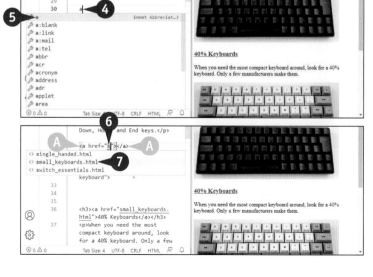

B The page name appears.

8 Drag across the closing `</a>` tag to select it.

9 Drag the selected tag to after the end of the `<img>` tag.

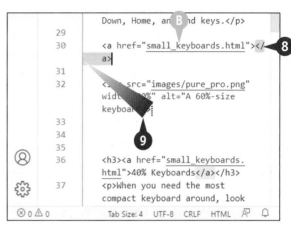

C The tag appears in its new location, now making the `<img>` tag the hyperlink's display element.

D Optionally, delete any extra space.

10 Click **Refresh** (🔄).

The web page refreshes.

11 Move the pointer over the image (not shown).

E The link pointer appears.

F The link destination appears.

You can click the link to display the destination page.

How can I make an image link more obvious to the visitor?
When the visitor moves the pointer over the image, the link pointer and the link address give them visual cues to the link's presence. To make the link more obvious, consider adding the `title` attribute to the link with text that will appear in a ScreenTip when the pointer is over the image. You can also simply add text nearby telling the reader to click the image.

Create Multiple Links from an Image

As well as letting you use an image as the clickable element for a link, HTML enables you to use different areas of the same image for different links. An image that handles multiple links like this is called an *image map*. You can define rectangular, circular, and polygonal areas.

This section demonstrates creating a straightforward image map whose left half and right half trigger different links. You can use any image, but normally you would pick an image that has identifiably different content in each area you will map to a different destination.

Create Multiple Links from an Image

Note: Before starting the steps, prepare the image you will use for the map. See the tip.

1. In Visual Studio Code, open the file you want to use.

2. Open the file in a browser window.

3. In Visual Studio Code, click to place the insertion point where you will insert the image.

4. Type **img**.

    The expansion list of img tags appears.

5. Click **img**.

    The `<img>` tag appears, including the src attribute and the alt attribute:

    `<img src="" alt="">`

6. With the insertion point between the double quotation marks after `src=`, start typing the source path.

    The expansion list appears.

7. Click the appropriate entry.

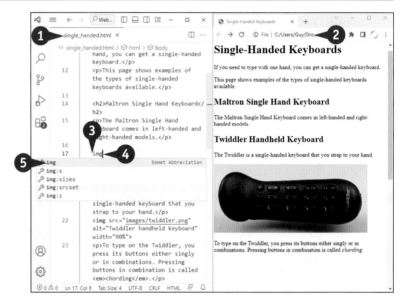

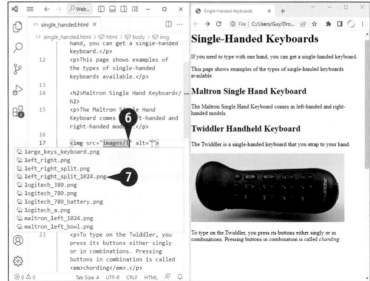

104

The image's filename appears.

8 Click between the double quotation marks after `alt=`, and then type the alternative text for the image.

9 Add the `width` attribute with a suitable value.

10 Add the `height` attribute with a suitable value.

11 Type the `usemap` attribute and assign to it the name you will give the map — for example:

`usemap="#kbmap"`

12 Click **Refresh** (⟳).

The web page refreshes.

13 Click to place the insertion point where you want to start the map definition, and then start typing **map**.

The expansions list appears.

14 Click **map**.

The opening `<map>` tag and closing `</map>` tag appear:

`<map name = "">` `</map>`

15 Inside the double quotation marks, type the map name you used in step **11**, without the #:

`<map name = "kbmap"></map>`

16 Press `Tab` to move the insertion point to just before the `</map>` tag, and then press `Enter` several times to add blank lines before the `</map>` tag.

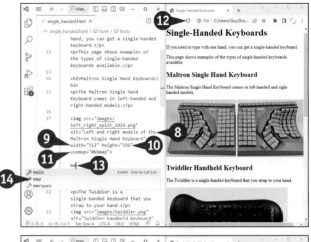

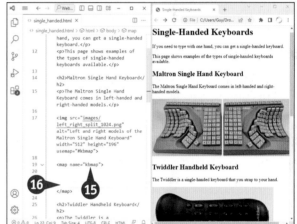

continued ▶

TIP

How do I prepare an image for use as an image map?
If necessary, create a resized version of the image, as discussed in Chapter 4. Then open that version in your graphics app and use the app's selection tools to work out the areas you will link. For a rectangle, you need four values: the horizontal and vertical coordinates of the upper-left corner and lower-right corner. For a circle, you need three values: the horizontal and vertical coordinates of the midpoint and then the radius. For a polygon, you need as many pairs of horizontal and vertical coordinates as needed to outline the shape, assuming straight lines linking the vertices.

W hen creating an image map, you use an `area` tag to define each clickable area. You use the shape attribute of the `area` tag to specify the area's shape: `shape="rect"` creates a rectangle, `shape="circle"` creates a circle, and `shape="poly"` creates a polygon. You use the `coords` attribute to specify the coordinates for the area. For example, `shape="rect"` `coords="257,0,512,196"` specifies a rectangle whose upper-left corner is 257 pixels from the left edge of the image and 0 pixels from the top, and whose lower-right corner is 512 pixels from the left edge and 196 pixels from the top.

Create Multiple Links from an Image (continued)

17 On the first blank line, type **area**.

The expansions list appears.

18 Click **area.r**.

Visual Studio Code inserts the basis of a tag for a rectangle area:

```
<area shape="rect" coords=
"" href="" alt ="">
```

19 With the insertion point between the double quotation marks after `coords`, type the pixel coordinates of the rectangle — for example:

```
coords="0,0,256,196"
```

20 Press Tab to move the insertion point to between the double quotation marks after `href`, and then enter the destination page by typing or by using the expansion list.

21 Press Tab to move the insertion point to between the double quotation marks after `alt`, and then type the alt text.

22 Press ➡ to move the insertion point past the closing double quotation marks, and then type the `title` attribute and text to assign to it.

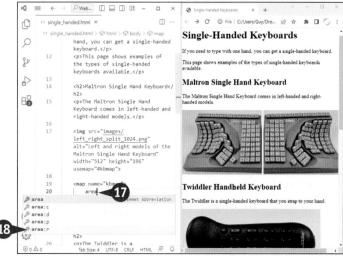

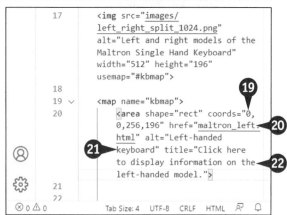

23 On the next blank line, repeat steps **17** to **22** to create the second area.

This time, specify the coordinates, destination, alternative text, and title for the second area.

The example uses the following code:

```
<area shape = "rect"
coords="257,0,512,196"
href="maltron_right.html"
alt="Right-handed keyboard"
title="Click here to
display information on the
right-handed model."
```

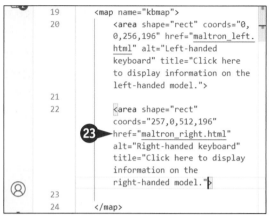

24 Click **Refresh** (⟳).

The web page refreshes.

25 Move the pointer over the image.

Ⓐ The ScreenTip for that area appears.

Ⓑ The destination URL for that area appears.

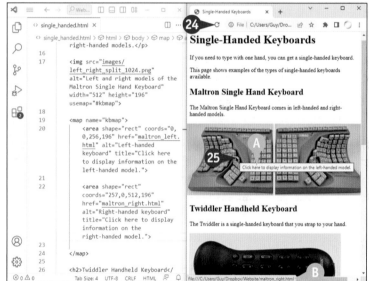

TIPS

Can I create overlapping areas in an image map?

No. If the areas overlap, only the areas defined before the overlap occurs will work.

Must I map the whole of the image?

No, you need not map the whole image. Simply define the areas you want to map, and leave the rest of the image unmapped.

Include an Audio File in a Web Page

HTML's `audio` element enables you to include an audio file in a web page. You can set the audio file to play automatically, though some browsers disable or mute autoplay. Generally, it is better to display controls that let the visitor control playback.

You can use three types of audio files: MP3 files, WAV files, and Ogg Vorbis files. Chrome, Firefox, Edge, and Opera support all three types; Safari does not support Ogg Vorbis. MP3 files are generally the best choice, because MP3 is a compressed format, whereas WAV is not.

Link an Audio File

1 In Visual Studio Code, open the file you want to use.

2 Open the file in a browser window.

3 In Visual Studio Code, click to position the insertion point where you want to place the audio file.

4 Type **au**.

The expansions list opens.

5 Click **audio**.

A The opening `<audio>` tag and closing `</audio>` tag appear, with the `src` attribute between them.

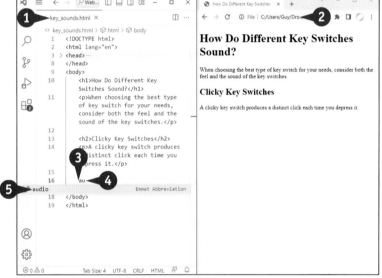

6 With the insertion point between the double quotation marks after `src=`, start typing the path to the audio file.

The expansions list appears.

7 Click the file.

The filename appears.

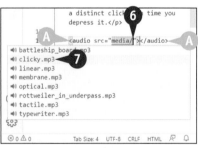

8 Press ➡ to move the insertion point past the closing double quotation marks, and then type a space (not shown).

9 Type **controls**.

10 Click before the `</audio>` tag.

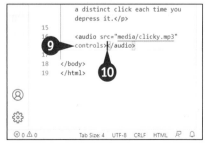

108

11 Type text for the browser to display if it cannot play the audio file — for example, *Your browser cannot play this audio.*

Note: Text you type between the opening `<audio>` tag and the closing `</audio>` tag appears only if the browser cannot play the audio file.

12 Click **Refresh** (⟳).

B The audio control appears if the browser can play the audio.

13 Click **Play** (▶).

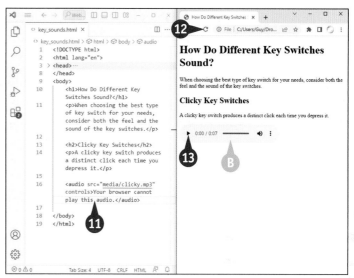

The audio starts playing.

C You can click **Volume** (◀)) to adjust the volume.

Note: The audio control has a different appearance in different browsers, but its icons are generally easy to understand.

Note: To make the audio play automatically, add the `autoplay` attribute to the opening `<audio>` tag — for example, `<audio src="media.tactile.mp3" autoplay controls>`. Omit the `controls` attribute if you do not want to display the controls.

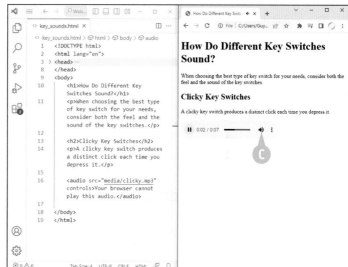

TIP

Should I use autoplay for audio?

Needs and circumstances vary, but generally it is best to use autoplay for audio only if the visitor is expecting audio to play on the page — for example, if they have followed a link to listen to a song. Otherwise, the experience of audio blaring unexpectedly and perhaps indiscreetly provokes few positive reactions among visitors.

Remember also that some browsers suppress autoplay because it is so often unwelcome. Given this, always include the `controls` attribute to display the playback controls so that the visitor can play the audio, pause it, and adjust the volume.

Include a Video File in a Web Page

HTML's `video` element allows you to include a video file in a web page. As with audio, you can set the video file to play automatically, but some browsers disable or mute autoplay. If you choose to use autoplay for a video, you may want to mute playback. This way, you can make the video's presence, and perhaps its appeal, clear to the visitor without blasting unwanted audio at them.

Include a Video File in a Web Page

1 In Visual Studio Code, open the file you want to use.

2 Open the file in a browser window.

3 In Visual Studio Code, click to position the insertion point where you want to place the video file.

4 Type **vi**.

The expansions list opens.

5 Click **video**.

Ⓐ The opening `<video>` tag and closing `</video>` tag appear, with the `src` attribute between them.

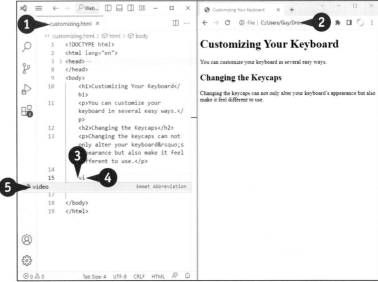

6 With the insertion point between the double quotation marks after `src=`, start typing the path to the video file.

The expansions list appears.

7 Click the file.

The filename appears.

8 Press ➡ to move the insertion point past the closing double quotation marks, and then type a space (not shown).

9 Type **controls**.

10 Type a space, **width=**, and the width — for example:

`width="90%"`

11 Click before the `</video>` tag.

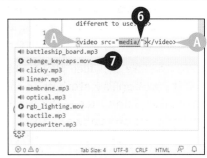

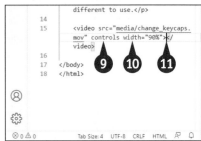

12 Type text for the browser to display if it cannot play the video file — for example, *Your browser cannot play this video*.

Note: Text you type between the opening `<video>` tag and the closing `</audio>` tag appears only if the browser cannot play the video file.

13 Click **Refresh** (⟳).

B The video appears if the browser can play it.

14 Click **Play** (▶).

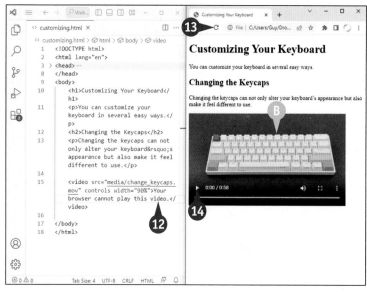

The audio starts playing.

C You can click **Volume** (◀)) to adjust the volume.

D You can click **Full Screen** (such as ▣ or ▣) to expand the video to full screen.

Note: The video control has a different appearance in different browsers, but its icons are generally easy to understand.

Note: To make the video play automatically, add the `autoplay` attribute to the opening `<video>` tag — for example, `<video src="intro1.mov" autoplay controls>`. Omit the `controls` attribute if you do not want to display the controls.

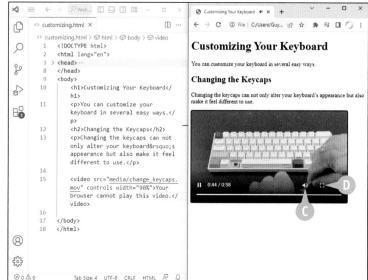

TIP

What movie formats can I use?
HTML directly supports the MP4 format, also known as MPEG-4; the Ogg video format; and the WebM format. MP4 has near-universal compatibility, so it is a good choice for general use; it is also the format that YouTube recommends.

Embed a YouTube Video in a Web Page

Instead of placing a video file hosted on your own website on one of your web pages, you can embed a video file hosted on YouTube on the web page. To embed a YouTube video, you place an `iframe` element on the web page and set its source to the appropriate URL on YouTube.

If the video is your own, start by uploading it to your YouTube account, setting its details, and publishing it. If the video is someone else's, display it on YouTube. Either way, get the video's YouTube ID, as explained in the tip.

Embed a YouTube Video in a Web Page

1 In Visual Studio Code, open the file you want to use.

2 Open the file in a browser window.

3 In Visual Studio Code, click to place the insertion point where you want to embed the video.

4 Type **i**.

The expansions list appears.

5 Click **iframe**.

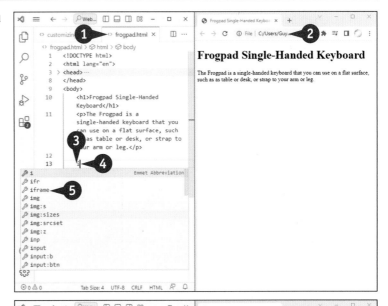

Visual Studio Code inserts the opening `<iframe>` tag, the `src` attribute and `frameborder` attribute, and the closing `</iframe>` tag.

6 With the insertion point between the double quotation marks after `src=`, enter the YouTube URL for embedding the video. This consists of the YouTube domain, the `embed` folder, and the video's YouTube ID — for example:

`www.youtube.com/embed/`
`9CzCDziLsro`

7 Click **Refresh** (C).

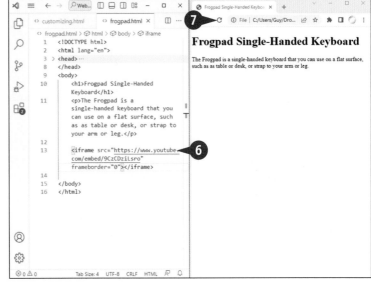

🅐 The embedded video appears.

8 Press → to move the insertion point to after the closing double quotation marks, and then type a space (not shown).

9 Type **width=** and a suitable width in pixels, followed by a space, **height=**, and a suitable height in pixels — for example:

width="500" height="375"

10 Click **Refresh** (🔄).

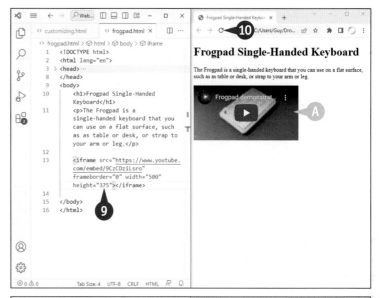

🅑 The video appears at the size you specified.

11 Click **Play** (▶) (not shown).

The video plays.

🅒 You can click **Volume** (🔊) to adjust the volume.

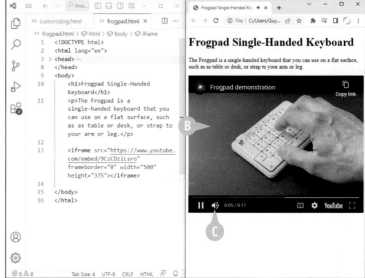

TIP

Where do I find the video's YouTube ID?
If you have just published the video, look in the Video Link box in the Video Published dialog box. If you published the video a while ago, go to the Channel Content page for your YouTube account, move the pointer over the video, and then click **Details** (✏) to display the Video Details screen; then look at the Video Link readout on the right side. If the video is not yours, display the video for playing, click the address box, and read the part of the URL after v=. For example, in the URL www.youtube.com/watch?v=9CzCDziLsro, the video's ID is 9CzCDziLsro.

CHAPTER 6

Creating Lists and Tables

HTML enables you to create lists, such as bulleted and numbered lists, and tables that consist of rows and columns. Lists are great for presenting discrete topics or step-by-step instructions, whereas tables let you not only lay out information in a clear and logical manner, using borders and gridlines to delineate the table visually, but also implement special layout effects.

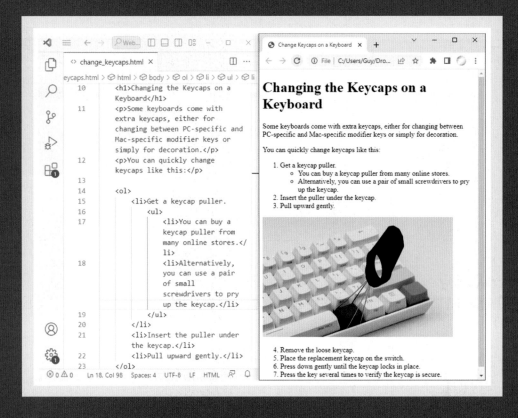

Grasp the Different Types of Lists

When you need to present itemized information on a web page, you can use a list. HTML enables you to create three types of lists — numbered lists, bulleted lists, and definition lists — and to create complex lists by nesting those lists with each other. For example, you might create a bulleted sublist within a numbered list, or you might create a numbered sublist using different numbering within another numbered list.

This section explains the list types and illustrates their differences. The following four sections show you how to create numbered lists, bulleted lists, definition lists, and nested lists.

Numbered Lists

In HTML, a numbered list is called an *ordered list*, because the items appear in a specific order, such as a list of numbered steps to accomplish a task.

To start a numbered list, you enter the opening `<ol>` tag; to end the list, you enter the closing `</ol>` tag:

```
<ol>
</ol>
```

Between these tags, you enter each list item, beginning with the opening `<li>` tag and ending with the closing `</li>` tag, with the item's text between them. For example, the following code produces the three-step numbered list shown in the nearby illustration.

```
<ol>
    <li>Unplug your computer from power.</li>
```

Ordered List

1. Unplug your computer from power.
2. Connect the keyboard to the USB port.
3. Connect the computer to power again.

```
    <li>Connect the keyboard to the USB port.</li>
    <li>Connect the computer to power again.</li>
</ol>
```

The browser automatically displays the numbers for the items, starting with 1, unless you specify a different number by including the `start` attribute in the `<ol>` tag — for example, `<ol start="5">`. You can specify a different numbering type, such as a-b-c or i-ii-iii, by including the `type` attribute in the `<ol>` tag — for example, `<ol type="a">` for lowercase a-b-c numbering.

Bulleted Lists

In HTML, a bulleted list is called an *unordered list*, since the items have no numerical order.

To start a bulleted list, you enter the opening `<ul>` tag; to end the list, you enter the closing `</ul>` tag:

```
<ul>
</ul>
```

Between these tags, you enter each list item, again beginning with the opening `<li>` tag and ending with the closing `</li>` tag, with the item's text between them. For example, the following code creates the four-bullet list shown in the nearby illustration:

```
<ul>
    <li>Clicky</li>
    <li>Tactile</li>
    <li>Linear</li>
    <li>Optical</li>
</ul>
```

Unordered List

- Clicky
- Tactile
- Linear
- Optical

The browser automatically displays the bullet point for each item, using a default bullet, a solid circle. You can specify a different bullet by including the `type` attribute in the `<ul>` tag — for example, `type="square"` for filled-in squares.

Definition Lists

A *definition list* is a list that consists of pairs of items, such as a term and its definition in a glossary or lexicon.

To start a definition list, you enter the opening `<dl>` tag; to end the list, you enter the closing `</dl>` tag:

```
<dl>
</dl>
```

Between these tags, you enter each pair of terms — first the "definition term" — the term to be defined — between an opening `<dt>` tag and a closing `</dt>` tag and second the "definition description" between an opening `<dd>` tag and a closing `</dd>` tag. For example, the following code creates the two-term list shown in the nearby illustration:

```
<dl>
    <dt>tenkey</dt>
    <dd>The section of a computer keyboard that contains the number keys and
arrow keys</dd>
    <dt>tenkeyless</dt>
    <dd>Of a keyboard, not having a tenkey section</dd>
</dl>
```

Definition List

tenkey
> The section of a computer keyboard that contains the number keys and arrow keys

tenkeyless
> Of a keyboard, not having a tenkey section

Nested Lists

When you need a complex list, you can nest any of the three kinds of list within any other list. For example, the following code creates the numbered list with bulleted subitems shown in the nearby illustration.

```
<ol>
    <li>Unplug your computer
from power.</li>
    <li>Connect the keyboard
to the USB port.
        <ul type="square">
            <li>Use a USB adapter if necessary.</li>
            <li>Use a USB port on the computer if possible.</li>
        </ul>
    </li>
    <li>Connect the computer to power again.</li>
</ol>
```

Nested List

1. Unplug your computer from power.
2. Connect the keyboard to the USB port.
   - Use a USB adapter if necessary.
   - Use a USB port on the computer if possible.
3. Connect the computer to power again.

Create a Numbered List

HTML enables you to create numbered lists, which HTML calls *ordered lists*, by using the `ol` element. You start the list with the opening `<ol>` tag and end it with the closing `</ol>` tag. Between these tags, you create a list item, `li`, element for each numbered item, placing the item's text between an opening `<li>` tag and a closing `</li>` tag.

The browser automatically starts numbering at the first item in the list. You can change the starting number for a list manually. You can also use different types of numbering, as explained in the tip.

Create a Numbered List

1 In Visual Studio Code, open the file in which you want to create a numbered list.

2 Open the file in a browser window.

3 In Visual Studio Code, click to place the insertion point where you want to start the list.

4 Type **o**.

The expansions list appears.

5 Click **ol.**

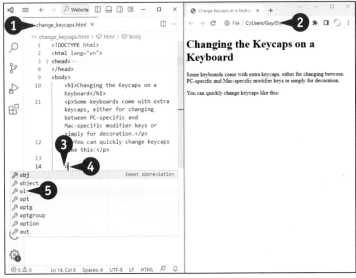

A Visual Studio Code inserts the opening `<ol>` tag and closing `</ol>` tag, placing the insertion point between them.

6 Press Enter to add a blank line between the codes (not shown).

7 Click to place the insertion point on the blank line.

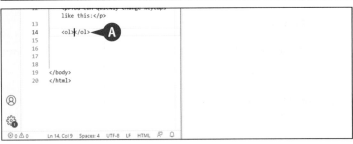

8 Type **li**, and then click **li** on the expansions list.

B Visual Studio Code inserts the opening `<li>` tag and closing `</li>` tag, placing the insertion point between them.

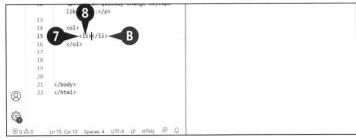

9 Type the text for the list item.

10 Press <kbd>Enter</kbd>, and then repeat steps **8** and **9** to add other list items.

11 Click **Refresh** (⟳).

The web page refreshes.

C The numbered list appears.

12 Click to place the insertion point on the line after the closing `</ol>` tag.

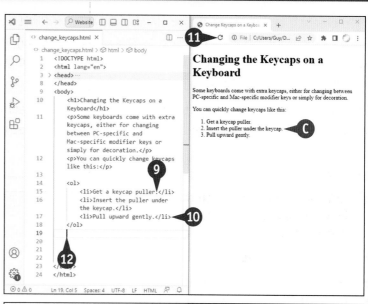

13 Insert an `img` element by using the techniques you learned in Chapter 4.

14 After the closing `>` of the `<img>` tag, repeat steps **4** to **9** to insert another `ol` element. Add the `start=` attribute to the opening `<ol>` tag and specify the value needed for the next list item — for example:

`<ol start="4">`

15 Click **Refresh** (⟳).

The web page refreshes.

D The image appears.

E The second numbered list appears, starting at the number you specified.

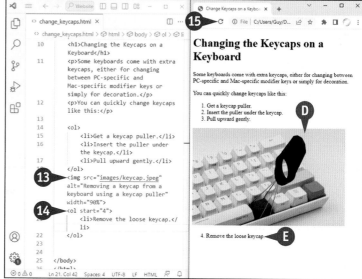

TIP

What numbering types can I use for an ordered list?
HTML lets you use five types of numbering in ordered lists by including the `type` attribute with the appropriate keyword in the opening `<ol>` tag. Use `type="1"` or omit the `type` argument to create decimal numbering: 1, 2, 3. Use `type="a"` for lowercase letter numbering: a, b, c. Use `type="A"` for uppercase letter numbering: A, B, C. Use `type="i"` for lowercase Roman numerals: i, ii, iii. Use `type="I"` for uppercase Roman numerals: I, II, III.

Create a Bulleted List

To create a bulleted list, which HTML calls an *unordered list*, you use the `ul` element. You start the list by entering the opening `<ul>` tag and end it with the closing `</ul>` tag. Between these tags, you create a list item, `li`, element for each bulleted paragraph. You place the list item's text between an opening `<li>` tag and a closing `</li>` tag.

The browser automatically displays a default bullet, a "disc" or filled-in circle, before each `li` element. You can specify a different type of bullet, as explained in the tip.

Create a Bulleted List

1 In Visual Studio Code, open the file in which you want to create the bulleted list.

2 Open the file in a browser window.

3 In Visual Studio Code, click to place the insertion point where you want to start the bulleted list.

4 Type **u**.

The expansions list appears.

5 Click **ul**.

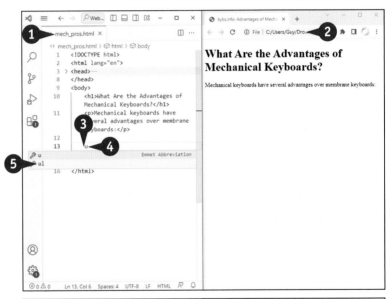

A Visual Studio Code inserts the opening `<ul>` tag and closing `</ul>` tag, placing the insertion point between them.

6 Press Enter to add a blank line between the codes (not shown).

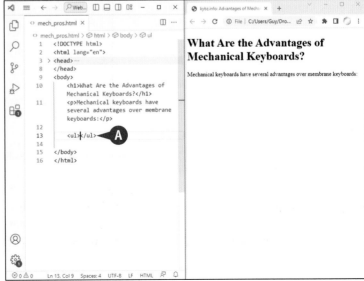

7 Click to place the insertion point on the blank line.

8 Type **li**, and then click **li** on the expansions list.

B Visual Studio Code inserts the opening `<li>` tag and closing `</li>` tag, placing the insertion point between them.

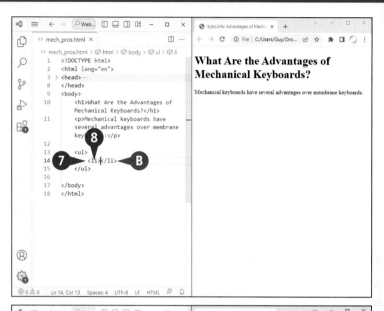

9 Type the text for the list item.

10 Press Enter, and then repeat steps **8** and **9** to add other list items.

11 Click **Refresh** (⟳).

The web page refreshes.

C The bulleted list appears.

TIP

How do I specify different types of bullets?

HTML enables you to use three types of bullets in an unordered list: disc, the default, a filled-in circle; circle, an empty circle; and square, a filled-in square. To specify the bullet type, include the `type` attribute in the opening `<ul>` tag: `<ul type="disc">`, `<ul type="circle">`, or `<ul type="square">`. Because disc is the default type, you can omit the `type` attribute if you want disc bullets.

Create a Definition List

HTML's definition list enables you to present a list of terms along with their definitions or explanations. You start the list by entering the opening `<dl>` tag and end it with the closing `</dl>` tag. Between these tags, you enter each pair of a definition term and its definition description. The definition term goes between an opening `<dt>` tag and a closing `</dt>` tag, while the definition description goes between an opening `<dd>` tag and a closing `</dd>` tag.

Create a Definition List

1 In Visual Studio Code, open the file in which you want to create the definition list.

2 Open the file in a browser window.

3 In Visual Studio Code, click to place the insertion point where you want to start the definition list.

4 Type **d**.

The expansions list appears.

5 Click **dl**.

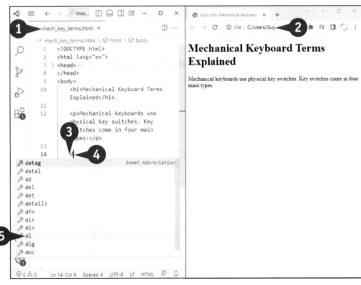

A Visual Studio Code inserts the opening `<dl>` tag and closing `</dl>` tag, placing the insertion point between them.

6 Press Enter twice to add two blank lines between the codes (not shown).

7 Click to place the insertion point on the first blank line.

8 Type **dt**, and then click **dt** on the expansions list.

B Visual Studio Code inserts the opening `<dt>` tag and closing `</dt>` tag, placing the insertion point between them.

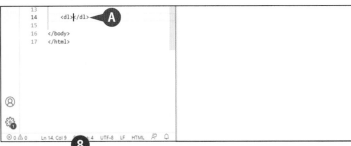

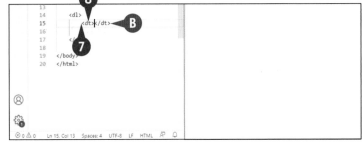

9 Type the text for the definition term.

10 Type **dd**, and then click **dd** on the expansions list.

Visual Studio Code inserts the opening `<dd>` tag and closing `</dd>` tag, placing the insertion point between them.

11 Type the text of the definition description.

12 Click **Refresh** (🔄).

The web page refreshes.

C The definition list appears.

13 Click before the closing `</dd>` tag.

14 Repeat steps **8** to **11** to enter further definition pairs.

15 Click **Refresh** (🔄).

The web page refreshes.

D The new definition pairs appear in the list.

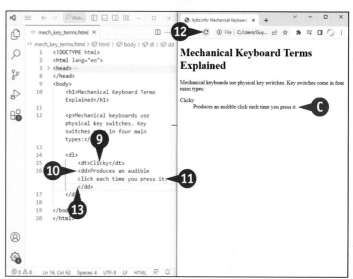

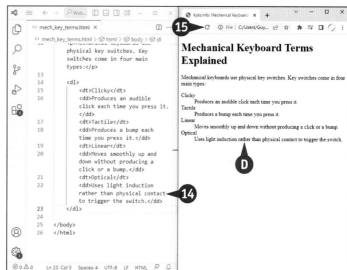

TIP

How can I list two separate definition description items for the same definition term?
Just use two dd elements in the appropriate place in the definition list. For example:

```
<dl>
    <dt>Course</dt>
    <dd>Coding 101</dd>
    <dt>Faculty</dt>
    <dd>Bill Sykes</dd>
    <dd>Dianne Opta</dd>
</dl>
```

Nest One List Inside Another List

HTML allows you to nest any list type within any list type. For example, you can nest a bulleted list inside a numbered list, inside a definition list, or inside another bulleted list. You can nest lists several levels deep if you need to. Nesting enables you to create complex lists to convey information clearly in your web pages.

The browser indicates the list hierarchy by adding indentation for each level of nesting. For a nested bulleted list, the browser shows a circle bullet rather than the disc bullet by default. This helps make nested bulleted lists easier to identify visually.

Nest One List Inside Another List

1 In Visual Studio Code, open the file in which you want to create the complex list.

2 Open the file in a browser window.

3 In Visual Studio Code, create the outermost list using the techniques explained earlier in this chapter.

The example uses a numbered list as the outermost list.

4 Click to place the insertion point before the closing `</li>` tag of the list item after which you want to place the nested list.

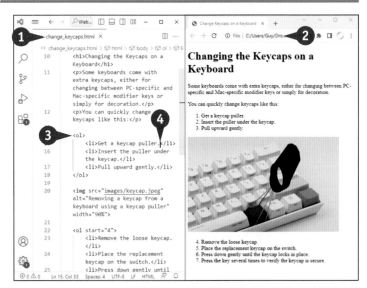

5 Press Enter to create a blank line (not shown).

6 Type the two-letter identifier for the type of list you want to nest — **ul**, **ol**, or **dl** — and then click the appropriate item on the expansions list.

This example uses **ul** to nest a bulleted list within the numbered list.

A Visual Studio Code inserts the opening tag and closing tag for the element, placing the insertion point between them.

7 Press Enter to create a blank line (not shown).

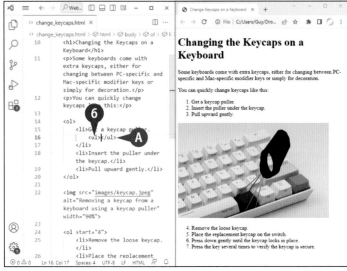

8 Type **li** and then click **li** on the expansions list.

Visual Studio Code inserts the opening `<li>` tag and closing `</li>` tag, placing the insertion point between them.

9 Type the first list item.

10 Repeat steps **8** and **9** to add further list items, as needed.

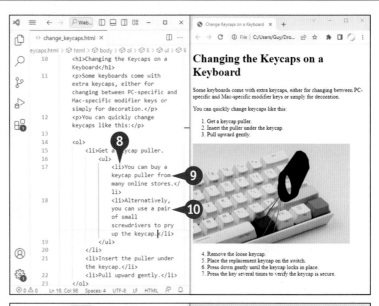

11 Click **Refresh** (⟳).

The web page refreshes.

B The nested list appears.

The indent indicates that the nested list is subordinate to the outer list.

C By default, the browser displays a circle for a nested bulleted list. You can specify a disc by using `<ul type="disc">` or a square by using `<ul type="square">`.

TIP

Do I need to indent the HTML code for nested lists?
No. Any indents in HTML code are for the convenience of humans rather than computers. Indenting a nested list simply makes your HTML easier to read because you can more easily see where the nested elements start and end. Because of this increase in readability, indenting code is generally recommended as good practice. Visual Studio Code helps further by displaying vertical lines to indicate the extent of lists and list items.

Learn the HTML for Tables

HTML enables you to create tables that consist of cells formed by the intersection of rows and columns. Tables can be great for laying out complex information clearly and logically in your web pages.

In this section, you learn what elements HTML uses for tables and how to arrange those elements to create tables. In the following sections, you put this knowledge into effect, creating tables and formatting them.

Identify the Components of a Table

A table consists of four main elements, identified in the nearby illustration and explained in the following list:

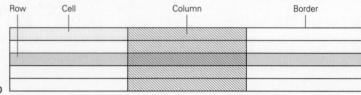

- **Row.** A row is a horizontal line of cells. The top row of the table is often a header row.

- **Cell.** A cell is one of the rectangles that makes up a table. A cell is formed by the intersection of a row and a column.

- **Column.** A column is a vertical stack of cells.

- **Border.** The border is the rectangle around the outside of each cell and around the outside of the table. The border is invisible unless you format it to be visible.

Understanding the HTML Elements for a Table

To create a table, you place a table element on the page. The table element consists of an opening `<table>` tag and a closing `</table>` tag, like this:

```
<table>
</table>
```

The table element acts as a container for the table's rows. To create a row, you place a tr element inside the table element, like this:

```
<table>
    <tr>
    </tr>
</table>
```

A tr element contains the cells that appear in that row. These cells can be either *table headers*, cells you would typically use for displaying information such as titles, or *table data*, regular cells for nontitle text or other content.

Table headers use the th element, which has an opening `<th>` tag and a closing `</th>` tag. The following example contains just a two-cell row of table headers:

```
<table>
    <tr>
        <th>Header 1</th>
        <th>Header 2</th>
    </tr>
</table>
```

Table data cells use the `td` element, which has an opening `<td>` tag and a closing `</td>` tag. Continuing the example, the following code produces a two-row, two-column table with one row of table headers and one row of table data:

```
<table>
    <tr>
        <th>Header 1</th>
        <th>Header 2</th>
    </tr>
    <tr>
        <td>Data 1</td>
        <td>Data 2</td>
    </tr>
</table>
```

Displayed in a browser, this table appears without a border by default, which makes it hard to determine the cell boundaries and the extent of the table, as you can see in the nearby illustration.

Adding a border to the `<table>` tag, as in the following example, places a border around the outside of the table, as shown nearby. Normally, you would use internal or external CSS to apply suitable borders to the table, as discussed in Chapter 9; but this example uses an inline style for convenience:

```
<table style="border: 1px solid black;">
```

Adding a border to each of the table header cells and table data cells, as in the following example, enables you to see where the cells end:

```
<table style="border: 1px solid black;">
    <tr>
        <th style="border: 1px solid blue;">Header
1</th>
        <th style="border: 1px solid blue;">Header
2</th>
    </tr>
    <tr>
        <td style="border: 1px solid blue;">Data
1</td>
        <td style="border: 1px solid blue;">Data
2</td>
    </tr>
</table>
```

Create a Table

To create a table in HTML, you insert a `table` element at the appropriate point in the web page. You then insert a table row, `tr`, element to create each row in the table before populating the rows with the table header, `th`, and table data, `td`, elements that form the cells. The number of `th` elements or `td` elements in a row controls how many columns it contains.

Create a Table

1. In Visual Studio Code, open the file in which you want to create the table.

2. Open the file in a browser window.

3. In Visual Studio Code, click to place the insertion point where you want to insert the table.

4. Type **t.**

   The expansions list appears.

5. Click **table**.

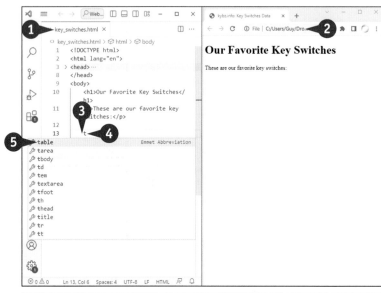

Visual Studio Code inserts the opening `<table>` tag and closing `</table>` tag, placing the insertion point between them.

6. Press Enter to add a blank line (not shown).

7. Type **tr**, and then click **tr** on the expansions list.

   Visual Studio Code inserts the opening `<tr>` tag and the closing `</tr>` tag, placing the insertion point between them.

8. Press Enter to add a blank line (not shown).

9. Type **th**, and then click **th** on the expansions list.

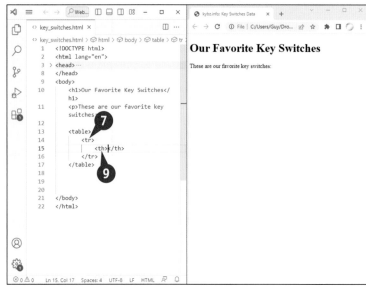

Visual Studio Code inserts the opening `<th>` tag and the closing `</th>` tag, placing the insertion point between them.

10 Type the text for the first table header.

11 Click after the closing `</th>` tag, and then follow steps **8** to **10** to add further table header cells, as needed.

12 Click **Refresh** (⟳).

The web page refreshes.

Ⓐ The table headers appear.

13 Click after the closing `</tr>` tag and press Enter to create a blank line.

14 Follow steps **7** to **11** to create a new row and populate it. This time, type **td** to create table data cells rather than table header cells.

15 Click **Refresh** (⟳).

The web page refreshes.

Ⓑ The table cells appear.

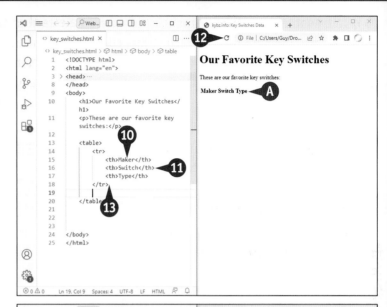

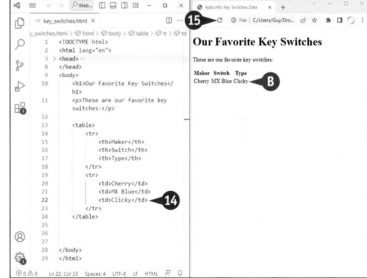

TIP

How can I add a border to the table?

You can quickly add a border by adding the `style` attribute to the opening `<table>` tag. For example, changing the tag to `<table style="border: 1px solid black;">` produces a 1-pixel solid black border around the table. For more information, see the section "Format Table Borders," later in this chapter.

Add Rows or Columns to a Table

HTML enables you to add rows or columns to a table you have inserted in a web page. To add a row, you create a new `tr` element at the appropriate place in the table and then populate it with either table header cells or table data cells. To add a column, you add table header cells or table data cells at the appropriate point in each existing row.

Add Rows or Columns to a Table

1 In Visual Studio Code, open the file containing the table to which you want to add rows or columns.

2 Open the file in a browser window.

3 In Visual Studio Code, click to place the insertion point where you want to insert a row — before the first opening `<tr>` tag, between a closing `</tr>` tag and the next opening `<tr>` tag, or after the last closing `</tr>` tag.

The example illustrates adding a new row after the last existing row.

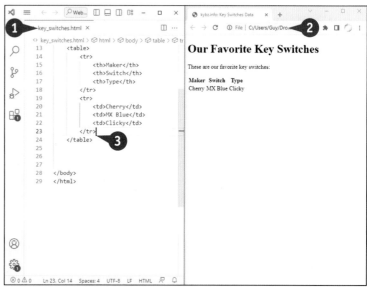

4 Press `Enter` to create a blank line (not shown).

5 Type **tr**, and then click **tr** on the expansions list.

Visual Studio Code inserts the opening `<tr>` tag and the closing `</tr>` tag, placing the insertion point between them.

6 Press `Enter` to add a blank line (not shown).

7 Type **td** and press `Tab` to enter the `<td>` tag and `</td>` tag, and then type the text contents between them.

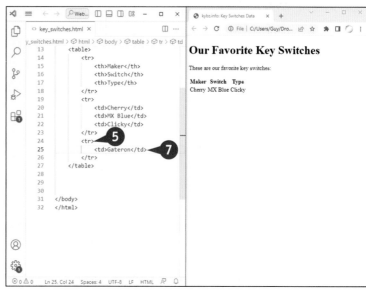

8 On subsequent lines, enter the other cells for the row.

9 Click **Refresh** (↻).

The web page refreshes.

A The new row of cells appears in the table.

10 Click at the point in the first row where you want to add a column — before the first opening `<th>` or `<td>` tag, between a closing `</th>` or `</td>` tag and the next opening `<th>` or `<td>` tag, or after the last closing `</th>` or `</td>` tag.

The example adds a new column after the last existing column.

11 Press Enter to create a blank line, as needed, and then enter the tags and contents for the new cell on that line.

12 Repeat step **11** to enter the new cell for each other row.

13 Click **Refresh** (↻).

The web page refreshes.

B The new column appears.

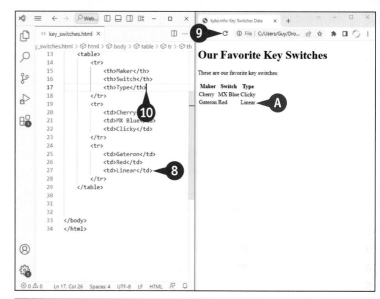

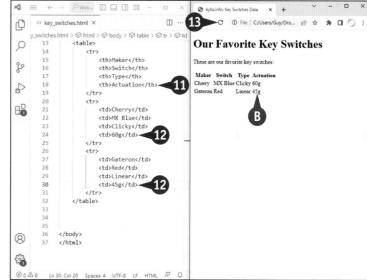

TIP

What happens if the rows contain different numbers of cells?
HTML handles the table layout as elegantly as possible, leaving blank space in the column where the cell is missing. The missing cell or cells will be at the right end of the row. For example, if the first row of a table contains five cells but the second row contains only three cells, the last two columns in the second row will be blank.

Specify Table Width and Column Width

HTML enables you to specify table width by including the `style` attribute in the opening `<table>` tag and specifying the width as part of the style. If you do not specify the width, the browser displays the table as compactly as possible, which can help tables fit on smaller screens. You can specify either a fixed measurement or a measurement based on the available space.

Similarly, you can control column width by including the `style` attribute in the opening `<th>` tag or `<td>` tag for a cell in the column and specifying the width as part of the style.

Specify Table Width and Column Width

Note: Normally, you would use internal or external CSS to control table width and column width, as discussed in Chapter 9. This example uses inline styles for simplicity.

1. In Visual Studio Code, open the file containing the table you want to affect.

2. Open the file in a browser window.

Ⓐ The browser displays the table compactly.

3. In Visual Studio Code, click to place the insertion point before the closing > in the opening `<table>` tag.

4. Type a space and then **style="width:100%"**.

Note: Specifying `width:100%` makes the table take up 100 percent of the width of the window.

5. Click **Refresh** (⟳).

   The web page refreshes.

Ⓑ The table now takes up the full width of the window.

6. In Visual Studio Code, click to place the insertion point before the closing > of the opening `<th>` tag or `<td>` tag of a cell in the column whose size you want to set.

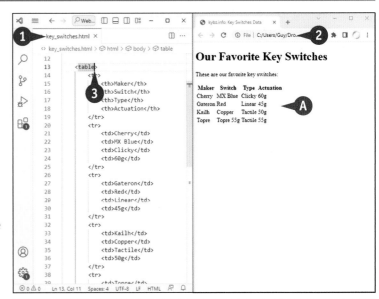

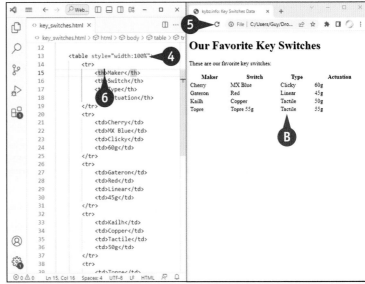

7 Type a space followed by **style=width"**, the width you want to use, and then **"**.

For example, type `style= "width:15%"` to make the column containing the cell occupy 15 percent of the width of the table.

8 Click **Refresh** (⟳).

The web page refreshes.

C The width of the column you changed now occupies the amount of space you specified.

9 Add the `style` attribute to a cell in each other column whose width you want to set.

10 Click **Refresh** (⟳).

The web page refreshes.

The column width change as specified.

TIPS

What happens if I specify different widths for multiple cells in the same column?
The browser implements the widest width specified, so all the cells in the column receive that width.

How do I control the height of a row?
Include the `style` attribute in the opening `<tr>` tag for the row and specify the height in pixels. For example, `<tr style="height:225px">` assigns the height 225 pixels to the row.

Format Table Borders

By default, HTML tables appear with invisible borders, which can be helpful for achieving layout effects. But for many tables, you will likely want to have visible borders. To get them, you need to tell HTML how to format the borders. You do this by adding the `style` attribute to the opening tag for the appropriate part of the table, such as the `table` element itself or a `td` element, and specifying the style formatting to use. You can either display separate borders for the table itself and for individual cells or collapse table and cell borders to a single line.

Format Table Borders

Note: Normally, you would use CSS to format table borders, as discussed in Chapter 9. This example uses inline styles for simplicity.

1. In Visual Studio Code, open the file containing the table whose borders you want to format.

2. Open the file in a browser window.

A. The browser displays the table with no borders by default.

3. In Visual Studio Code, click to place the insertion point before the closing > in the opening <table> tag.

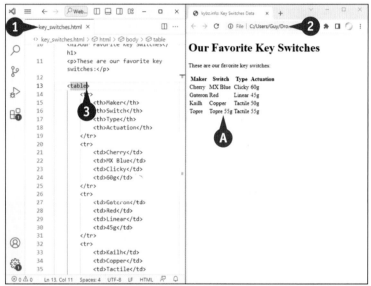

4. Type a space, followed by `style=` and the formatting inside double quotation marks, such as `"border:1px solid blue"`, so the tag looks like this:

`<table style="border: 1px solid blue">`

5. Click **Refresh** (↻).

   The web page refreshes.

B. The border appears around the table.

6. Click to place the insertion point before the closing > in the opening <th> tag or <td> tag for a cell you want to format.

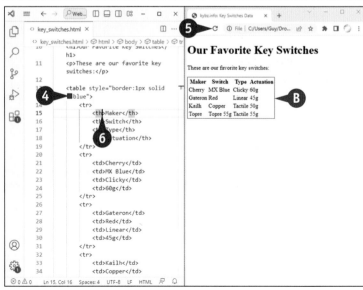

7 Type a space, followed by `style=` and the formatting inside double quotation marks, such as `"border:1px solid blue"`, so the tag looks like this:

```
<th style="border:1px solid
blue">
```

8 Repeat steps **6** and **7** for each other cell you want to format.

9 Click **Refresh** (↻).

The web page refreshes.

⊙ The cell borders appear.

⊙ A gap appears between the table border and the cell border and between the borders of adjacent cells.

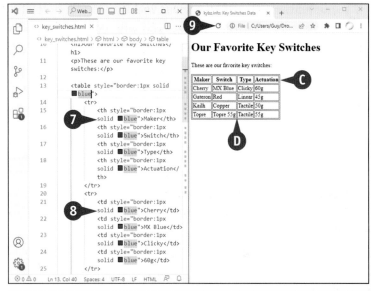

10 Type a semicolon and `border-collapse:collapse`, adding it to the opening `<table>` tag, so the tag looks like this:

```
<table style="border:
1px solid blue;border-
collapse:collapse">
```

11 Click **Refresh** (↻).

The web page refreshes.

⊙ The borders appear collapsed to a single line.

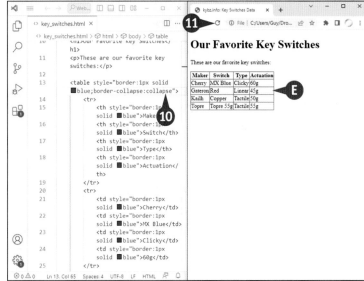

TIP

What are the key terms for formatting borders?
Start by specifying the width in pixels — for example, `1px` or `2px`. Next, specify the line style by using `solid`, `dotted`, `dashed`, `double`, `groove`, `ridge`, `inset`, or `outset`; use `none` to have no border, or `hidden` to hide the border. Then specify the color, either using a color name — such as `red`, `darksalmon`, or `lightgoldenrodyellow` — or using a hexadecimal value, such as `#00D2D2`.

Adjust Table Padding and Spacing

By default, HTML places borders tightly around cells and tables, but it enables you to change the distance by adjusting two parameters, padding and spacing. *Padding* is the space between the edge of a cell and the cell content; HTML sets padding to 1 pixel by default. You can adjust padding in all directions at once by setting the `cellpadding` attribute. *Spacing* is the space between one cell and the next cell; HTML sets spacing to 2 pixels by default. You can adjust spacing for a whole table by setting the `cellspacing` attribute.

Adjust Table Padding and Spacing

1 In Visual Studio Code, open the file containing the table whose padding and spacing you want to change.

2 Open the file in a browser window.

The example table has its borders collapsed, which prevents the space between the table borders and cell borders from appearing.

3 If your table has the borders collapsed, select the `border-collapse:collapse` text and press Del to delete the text.

4 Click **Refresh** (⟳).

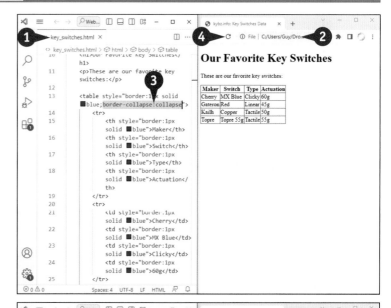

The web page refreshes.

Ⓐ The borders that were collapsed appear.

5 Click to place the insertion point before the closing > in the opening `<table>` tag.

6 Type **cellpadding=** and the value for the number of pixels inside double quotation marks. For example, the following code adds 10 pixels of padding:

```
cellpadding="10"
```

7 Click **Refresh** (⟳).

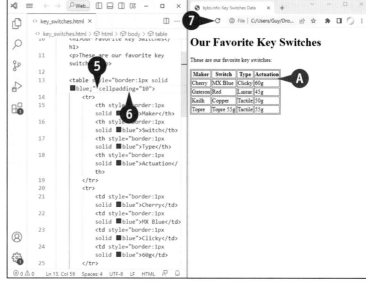

The web page refreshes.

B 10 pixels of padding appears between each cell border and the cell content.

8 In Visual Studio Code, type **cellspacing=** and the value for the number of pixels inside double quotation marks. For example, the following code adds 20 pixels of spacing between cells:

```
cellspacing="20"
```

9 Click **Refresh** (⟳).

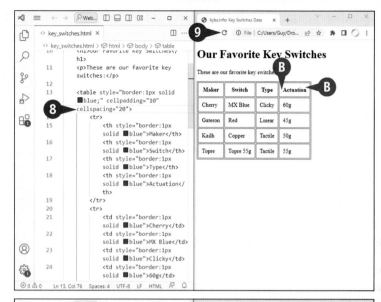

The web page refreshes.

C 20 pixels of space appears between the cell borders.

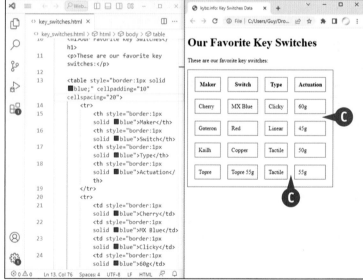

TIP

How can I set different amounts of padding for the different sides of cells?
The best way to set different amounts of padding for the top, bottom, left, and right sides of a cell or cells, is to use CSS, as explained in Chapter 9. CSS enables you to set padding for all sides simultaneously by using the `padding` attribute or for sides individually by using the `padding-top`, `padding-bottom`, `padding-left`, and `padding-right` attributes.

137

Create Groups of Columns

HTML enables you to create groups of columns within a table. Column groups can be helpful for applying different formatting to different sets of columns.

To create a column group, you use a `colgroup` element, which begins with an opening `<colgroup>` tag and ends with a closing `</colgroup>` tag. Within the column group, you create a `col` element and use its `span` attribute to specify how many columns to span.

Create Groups of Columns

1 In Visual Studio Code, open the file containing the table in which you want to create the column group.

2 Open the file in a browser window.

3 In Visual Studio Code, click to place the insertion point immediately after the opening `<table>` tag.

4 Press Enter to create a blank line (not shown).

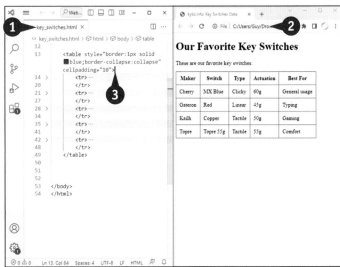

5 Type **co**.

The expansions list opens.

6 Click **colgroup**.

A Visual Studio Code inserts the opening `<colgroup>` tag and the closing `</colgroup>` tag, placing the insertion point between them.

7 Press Enter twice to create a blank line (not shown).

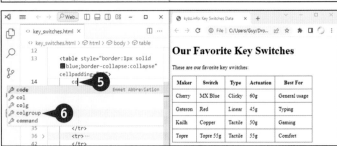

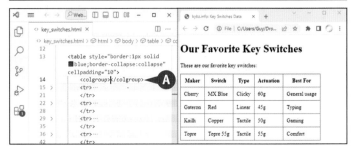

8 Click the blank line and type the definition for the `col` element, which specifies the columns for the column group and the formatting to apply, as shown next. Here, `span="2"` makes the group contain the first two columns, while the `style` attribute applies the background color.

```
<col span="2" style=
"background-color:
lightsteelblue;">
```

9 Click **Refresh** (⟳).

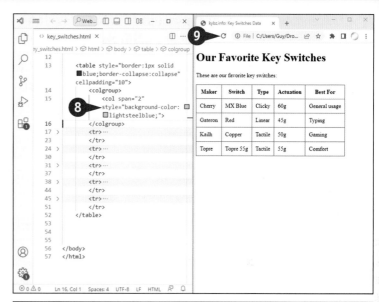

The web page refreshes.

Ⓑ The first two columns are now part of the column group and display the light steel-blue background color.

TIP

Can I create a group of rows in a table?

Yes. You can split a table into three sections: a section containing header rows, the body section, and a section containing footer rows. Create the header section by placing an opening `<thead>` tag before the opening `<tr>` tag for the first row in the section and a closing `</thead>` tag after the closing `</tr>` code for the last row in the section. Similarly, wrap the body section in an opening `<tbody>` tag and a closing `</tbody>` tag, and enclose the footer section in an opening `<tfoot>` tag and a closing `</tfoot>` tag.

Align Tables, Rows, and Cells

H TML enables you to control alignment for tables, rows, and cells. You can align a table horizontally on a page. You can align the contents of cells horizontally. You can also align the contents of either cells or whole rows vertically.

To control horizontal alignment, you set the `align` attribute of the appropriate element. To control vertical alignment, you set the `valign` attribute.

Align Tables, Rows, and Cells

1. In Visual Studio Code, open the file containing the table whose alignment you want to adjust.

2. Open the file in a browser window.

A. The table is aligned left on the web page.

B. The table headers are centered.

C. The table data cells are aligned left.

3. In Visual Studio Code, click to place the insertion point before the closing > in the opening <table> tag.

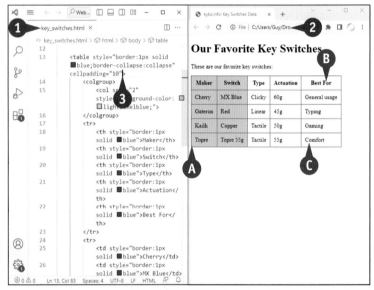

4. Type a space followed by **align=** and **left**, **center**, or **right** inside double quotation marks — for example:

```
<table align="center">
```

5. Click **Refresh** (C).

The web page refreshes.

D. The table takes on the new alignment — in this case, center alignment.

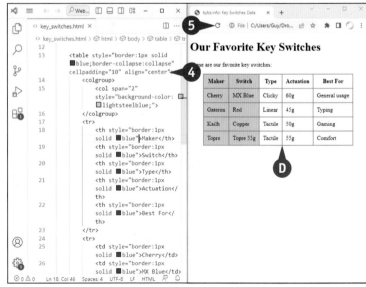

6 In Visual Studio Code, click to place the insertion point before the closing > in the opening `<th>` tag or `<td>` tag for the cell whose alignment you want to change.

7 Type a space followed by **align=** and **left**, **center**, or **right** inside double quotation marks — for example:

```
<td align="right">
```

8 Click **Refresh** (⟳).

The web page refreshes.

E The cell's content takes on the new alignment — in this case, right alignment.

Note: If you need to change the alignment of the other cells in the column, repeat steps **6** and **7** for each cell.

Note: Normally, you would use CSS to control the alignment of cells, rows, and tables. See Chapter 9 for details.

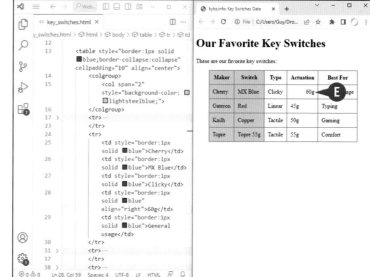

TIP

How do I control vertical alignment in table cells?
To control vertical alignment, add the `valign` attribute to the opening tag of the appropriate element and specify `top`, `middle`, or `bottom`, as appropriate. For example, to apply top alignment to all the cells in a row, you could use `<tr valign="top">`; to apply bottom alignment to a table header cell, you could use `<th valign="bottom">`.

Create Cells That Span Rows or Columns

HTML lets you create cells that span two or more rows vertically or two or more columns horizontally. To create a cell that spans multiple rows, you include the `rowspan` attribute in the opening tag of the appropriate cell, specifying the number of rows the cell should span, and reduce the number of cells in the subsequent rows accordingly. Similarly, to create a cell that spans multiple columns, you include the `colspan` attribute in the opening tag of the appropriate cell, specifying the number of columns the row should span, and reduce the number of cells in that row accordingly.

Create Spanner Cells

In your HTML file, create the table as usual by entering an opening `<table>` tag and a closing `</table>` tag. The example table shown here has a 3-pixel solid purple border, 10 pixels of cell padding, and 4 pixels of cell spacing.

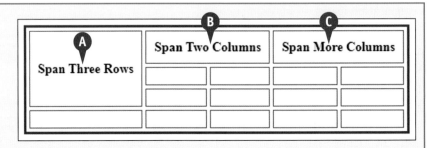

```
<table style="border:3px solid purple; cellpadding="10" cellspacing="4">
</table>
```

Between the `<table>` tag and the `</table>` tags, create the rows and cells using the techniques explained earlier in this chapter. When you reach the cell where you want to create a spanner cell, include the `rowspan` attribute or the `colspan` attribute, as appropriate, and assign the number of columns to it. For example, the second statement creates a three-row spanner cell (A), whereas the third statement and fourth statement each create a two-column spanner cell (B, C).

```
<tr>
    <th rowspan="3" style="border:1px solid blue">Span Three Rows</th>
    <th colspan="2" style="border:1px solid blue">Span Two Columns</th>
    <th colspan="2" style="border:1px solid blue">Span More Columns</th>
</tr>
```

This row is five cells wide — one cell for the row spanner plus two cells for each of the two column spanners. Each other row in the table must contain a total of five cells, but the row spanner cell occupies the first cell in the second row and third row, so each of these rows needs only four cells defined:

```
<tr>
    <td style="border:1px solid blue"></td>
    <td style="border:1px solid blue"></td>
    <td style="border:1px solid blue"></td>
    <td style="border:1px solid blue"></td>
</tr>
```

The final row of the table needs five cells defined.

Set a Background Color or Image for a Table

To make a table more attractive or to give it a distinctive look, you can set a background color or background image for it. To apply a background color to a table, you include the `style` attribute in the opening `<table>` tag and specify `background-color` and the color. To apply an image, you include the `style` attribute in the opening `<table>` tag and specify `background-image` and the path to the image.

Set a Background Color for a Table

In the HTML file, create the table as usual by entering an opening `<table>` tag and a closing `</table>` tag. In the `<table>` tag, include the `style`

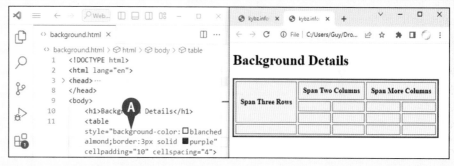

attribute, and specify `background-color` and the color (A). You can use either the color name, such as `blanched-almond`, or the hexadecimal code, such as `#33333` for the Gray20 light gray.

```
<table style="background-color:blanchedalmond;border:3px solid purple;"
cellpadding="10" cellspacing="4">
```

Set a Background Image for a Table

To set a background image, include the `style` attribute in the opening `<table>` tag and specify `background-image` followed by `URL` and the path to the image file, delimited by single quotes, inside parentheses. For example, the following `<table>` tag includes the image named `realforce.jpeg` stored in the `images` folder:

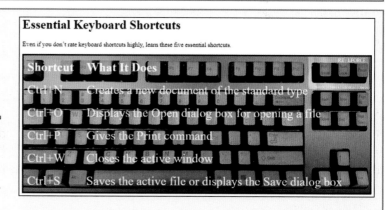

```
<table style="background-image:url('images/realforce.jpeg'); background-
repeat:no-repeat; background-size:cover;border: 3px solid black">
```

As you can see in the example, you can set various parameters to control how the image file appears. Setting `background-repeat` to `no-repeat` tells the browser to display the image without tiling it, and setting `background-size` to `cover` makes the image the right size to occupy all the space in the table.

Nest One Table Inside Another Table

HTML enables you to nest one table inside another table. You may find this capability useful when you need to create complex table layouts in your web pages.

To nest a table, you place the nested `table` element within the appropriate cell of the outer table. The outer table is sometimes called the *parent table*, and the nested table is called the *child table*.

Nest One Table Inside Another Table

1. In Visual Studio Code, open the file in which you want to create a nested table.

2. Open the file in a browser window.

3. In Visual Studio Code, click to place the insertion point where you want the outer table to appear.

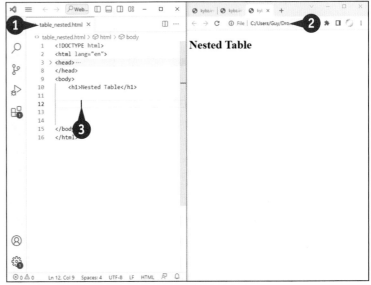

4. Create the outer table using the techniques explained in the section "Create a Table," earlier in this chapter: First, insert the `table` element, and then insert `tr` elements and populate them with `th` elements and `td` elements, as needed.

5. Click **Refresh** (⟳).

    The web page refreshes.

    Ⓐ The sample outer table has an outside border so it is easy to see the space the table occupies.

    Ⓑ Similarly, the cells also have borders.

6. Click to place the insertion point between the tags for the cell in which you want to nest a table.

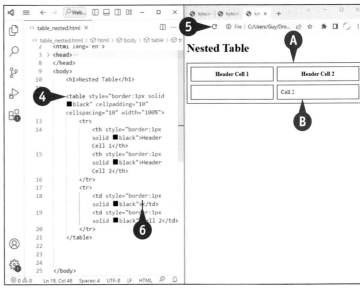

144

⑦ Create the nested table, again using the techniques explained in the section "Create a Table," earlier in this chapter: First, insert the table element, and then insert tr elements and populate them with th elements and td elements, as needed.

⑧ Click **Refresh** (C).

The web page refreshes.

🅒 The sample nested table has a red outside border.

🅓 The cells of the nested table have a blue outside border.

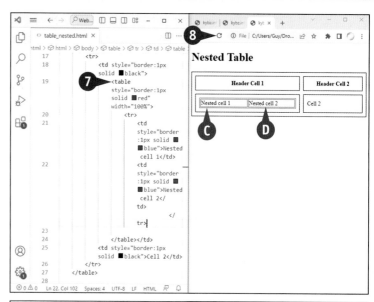

⑨ Add further cells to the nested table, as needed.

⑩ Click **Refresh** (C).

The web page refreshes.

🅔 The cells appear in the nested table.

🅕 The outer table resizes as needed to accommodate the nested table.

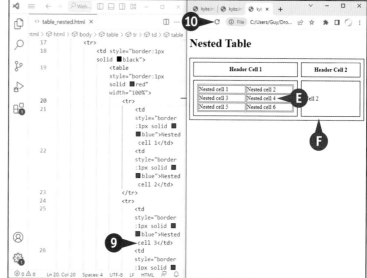

TIP

How many levels deep can I nest tables?

In theory, you can nest tables to however many levels deep you need. But in practice, it is usually best to limit nesting to two or three levels. Deeply nested tables can make your code hard to read and maintain and can make the page load more slowly, because the browser has to render all the nested tables. Deep nesting may also cause issues with accessibility features or accessibility hardware.

Getting Started with CSS

In this chapter, you start working with Cascading Style Sheets, CSS. After learning how CSS works and how to distinguish inline, internal, and external CSS, you start using these types of CSS to apply formatting. You then move on to working with element selectors, class selectors, and ID selectors.

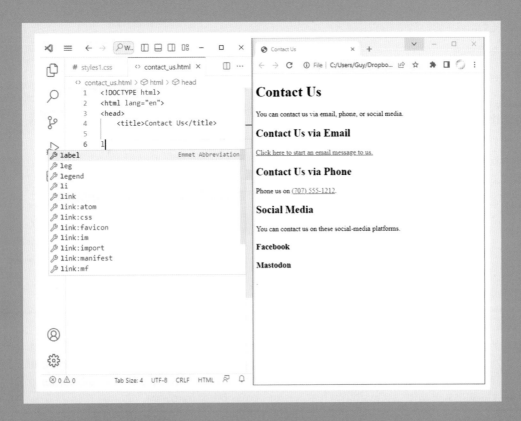

Grasp How CSS Works

Cascading Style Sheets, usually abbreviated to CSS, is a style sheet language used to describe how to display documents written in HTML, such as web pages, and other markup languages. CSS works by implementing a series of rules that control the display of the elements that make up the web page. CSS rules can apply either to specific elements or to groups of elements, as needed. CSS rules can be defined in three locations: first, inline, meaning inside the element; second, internally, meaning elsewhere in the same HTML document; or third, externally, meaning in a separate file linked to the document.

The CSS Cascade

You can use CSS in three ways in your web pages: as inline CSS, as internal CSS, and as external CSS. The following subsections explain each type.

The nearby diagram illustrates how CSS "cascades" down the three levels of CSS — inline CSS at the top, internal CSS next, and external CSS third — to the base, where the browser settings implemented by the user are. Style information set by inline CSS flows down from the top level to the middle level, overriding any style information set by internal CSS. In turn, style information set by internal CSS flows down from the middle level to the bottom level, overriding any style information set by external CSS. Again in turn, the external CSS overrides the user's browser settings.

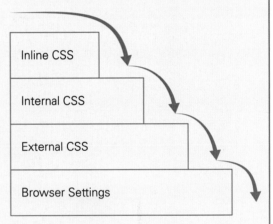

Inline CSS

Inline CSS is style formatting that you define directly in an HTML element by including the `style` attribute in the element's opening tag and specifying the formatting you want. You have used inline CSS in some of the examples earlier in the book. For example, the following statement includes the `style` attribute in the opening `<table>` tag and assigns border formatting to it, producing a border that is 1 pixel wide, a solid line, and blue:

```
<table style="border:1px solid blue">
```

As you can see, the `style` definition goes within double quotation marks. If you need to specify more than one type of formatting in the same `style` definition, you use semicolons to separate the style type. For example, the following statement adds the `border-collapse` property, setting it to `collapse`, which collapses the table and cell borders to a single line instead of having them appear as separate lines:

```
<table style="border:1px solid blue;border-collapse:collapse">
```

Internal CSS

Internal CSS is style formatting that you define within the HTML file but not within a particular element. Internal CSS applies to the HTML file as a whole rather than to a particular element.

To create an internal style sheet, you place a `style` element in the `head` section of the web page and define the styles within the `style` element. The following example shows an internal style sheet containing a definition for the `h1` style and the `p` style:

```
<head>
    <title>Internal Mechanisms</title>
    <style>
        h1 {
            font-size: 28px;
            color:blueviolet;
            text-align: center;
        }

        p {
            color:black;
            font-size: 14px;
            line-height: 1.5;
        }
    </style>
</head>
```

External CSS

External CSS is a style sheet that you create in a separate file and then link to the HTML documents to which you want to apply it. An external CSS file has the .css file extension.

How Should You Use Inline, Internal, and External CSS?

To format your HTML files efficiently, use external CSS to apply as much formatting as possible. The advantage of external CSS is that, when you need to update the formatting of your HTML documents, you need change only the CSS file rather than having to change the individual document files. The documents automatically pick up the changes you make to the CSS file.

Using external CSS also enables you to separate the task of creating the CSS from the task of creating the HTML. For example, your company might have a designer create the external CSS to implement the company's design standards while you and your developer colleagues create the HTML pages.

Use internal CSS when you need to override your external CSS formatting throughout a document. Use inline CSS when you need to override either your internal CSS formatting or your external CSS formatting for a single element in the document.

Format Elements with Inline CSS

When you need to apply specific formatting to individual elements in your documents, you can use inline CSS. Inline CSS essentially means creating a mini style sheet within a particular element, such as a heading or a list item. To implement inline CSS, you add the `style` attribute to the opening tag for the element and then specify the style formatting.

Using inline CSS is labor-intensive and makes your web pages harder to keep updated, so you should use inline CSS only when absolutely necessary to produce the effects you require.

Format Elements with Inline CSS

1 In Visual Studio Code, open the file in which you want to apply formatting with inline CSS.

2 Open the file in a browser window.

3 In Visual Studio Code, click before the closing > of the opening tag of the element you want to format.

4 Type a space followed by **s**.

The expansions list appears.

5 Click **style**.

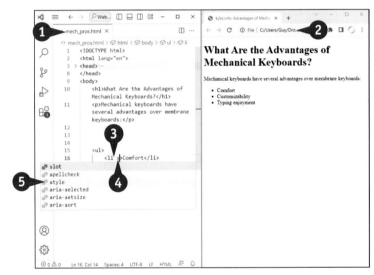

A Visual Studio Code inserts the `style` attribute, placing the insertion point within double quotation marks after it, and displays the property list.

6 Click the property you want to format. This example uses **color**.

B Visual Studio Code inserts the property. If appropriate, it displays the values list. In the example, Visual Studio Code displays a list of colors.

7 If the value you want appears, click it. Otherwise, type the value.

150

C The value appears.

D Visual Studio Code enters a semicolon, ;, in case you need to continue the style definition.

8 Click **Refresh** (⟳).

The web page refreshes.

E The formatting appears.

9 Click to place the insertion point after the semicolon.

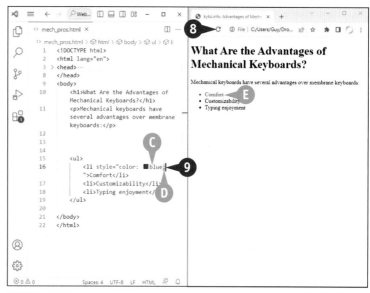

10 Start typing the name of the property you want to use, and then click the property on the property list.

For example, type **fo** and then click **font-weight**.

11 If the values list appears, click the value. Otherwise, type the value.

For example, you might specify **bold** for `font-weight`.

12 Click **Refresh** (⟳).

The web page refreshes.

F The formatting appears.

TIP

How can I use inline CSS most effectively?

Perhaps counterintuitively, the most effective way to use inline CSS is to avoid it wherever possible. Try to use inline CSS only when a particular element needs formatting that you will not apply to elements elsewhere. For example, if one `h1` element requires a special look, inline CSS may be a good solution. But if multiple, though not all, `h1` elements require that special look, a class selector or ID selector is a better solution.

Format a Page Using Internal CSS

W hen you need to apply special formatting right through an HTML document, overwriting the formatting applied by external CSS, you can use internal CSS. To implement internal CSS, you add a `style` element to the `head` section of the HTML document and create the style definitions in it. The browser then prioritizes those style definitions over style definitions using the same names in a linked external CSS. However, any inline CSS in the HTML document's elements overrides the internal CSS.

Format a Page Using Internal CSS

1 In Visual Studio Code, open the file in which you want to create an internal style sheet.

2 Open the file in a browser window.

3 In Visual Studio Code, click at the point in the `head` section where you want to place the internal style sheet.

4 Type a space followed by **st**.

The expansions list appears.

5 Click **style**.

Visual Studio Code inserts the opening <style> tag and closing </style> tag, placing the insertion point between them.

6 Press Enter to create a blank line between the tags (not shown).

7 On the blank line, type the name of the first style you want to define, followed by a space and an opening brace — for example:

`h2 {`

A Visual Studio Code inserts the closing brace to match.

8 Press Enter to create a blank line between the braces (not shown).

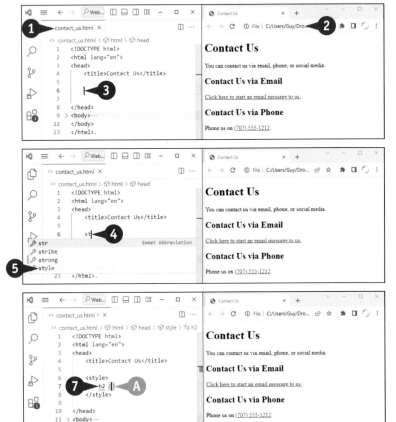

9 On the blank line, start typing the name of the property you want to set first.

The property list appears.

10 Click the property.

B Visual Studio Code inserts the property. If appropriate, it displays the values list. In the example, Visual Studio Code displays a list of colors.

C Visual Studio Code enters a semicolon, ;, in case you need to continue the style definition.

11 If the value you want appears, click it. Otherwise, type the value.

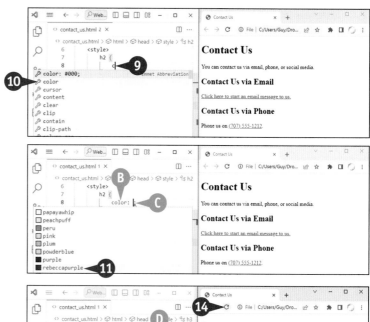

D The value appears.

12 On a new line, repeat steps **9** to **11** to specify further formatting, as needed.

13 Repeat steps **7** to **11** to define other styles, as needed.

14 Click **Refresh** (↻).

The web page refreshes.

E The formatting appears in all its glory or horror.

TIP

Does internal CSS have advantages over external CSS?

Yes, internal CSS has several advantages over external CSS. First, internal CSS enables you to easily override external CSS formatting. Second, internal CSS lets you see more easily what style formatting is being applied to the file — you do not need to open an external style sheet file. Third, your web pages will load a little faster because the browser does not have to request the style sheet file from the server. Fourth, a web page containing internal CSS is more portable than a page with external CSS, because you can move the page to a different location without having to make sure the external CSS is still accessible.

Create an External CSS File

In general, the most efficient way to format your web pages is by using external CSS files. You can use either a single external CSS file or multiple external CSS files for any HTML file. To create an external CSS file, you create a text file with the .css file extension and define the styles inside that file. You then link the external CSS file to the HTML files. See the next section, "Link an External CSS File to a Web Page," for instructions on linking.

Create an External CSS File

1 In Visual Studio Code, click **Explorer** (⟱).

The Explorer bar appears.

2 Move the pointer over the Website section of the Explorer bar.

The pop-up controls appear.

3 If you store your CSS files in a separate folder, click that folder (> changes to ∨).

Ⓐ You can create a new folder by clicking **New Folder** (⟱), typing the name, and then pressing Enter.

4 Click **New File** (⟱).

A text box for naming the new file appears.

5 Type the filename and press Enter.

The file appears, ready for you to work in it.

Note: To make your CSS file easy to read, you can include comment lines that explain the styles you define and their purpose.

6 Type **/*** to start a comment line.

7 Type the text of the comment. The example uses **top-level heading style.**

8 Type ***/** to end the comment line.

9 Press Enter and type **h** to begin defining the h1 style.

The style list appears.

10 Click **h1.**

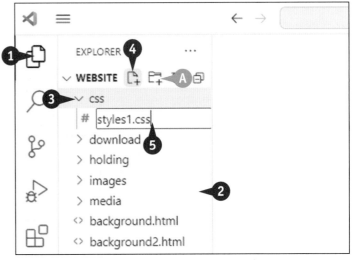

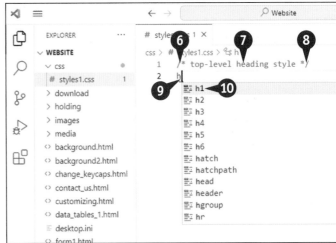

154

Visual Studio Code inserts h1.

⑪ Type a space, followed by **{**.

Visual Studio Code inserts the matching closing brace, **}**, positioning the insertion point between the braces.

⑫ Press **Enter** to create a new line (not shown).

⑬ Start typing the name of the first property you want to set.

The property list opens.

⑭ Click the property.

If appropriate, Visual Studio Code displays the values list.

⑮ If the value you want appears, click it.

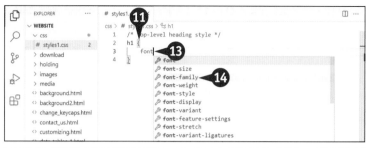

B Visual Studio Code enters the value you chose.

Note: If Visual Studio Code does not display the values list, type the value for the property.

⑯ On subsequent lines, enter further properties and values until you finish defining the style.

⑰ Create further styles, as needed.

TIP

Must I lay out the style properties on different lines, as in the example?

No. The layout shown is a convention optimized for readability and ease of maintenance. But you can put multiple properties on the same line if you prefer. For example, p {font-size: medium; font-weight: 500;color: burlywood; } — all on a single line — works fine.

Link an External CSS File to a Web Page

After creating an external CSS file, you link it to the web pages you want it to format. To make the link, you place a `<link>` tag in the header of each web page.

You can link multiple external CSS files to the same web page by using multiple `<link>` tags. For example, if all your web pages share a common core of styles, you might put those styles in one CSS file. You might then create other CSS files, each containing extra styles for a different type of web page or content.

Link an External CSS File to a Web Page

1 In Visual Studio Code, open the web page to which you want to link the external CSS file.

2 Open the file in a browser window.

3 In Visual Studio Code, click in the head section where you want to place the link.

4 Type **l.**

The expansions list appears.

5 Click **link.**

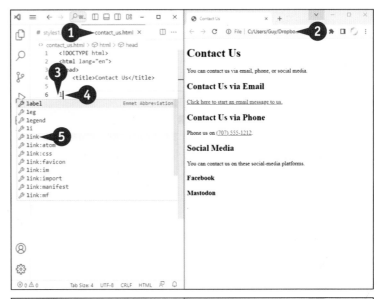

Visual Studio Code inserts the `<link>` tag, including the `rel` attribute set to `stylesheet` and the `href` attribute with no setting:

```
<link rel="stylesheet"
href="">
```

6 With the insertion point between the double quotation marks after `href=`, start typing the path to the external CSS file.

The expansions list appears.

7 Click the style sheet you want to link.

(A) Visual Studio Code enters the style sheet name in the code.

(8) Click to place the insertion point just before the closing > of the <link> tag (not shown).

(9) Type **type="text/css"**.

Note: Including type="text/css" in the link to an external CSS file is not strictly necessary, but it is considered good practice. Specifying the type of the linked file ensures that the browser knows it is a CSS file.

(10) Click **Refresh** (C).

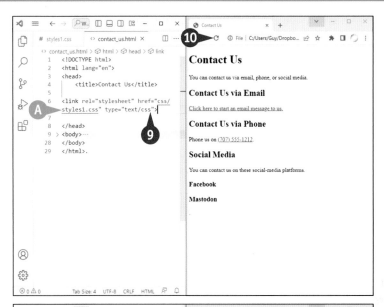

The web page refreshes.

(B) The web page now uses the styles from the style sheet you linked.

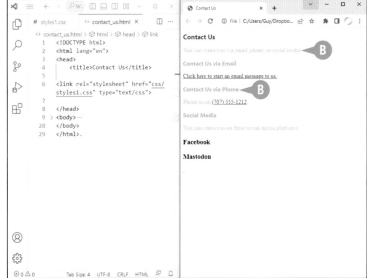

TIP

What happens if the same style is defined in multiple external CSS files linked to the same web page?
If the same style is defined twice or more in multiple external CSS linked to the same web page, the browser uses the last definition of the style. For example, if both the CSS files in the main text define the p style, the browser uses the p style definition from the second CSS file, because the browser encounters this file later in the code.

Distinguish Element, Class, and ID Selectors

To format your HTML documents, you apply styles to the appropriate parts of them using CSS. HTML enables you to apply styles to elements by using three primary types of selectors: element selectors, class selectors, and ID selectors.

This section explains and illustrates the differences between these three types of selectors. The sections "Apply Styles Using Element Selectors," "Apply Styles Using Class Selectors," and "Apply Styles Using ID Selectors," all later in this chapter, provide hands-on examples of working with each type of selector.

Element Selectors

An *element selector* enables you to select all instances of a particular HTML element in a web page. For example, if you want to apply a style to all the paragraph elements on a page, you can use the p selector. To specify an element selector, you simply use the name of the HTML element. For example, the following selector selects the h1 element and applies the aliceblue color:

```
h1 {
    color: aliceblue;
}
```

Class Selectors

A *class selector* allows you to target elements that have a particular class attribute. For example, if your HTML file contains elements with the class button, you can use that class to target those elements. To specify a class selector, you use the name of the class, preceded by a period, such as .button. The following example selects the .button class and applies the bisque color:

```
.button{
    color: bisque;
}
```

To work with class selectors, you may need to create a suitable class. See the subsection "Create a Class of Items in the HTML File," later in this chapter, for instructions on creating a class.

ID Selectors

An *ID selector* lets you target an element that has a unique ID attribute. To specify an ID selector, you use the ID name, preceded by #. For example, if you have assigned the ID keynote to a particular element, you can target that element by using the ID selector #keynote. The following example selects the keynote ID and applies the chartreuse color:

```
#keynote{
    color: chartreuse;
}
```

Apply Styles Using Element Selectors

W hen you need to apply a style to all the instances of a particular element in an HTML document, use an element selector. For example, to apply a style to all the instances of the p element in a document, you would use the p selector.

Using element selectors is the standard way of applying styles. Normally, you would use element selectors to apply most style formatting, using class selectors and ID selectors to apply special formatting to some elements, as needed.

Apply Styles Using Element Selectors

1 In Visual Studio Code, open the external CSS file to which you want to add the element selector.

2 In a browser window, open an HTML file to which you have attached the external CSS file.

3 In Visual Studio Code, click to place the insertion point where you want to create the element selector.

Ⓐ Optionally, type a comment about the element selector you will create.

4 Type the style name followed by a space and { — for example:

h2 {

Ⓑ Visual Studio Code inserts the matching closing brace, }.

5 Press Enter to create a blank line (not shown).

6 With the insertion point on the blank line, type the formatting for the style. This example uses text-align: center;:

```
h2 {
    text-align: center;
}
```

7 Click **Refresh** (⟳).

The web page refreshes.

Ⓒ The formatting applied by the element selector appears.

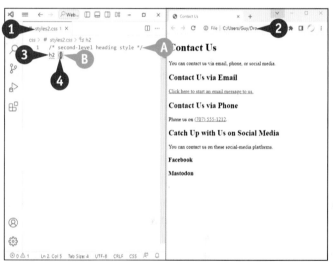

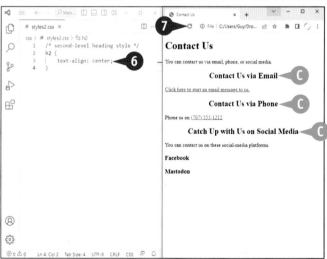

Apply Styles Using Class Selectors

When you need to apply a style to multiple elements of different types in an HTML document, you can assign the elements to a class and then use a class selector to apply the style. For example, if your document contained several key sections, each of which consisted of a heading and a paragraph of text, you could assign those headings and paragraphs to a class and then apply the style to the class.

This example uses an external CSS, which it assumes you have connected to the HTML file you want to format.

Apply Styles Using Class Selectors

Create a Class of Items in the HTML File

1 In Visual Studio Code, open the file that you will format using class selectors.

2 Open the file in a browser window.

3 In Visual Studio Code, click to place the insertion point just before the closing > of the opening tag for the element you want to format.

4 Type a space and then **class=** and the class name in double quotation marks — for example:

`class="alignright"`

5 Repeat steps **3** and **4** for each other paragraph you want to assign to the class.

Create the Class Selector in the CSS File

1 In Visual Studio Code, open the external CSS file to which you want to add the class selector.

A Optionally, type a comment about the class selector you will create.

2 Click to place the insertion point where you want to create the class selector.

3 Type a period, the class selector name, and then **{** — for example:

`.alignright {`

B Visual Studio Code inserts the matching closing **}**.

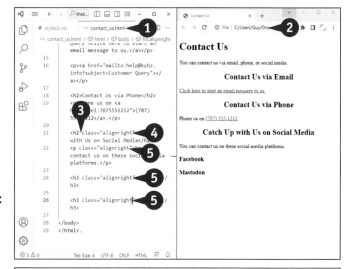

④ Press **Enter** to create a blank line (not shown).

⑤ Specify the formatting for the style, either by typing all the details or by choosing items from the lists that Visual Studio Code displays as you type. For the example shown, you might type **tex**, click **text-align** on the properties list, and then click **right** on the values list.

⑥ Click **Refresh** (↻).

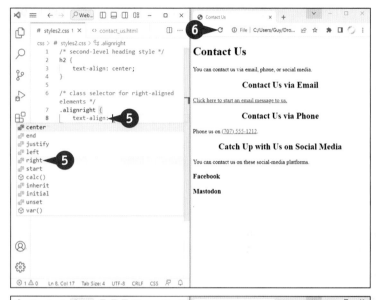

The web page refreshes.

Ⓒ The elements you assigned to the class take on the class's formatting. In the example, the elements become right-aligned.

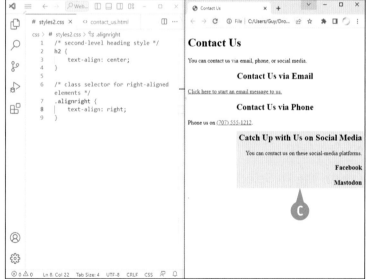

What restrictions are there on using class selectors?
- Class names must begin with a letter, with an underscore, or with a hyphen; they cannot begin with a number.
- Class names cannot contains spaces, but you can use hyphens or underscores to separate words.
- Each class name within an HTML document must be unique.

Apply Styles Using ID Selectors

When you need to apply a style to a single element in an HTML file, use an ID selector to identify that element. First, in the HTML file, you add the id attribute to the opening tag for the element and assign a name unique within the file. Then you add the ID selector to the CSS for the file.

Formatting a single element using an ID selector is more convenient than formatting the element using inline CSS because the ID selector's formatting can be in an external style sheet that you can apply to as many HTML files as needed.

Apply Styles Using ID Selectors

Assign an ID to an Element in the HTML File

1. In Visual Studio Code, open the file containing the element you will format with an ID selector.

2. Open the file in a browser window.

3. In Visual Studio Code, click to place the insertion point just before the closing > of the opening tag for the element you want to format.

4. Type a space and then **id=** and the id name in double quotation marks — for example:

   id="takeaway"

Create the ID Selector in the CSS File

1. In Visual Studio Code, open the external CSS file to which you want to add the ID selector.

A. Optionally, type a comment about the ID selector you will create.

2. Click to place the insertion point where you want to create the ID selector.

3. Type a #, the ID selector name, and then { — for example:

   #takeaway {

B. Visual Studio Code inserts the matching closing }.

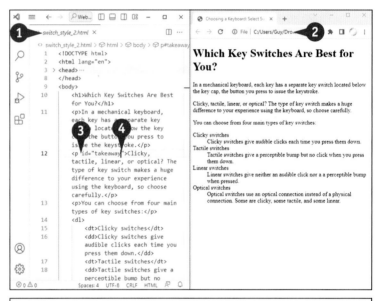

④ Press **Enter** to create a blank line (not shown).

⑤ Specify the formatting for the style, either by typing all the details or by choosing items from the lists that Visual Studio Code displays as you type. The example uses this code to display the element in a heavy font with a 5-pixel blue border around the text with 20 pixels of space between the two.

```
#takeaway {
    font-weight: 900;
    padding: 20px;
    border: 5px solid
blue;
}
```

⑥ Click **Refresh** (⟳).

The web page refreshes.

Ⓒ The element marked with the ID takes on the formatting.

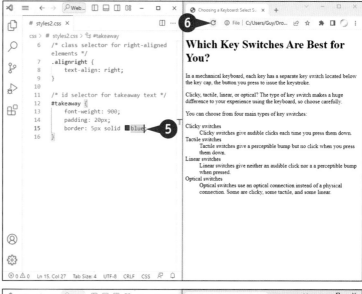

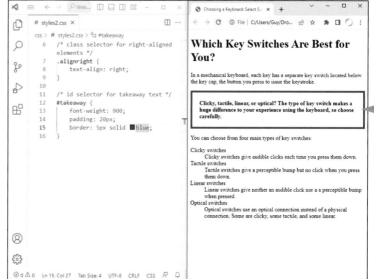

What happens if I use IDs that are not unique in an HTML document?
IDs that are repeated in an HTML document, rather than being unique, can cause two main problems. First, CSS will select only the first element that uses the ID; it will ignore subsequent elements with the repeated ID, so they do not receive the formatting you intended. Second, because assistive technologies rely on unique IDs to navigate pages and interact with them, screen readers and other assistive technologies may not work correctly, making it harder for users with disabilities to use your web pages.

Formatting Text with CSS

CSS enables you to format the text in your web pages to make them look the way you want. Basic formatting includes the font family, the font size and font weight, and the font color. More advanced formatting includes line height and letter spacing, superscripts and subscripts, and text shadows. You can also insert special characters and emojis in your pages.

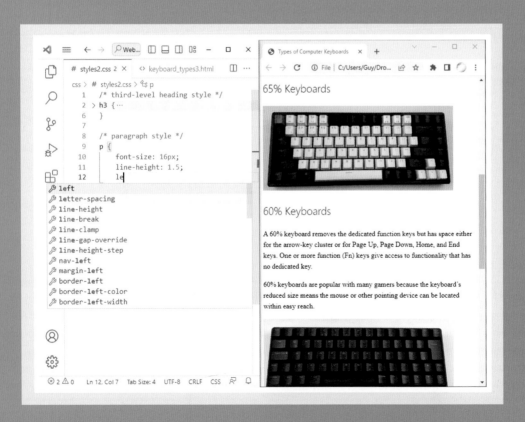

Understanding Fonts and How to Use Them

Working with fonts is a crucial part of web development, because fonts control the appearance of text on your web pages and can help convey your website's message, tone, and style. CSS gives you a wide variety of ways to control fonts and text styling, from essential properties such as font family and font size to more specialized properties such as superscripts, subscripts, and text shadows.

This section gives you an overview of the font properties you can control. The following sections show you how to effect changes in the properties.

Font Families

A *font family* is a set of typefaces that share a common design. For example, serif fonts have serifs, small projections finishing off the strokes of their letters, whereas sans-serif fonts have no serifs. Times New Roman and Baskerville are examples of serif fonts; Arial and Helvetica are examples of sans-serif fonts.

To specify the typeface used for text on a web page, you use the `font-family` property to set the font family. You can provide several values for `font-family` to specify fallback fonts in order of preference. For example, the following code specifies Helvetica, Arial, and sans-serif for the font family for the `body` element:

```
body {
    font-family: Helvetica, Arial,
sans-serif;
}
```

Here, if the web browser does not have Helvetica, it will fall back to Arial; if it does not have Arial either, it will fall back to the sans-serif font. The text will be displayed in some form, because the browser always has a serif font and a sans-serif font available.

Font Size

The `font-size` property enables you to set the font size using either a fixed measurement or a relative measurement. A fixed measurement can use various units, such as pixels, denoted by `px`; typographical ems, denoted by `em`; root ems, units relative to the root font size of the document, denoted by `rem`; or percentages of the default size, denoted by `%`. A relative measurement uses a comparative value such as `x-small`, `medium`, `large`, or `xx-large`.

The following example specifies a large font size for the body element:

```
body {
    font-size: large;
}
```

Sizing in root ems makes the font sizes relative to the font you set for the `body` element of the HTML document. For example, the following style definition sets the `font-size` property of the body element to `16px`:

```
body {
    font-size: 16px;
}
```

This makes a root em for the document also `16px`. You can then specify font sizes for other elements in root ems. For example, the following style definition sets the `font-size` property for the p element to `1rem`, making it `16px` as well:

```
p {
    font-size: 1rem;
}
```

Similarly, you might use `font-size: 1.5rem` to set a 24-pixel font size for another element in the same document.

Sizing using root ems enables you to easily adjust font sizes throughout a document: You need change only the pixel value of the `font-size` property of the `body` element. The other elements then change size automatically.

Font Weight

The `font-weight` property enables you to control the weight — the thickness or boldness — of the font characters. You can set `font-weight` either to a keyword value — `lighter`, `normal`, `bold`, or `bolder` — or to a number between `100`, which is lightest, and `900`, which is boldest. The following example specifies a `bold` font weight for the `h3` element:

```
h3 {
    font-weight: bold;
}
```

Font Color

The `color` property lets you specify the color for fonts and other objects. The following example specifies the `deepskyblue` color for the style:

```
h3 {
    color: deepskyblue;
}
```

See the section "Understanding Ways to Set Color in CSS" for an explanation of the different ways in which you can set color, such as by specifying the color name or by entering the RGB values.

Underlines, Overlines, and Strikethrough

CSS enables you to apply three types of text decoration: including underlines beneath the text, overlines above the text, and strikethrough across the text. You can choose from different styles of lines, such as solid, dotted, or wavy; set the color for the lines; and specify the line thickness. The following example specifies a solid red overline 5 pixels thick:

```
h4 {
    text-decoration: overline solid red 5px;
}
```

Using Custom Fonts from External Sources

As well as the built-in fonts provided by the browser, CSS enables you to use custom fonts from external sources. You can host the fonts on your web server, if you have permission to distribute them; or you can have the browser download the fonts from a font library.

See the section "Using Custom Fonts on Web Pages," later in this chapter, for information on deploying custom fonts on your web pages.

167

Specify the Font Family

The font family is often the best place to start the font formatting for a style. CSS enables you to specify your preferred font by name, but you can also provide a fallback list of fonts to use if the preferred font is not available.

To specify the font family, you include the `font-family` property in the style definition and set it to the appropriate font family or families.

Specify the Font Family

1 In Visual Studio Code, open the external CSS file you want to work on.

2 Also in Visual Studio Code, open an HTML file to which you have linked the external CSS file.

3 Open the HTML file in a browser window.

A In the example, the h3 elements use a serif font.

B Optionally, type a comment describing the style you are creating — for example:

```
/* third-level heading
style */
```

4 Start the style definition by typing the style name followed by a space and { — for example:

```
h3 {
```

Visual Studio Code automatically inserts the matching closing brace, }.

5 Press Enter to create a blank line (not shown).

6 Type **font**.

The expansions list appears.

7 Click **font-family**.

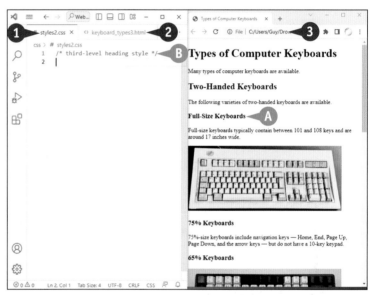

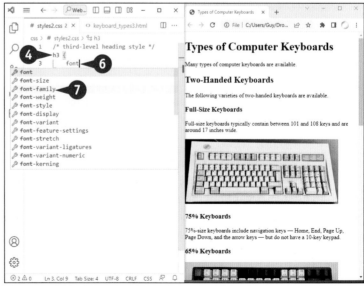

168

C Visual Studio Code inserts the
font-family property.

Visual Studio Code displays a list
of font families.

8 If the font family you want to
use appears, click it.

If not, type the details of the
font family you want. See the tip
for an example.

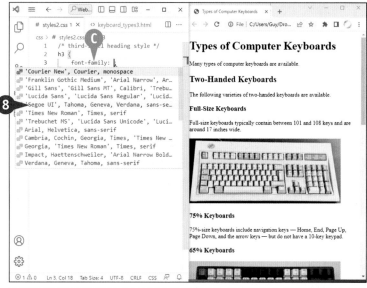

D The font-family property displays
the details of the font family you
chose.

9 Click **Refresh** (C).

The web page refreshes and displays
the new formatting.

E In the example, the h3 elements
change to a sans-serif font.

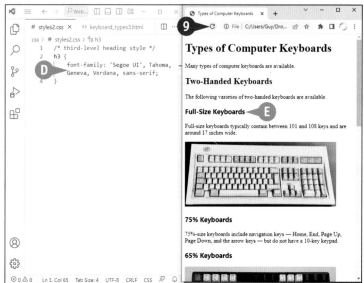

TIP

How do I enter the details for a font family?

Type the name of the font family. If the name includes any spaces or special characters, put the name in
double quotation marks — for example, font-family: "Helvetica Neue". If the name does not
contain spaces or special characters, enter the name unadorned — for example, font-family:
Helvetica. When providing a fallback stack of fonts, separate them with commas — for example,
font-family: "Helvetica Neue", Helvetica, sans-serif specifies Helvetica Neue font;
failing that, Helvetica; and failing that too, sans-serif font.

Set the Font Size and Font Weight

The font size and font weight can make a huge difference to how text appears on a web page. CSS enables you to specify the font size by including the `font-size` property and to control the font weight by using the `font-weight` property.

You can set `font-size` either to a specific height using a measurement unit such as pixels or typographical ems or to a relative size, such as `larger`. You can set `font-weight` either to a keyword value, such as `lighter` or `bolder`, or to a number between `100`, which is lightest, and `900`, which is boldest.

Set the Font Size and Font Weight

1 In Visual Studio Code, open the external CSS file you want to work on.

2 Also in Visual Studio Code, open an HTML file to which you have linked the external CSS file.

3 Open the HTML file in a browser window.

Note: If you are starting a new style, type the name, followed by a space and {. Visual Studio Code automatically enters the matching closing brace, }.

4 Click in the style where you want to add the font size.

5 Type **font**.

The expansions list appears.

6 Click **font-size**.

A Visual Studio Code inserts the `font-size` property.

Visual Studio Code displays a list of font sizes.

7 If the font size you want to use appears, click it. If not, type the font size. This example uses **24px**.

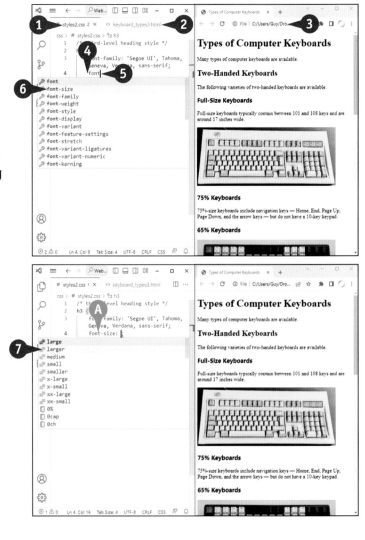

8 Click **Refresh** (⟳).

The web page refreshes.

B The change to the font size appears.

9 On a new line, type **font**.

The expansions list appears.

10 Click **font-weight**.

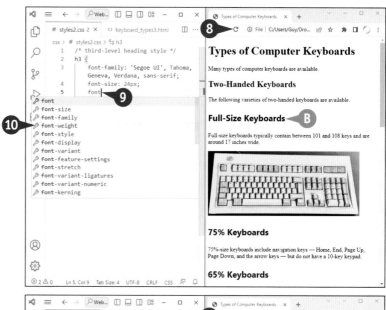

C Visual Studio Code inserts the `font-weight` property.

Visual Studio Code displays a list of font weights.

11 Click the font weight you want. The example uses **lighter**.

Visual Studio Code enters the font weight value in your code.

12 Click **Refresh** (⟳).

The web page refreshes.

D The change to the font weight appears.

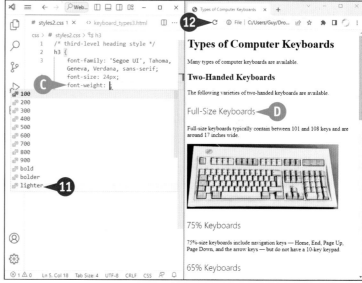

TIP

How do the numerical values for `font-weight` work?

`100` is the lightest weight and maps to `thin`; `400` is the standard font weight and maps to `normal`; and `900` is the heaviest weight and maps to `black`. The other values you can use are `200`, which maps to `lighter`; `300`, which maps to `light`; `500`, which maps to `medium`; `600`, which maps to `semi-bold`; `700`, which maps to `bold`; and `800`, which maps to `bolder`.

Adjust Line Height and Letter Spacing

CSS enables you to adjust line height and letter spacing in your HTML documents. To adjust line height, you set the `line-height` property in the style. You can use either a specific measurement, such as `24px` to make the line height 24 pixels, or a multiple of the font size, such as `1.5` to make the line height one and one-half times the font size.

To adjust letter spacing, you include the `letter-spacing` property in the style and specify the amount of space you want between each letter.

Adjust Line Height and Letter Spacing

1 In Visual Studio Code, open the external CSS file you want to work on.

2 Also in Visual Studio Code, open an HTML file to which you have linked the external CSS file.

3 Open the HTML file in a browser window.

Note: If you are starting a new style, type the name, followed by a space and {. Visual Studio Code automatically enters the matching closing brace, }.

4 Click in the style where you want to add the line height.

5 Type **li**.

The expansions list appears.

6 Click **line-height**.

Ⓐ Visual Studio Code inserts the `line-height` property.

Visual Studio Code displays the values list.

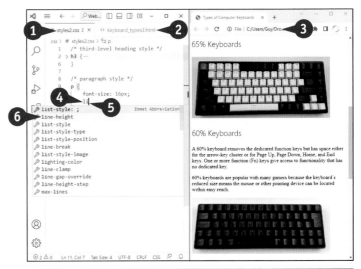

7 If the value you want appears, click it (not shown). Otherwise, type the value. This example uses the typed value **1.5** to make the line height one and one-half times the font size.

Ⓑ The font size is `16px`.

8 Click **Refresh** (⟳).

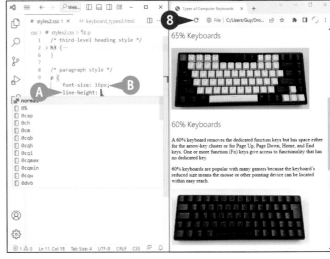

172

The web page refreshes.

C The line height of the p elements changes.

9 On a blank line within the style, type **le**.

The expansions list appears.

10 Click **letter-spacing**.

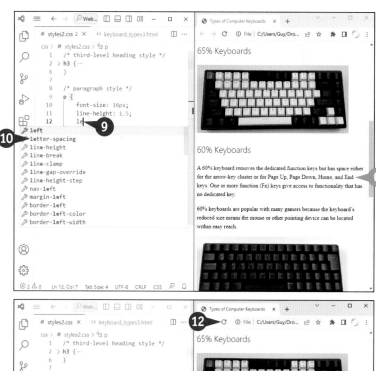

D Visual Studio Code inserts the letter-spacing property.

Visual Studio Code displays the values list.

11 Type the letter spacing you want. This example uses **2px** to apply two pixels of space between each letter.

12 Click **Refresh** (C).

The web page refreshes.

E The letter spacing of the p elements changes.

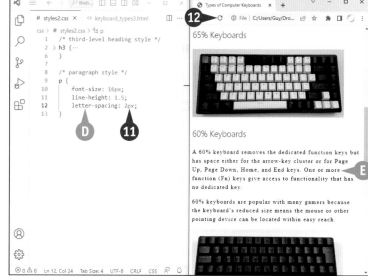

TIP

Should I set line-height to a pixel value or to a multiple of the font size?

Usually, setting line-height to a multiple of the font size gives better results, because it allows the line height to scale proportionally with the font size. This scaling makes it easier to maintain a consistent layout across different screen sizes.

This type of measurement is sometimes called a *unitless value*, because it does not use units, such as pixels or ems.

Create Superscripts and Subscripts

Some of your web pages may need superscript characters, such as m^2, or subscript characters, such as C_2H_6O. CSS enables you to display superscript characters by using the sup element and subscript characters by using the sub element.

Applying the sup element or the sub element produces a superscript or subscript with default settings. You can apply custom styles to produce exactly the superscripts and subscripts you prefer.

Create Superscripts and Subscripts

Add Superscripts and Subscripts to an HTML File

1 In Visual Studio Code, open the external CSS file you want to work on.

2 Also in Visual Studio Code, open an HTML file to which you have linked the external CSS file.

3 Open the HTML file in a browser window.

A The example HTML file contains a character that requires a superscript.

B It also contains a character that requires a subscript.

4 Click to place the insertion point before the character that requires superscript.

5 Type the opening <sup> tag.

6 Move the insertion point to after the character, and then type the closing </sup> tag.

7 Click before the character that requires subscript and type the opening <sub> tag.

8 Move the insertion point to after the character, and then type the closing </sub> tag.

9 Click **Refresh** ($\circlearrowright$).

The web page refreshes.

C The superscript appears.

D The subscript appears.

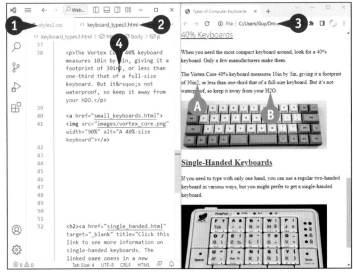

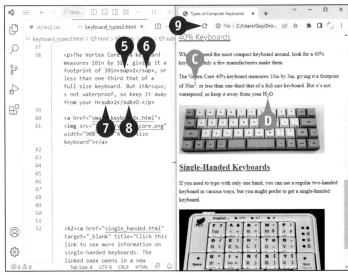

Configure the Superscript Style and Subscript Style

1 In Visual Studio Code, click the external CSS file's tab.

2 On a new line, type **sup**, a space, and **{**.

Visual Studio Code inserts the matching closing brace, **}**.

3 Press Enter to insert a blank line (not shown).

4 Type **v**.

The expansions list appears.

5 Click **vertical-align**.

Ⓔ Visual Studio Code inserts the `vertical-align` property.

The values list appears.

6 Click **super**.

Ⓕ The `super` value appears.

7 Type **font-size:** followed by the value you want. The example uses **0.6em**.

```
font-size: 0.6em;
```

8 Repeat steps **2** to **7** to define the `sub` style. Assign the `sub` value to the `vertical-align` property. Assign the same value to `font-size`. For example:

```
sub {
    vertical-align: sub;
    font-size: 0.6em;
}
```

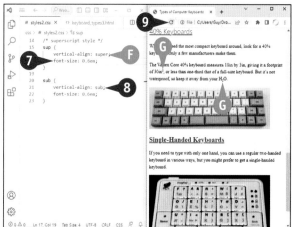

9 Click **Refresh** (⟳).

The web page refreshes.

Ⓖ The superscript and subscript take on the new formatting.

What else should I know about superscripts and subscripts?
To make sure your superscripts and subscripts appear exactly as you want them to, test your web pages on a variety of browsers. You may find that reducing the font size of superscripts and subscripts to your preferred size makes the characters small enough or light enough to become hard to see on the web page. If this happens and you do not want to increase the font size, try setting a heavier font weight or using a different font for the superscripts and subscripts.

How can I include equations in my web pages?
Look into Mathematical Markup Language, MathML, which is part of HTML5.

Understanding Ways to Set Color in CSS

CSS enables you to set color in several different ways. The most straightforward way is by using the color names built into CSS, such as red, green, and cornflowerblue. When you need a wider range of colors, you can specify a color by using a hexadecimal color code, an RGB or RGBA color value, or an HSL or HSLA color value. This section briefly explains these different methods.

Set Color by Using a Color Name

CSS has an extensive list of built-in colors that run the alphabetical gamut from aliceblue and antiquewhite all the way to yellow and yellowgreen. To use one of these colors, you simply specify it by name. The following example applies the saddlebrown color:

```
color: saddlebrown;
```

Set Color by Using a Hexadecimal Color Code

CSS lets you specify a color by using a hexadecimal color code. For example, the hexadecimal color code #800080 represents purple, the code #FFA500 represents orange, and the #4169E1 code represents royal blue. The following example applies royal blue:

```
color: #4169e1;
```

Set Color by Using an RGB or RGBA Color Value

RGB stands for Red, Green, Blue. RGB uses an additive color model that creates colors by adding different amounts of red, green, and blue light. An RGB value expresses the amount of red light, the amount of green light, and the amount of blue light, each as an integer in the range 0–255. For example, bright red is RGB(255, 0, 0) — the highest value for red, plus zero green and zero blue. The following example applies black:

```
color: rgb(0, 0, 0)
```

RGBA stands for Red, Green, Blue, Alpha, where the alpha value sets the transparency or opacity of the color, using a scale of 0–1, with 0 representing complete transparency and 1 representing total opacity. The following example applies semi-transparent red:

```
color: rgba(255, 0, 0, 0.5)
```

Set Color by Using an HSL or HSLA Color Value

HSL stands for Hue, Saturation, Lightness. Hue specifies the color's position on the color wheel, ranging from 0 degrees to 360 degrees. Saturation specifies the intensity of the color as a percentage, where 0% represents gray and 100% represents fully saturated color. Lightness specifies the brightness of the color as a percentage, where 0% is black, 100% is white, and 50% is the pure color. The following example applies a fully opaque blue color:

```
color: hsl(240, 100%, 50%);
```

HSLA stands for Hue, Saturation, Lightness, Alpha, where the alpha value sets the transparency or opacity of the color, using a scale of 0–1, with 0 representing complete transparency and 1 representing total opacity. The following example applies the previous blue color at 50% opacity:

```
color: hsla(240, 100%, 50%, 0.5)
```

Set Font Color

Changing the font color can be an easy and effective way to make your web pages look more visually appealing. CSS enables you to set the font color for text by using the methods explained in the previous section, "Understanding Ways to Set Color in CSS." This section illustrates setting the font color by specifying the color name.

Set Font Color

1 In Visual Studio Code, open the external CSS file in which you want to set font colors.

2 Also in Visual Studio Code, open an HTML file to which you have linked the external CSS file.

3 Open the HTML file in a browser window.

Note: If you are starting a new style, type the name, followed by a space and {. Visual Studio Code automatically enters the matching closing brace, }.

4 Click in the style where you want to add the color.

5 Type **co**.

The expansions list appears.

6 Click **color**.

Ⓐ Visual Studio Code inserts the color property.

The values list appears.

7 If you want to enter a color by name, click the name. Otherwise, type the hexadecimal code, RGB or RGBA code, or HSL or HSLA code for the color.

Ⓑ The color value appears in the code.

8 Click **Refresh** (↻).

The web page refreshes.

Ⓒ The element takes on the color formatting.

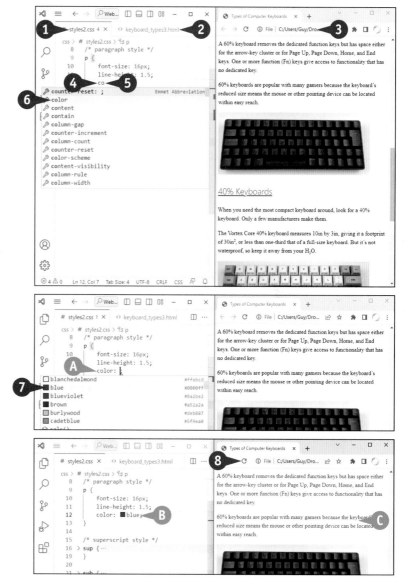

Apply Text Shadows

The text-shadow property in CSS lets you apply text shadows to a style. This property takes four arguments: h-shadow, v-shadow, blur-radius, and color. The h-shadow argument specifies the horizontal distance between the shadow and the text; a negative value moves the shadow to the left, whereas a positive value moves the shadow to the right. The v-shadow argument specifies the vertical distance between the shadow and the text; a negative value moves it up, and a positive value moves it down. The blur-radius argument specifies the degree of blur applied to the shadow. The color argument specifies the color.

Apply Text Shadows

1 In Visual Studio Code, open the external CSS file in which you want to apply text shadows.

2 Also in Visual Studio Code, open an HTML file to which you have linked the external CSS file.

3 Open the HTML file in a browser window.

Note: If you are starting a new style, type the name, followed by a space and {. Visual Studio Code automatically enters the matching closing brace, }.

4 Click in the style where you want to apply the text shadows.

5 Type **te**.

The expansions list appears.

6 Click **text-shadow**.

A Visual Studio Code inserts the text-shadow property.

Visual Studio Code displays the values list.

7 Type the horizontal distance. This example uses **3px**.

8 Type a space and the vertical distance. This example uses **6px**.

9 Type a space and the blur radius. This example uses **6px**.

10 Type a space and the color. This example uses **black**.

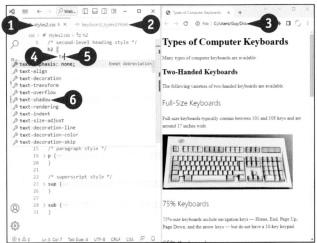

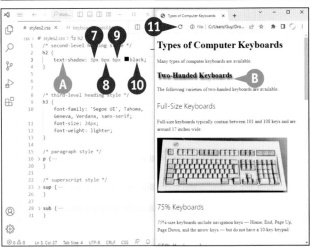

11 Click **Refresh** (⟳).

The web page refreshes.

B The text shadow appears.

Display Monospaced Font

CSS enables you to display monospaced font in your web pages. A *monospaced* font gives each character the same width rather than allowing the character width to vary. Monospaced font is useful for displaying information such as program code and for distinguishing technical terms from regular text.

To use a monospaced font, you can create a class selector for it in your CSS file and specify a suitable font family, such as Courier, with the system monospace font as a fallback. You can then use a span element to mark each relevant section of text as belonging to the class.

Display Monospaced Font

1 In Visual Studio Code, open the external CSS file in which you want to apply monospaced font.

2 Also in Visual Studio Code, open an HTML file to which you have linked the external CSS file.

3 Open the HTML file in a browser window.

4 In the CSS, type the name for the class selector — for example:

```
.mono {
```

5 Enter the font-family property and assign the monospace fonts — for example,

```
font-family: "Courier New",
Courier, monospace;
```

6 End the style definition with a closing brace, }.

7 Click the HTML file.

The HTML file becomes active.

8 Create a span element that encompasses each term. Assign the mono class to each span. For example:

```
<span class="mono">actuation
force</span>
```

9 Click **Refresh** (C).

The web page refreshes.

A The terms marked by the span elements appear in monospaced font.

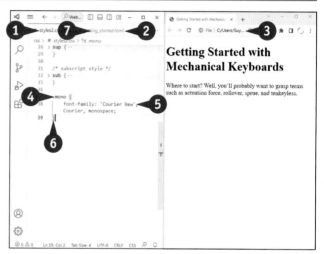

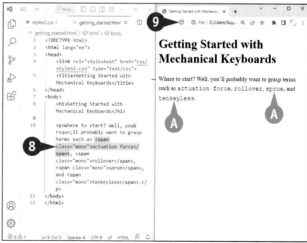

Apply Text Decoration

CSS provides the `text-decoration` property for applying "decoration" to text. You can use the `overline` value to apply a line above the text, use the `underline` value to apply an underline beneath the text, use the `linethrough` value to apply strikethrough, a line straight across the text. After specifying the line type, you can set its color, such as `chocolate` or `darksalmon`; set its style, such as `dashed`, `dotted`, `wavy`, or `solid`; and set its thickness.

Apply Text Decoration

1 In Visual Studio Code, open the external CSS file in which you want to define text decoration.

2 Also in Visual Studio Code, open an HTML file to which you have linked the external CSS file.

3 Open the HTML file in a browser window.

Note: If you are starting a new style, type the name, followed by a space and {. Visual Studio Code automatically enters the matching closing brace, }.

4 Click in the style where you want to apply the text decoration.

5 Type **te**.

The expansions list appears.

6 Click **text-decoration**.

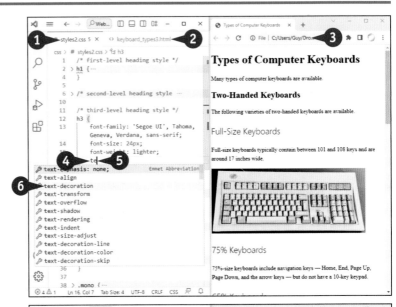

A Visual Studio Code enters the `text-decoration` property.

The values list appears.

7 Click **line-through**, **overline**, or **underline**, as needed. This example uses **underline**.

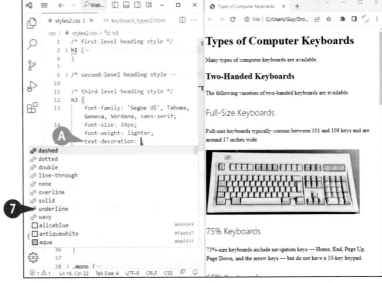

B Visual Studio Code inserts the code for the line type you clicked.

8 Click **Refresh** (C).

The web page refreshes.

C The line appears using default settings — a solid black line.

9 Type a space and the color for the line — for example:

```
text-decoration: underline red
```

10 Type another space and the line style — for example:

```
text-decoration: underline red wavy
```

11 Type another space and the line thickness — for example:

```
text-decoration: underline red wavy 5px
```

12 Click **Refresh** (C).

The web page refreshes.

D The line displays the formatting you specified.

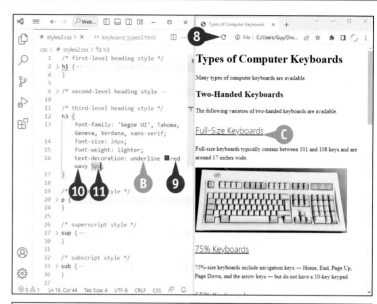

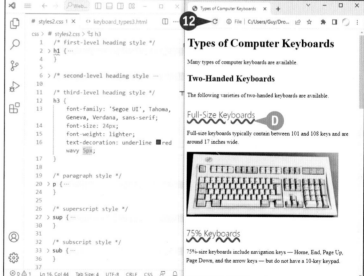

TIP

What is the `text-decoration-line` property for?
CSS gives you two ways to specify text decoration. The compact way is to use the `text-decoration` property as in the main text, specifying the line type as the first argument, the color as the second argument, the line style as the third, and the thickness as the fourth; the first argument is required, and the three others are optional. The longer-winded way is to use the `text-decoration-line` property to set the line type, the `text-decoration-color` property to set the color, the `text-decoration-style` property to set the style, and the `text-decoration-thickness` property to set the thickness.

Understanding HTML Entities

As well as regular characters that you can type using a keyboard, HTML enables you to include what are called *HTML entities* — special codes used to represent reserved characters and symbols. HTML entities typically consist of a special code or name entered between an ampersand symbol, &, and a semicolon, ;. For example, you can enter the HTML entity ∑ to enter the sum symbol, Σ, in an HTML document.

What Are HTML Entities?

HTML entities are codes you can enter in your HTML to represent characters and symbols that you cannot type directly into the HTML.

Some HTML entities are *reserved characters*, which means characters used in the HTML language. For example, HTML tags use the less-than symbol, <, and greater-than symbol, >, as delimiters, so HTML disallows the use of these characters for other purposes but provides the HTML entities < for inserting a less-than symbol and > for inserting a greater-than symbol in HTML documents. Similarly, because the HTML entities use the ampersand character, &, you cannot use the ampersand directly in an HTML document. Instead, you need to use the HTML entity, &.

Other HTML entities are characters that do not appear on standard computer keyboards. These entities cover everything from mathematical symbols and currency symbols to marks such as the pilcrow, ¶; and from characters in other languages, such as Greek, to invisible characters such as nonbreaking spaces.

Each HTML entity has an entity number, which starts with &#, and then has a unique number and ends with a semicolon, ;. Each of the more widely used HTML entities also has an entity name starting with & and ending with ;, which most people find easier to remember. For example, the Japanese yen symbol, ¥, has the entity number ¥ and the entity name ¥. If the entity has a name, you can enter either the name or the number in your HTML.

Widely Used HTML Entities

Table 8-1 lists the most widely used HTML entities. The table shows the entity's number and description, the entity's name if it has one, and how the entity appears — assuming it has a visible appearance.

Table 8-1:   Widely Used HTML Entities

Character	Entity Number	Entity Name	Description	Character	Entity Number	Entity Name	Description
N/A			Nonbreaking space	1	&#185;	&sup1;	Superscript 1
N/A	&#173;	&shy;	Soft hyphen, optional hyphen	2	&#178;	&sup2;	Superscript 2
&	&#32;	&amp;	Ampersand	3	&#179;	&sup3;	Superscript 3
'	&#8216;	&lsquo;	Left single quotation mark	´	&#180;	&acute;	Spacing acute
'	&#8217;	&rsquo;	Right single quotation mark	µ	&#181;	&micro;	Micro, mu
"	&#8220;	&ldquo;	Left double quotation mark	¶	&#182;	&para;	Paragraph
"	&#8221;	&rdquo;	Right double quotation mark	¸	&#184;	&cedil;	Spacing cedilla
<	@#60;	&lt;	Less-than sign, left angle bracket	º	&#186;	&ordm;	Masculine ordinal indicator
>	@#62;	&gt;	Greater-than sign, right angle bracket	¼	&#188;	&frac14;	Fraction 1/4
¢	&#162;	&cent;	Cent sign	½	&#189;	&frac12;	Fraction 1/2
£	&#163;	&pound;	Pound sign	¾	&#190;	&frac34;	Fraction 3/4
¥	&#165;	&yen;	Yen sign	¡	&#161;	&iexcl;	Inverted exclamation mark
¦	&#166;	&brvbar;	Broken vertical bar	¿	&#191;	&iquest;	Inverted question mark
§	&#167;	&sect;	Section	×	&#215;	&times;	Multiplication sign, times sign
¨	&#168;	&uml;	Spacing dieresis, umlaut	÷	&#247;	&divide;	Division sign
©	&#169;	&copy;	Copyright symbol	∏	&#8719;	&prod;	Product
ª	&#170;	&ordf;	Feminine ordinal indicator	∑	&#8721;	&sum;	Sum
«	&#171;	&laquo;	Left angle quotation mark	−	&#8722;	&minus;	Minus
»	&#187;	&raquo;	Right angle quotation mark	∗	&#8727;	&lowast;	Asterisk
¬	&#172;	&not;	Negation	√	&#8730;	&radic;	Square root
®	&#174;	&reg;	Registered trademark	∝	&#8733;	&prop;	Proportional to
¯	&#175;	&macr;	Spacing macron	∞	&#8734;	&infin;	Infinity
°	&#176;	&deg;	Degree symbol	α	&#945;	&alpha;	Lowercase alpha
±	&#177;	&plusmn;	Plus or minus	β	&#946;	&beta;	Lowercase beta
				γ	&#947;	&gamma;	Lowercase gamma
				δ	&#948;	&delta;	Lowercase delta
				ε	&#949;	&epsilon;	Lowercase epsilon

Insert Special Characters with HTML Entities

Once you know the HTML entity code for the special character you want to insert, you can quickly insert the code in a web page and display that character.

This section provides quick examples of inserting HTML entities. See the previous section, "Understanding HTML Entities," for a list of widely used HTML entity codes. For other entity codes, search online.

Insert Special Characters with HTML Entities

① In Visual Studio Code, open the HTML file you want to work on.

② Open the HTML file in a browser window.

③ Click where you want to insert the special character.

④ Type the entity name or entity code for the character. This example uses the entity name **—**, which inserts an em dash.

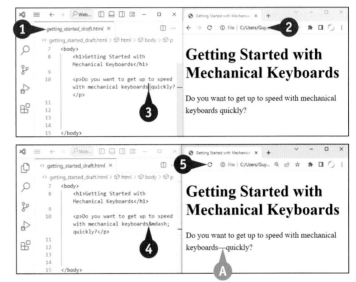

⑤ Click **Refresh** (🔄).

The web page refreshes.

Ⓐ The em dash appears.

⑥ Start a new paragraph and type the following text:

“Ready?”

⑦ Click **Refresh** (🔄).

The web page refreshes.

Ⓑ The left double quotation mark, specified by “, appears. You could use &#8220 instead.

Ⓒ The right double quotation mark, specified by ”, appears. You could use ” instead.

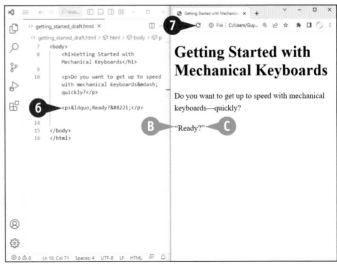

Note: A *nonbreaking space* is a space that keeps the preceding word and following word together even if they would otherwise be separated by a line breaking. For example, Acme Corporation ensures that the words appear on the same line.

Insert Emojis

Emojis, also called *emoticons* or *smileys*, started in instant messaging but have now colonized email, web pages, and other areas of online life. HTML enables you to insert an emoji in an HTML document by specifying the appropriate entity number in the Unicode character set called UTF-8, which contains most of the standard characters and symbols used in world languages.

To find the entity number, also called the *code point*, of the emoji you want to insert, visit an online site such as Emojipedia, `www.emojipedia.org`. Search or browse to locate the emoji, find the Codepoints readout, and copy the number.

Insert Emojis

1 In Visual Studio Code, open the HTML file you want to work on.

2 Open the HTML file in a browser window.

3 Click where you want to insert the emoji.

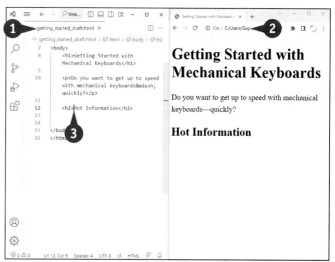

4 Type **&#x** followed by the emoji code point and a semicolon, **;**. For example, the code point for the fire emoji is 1F525, so the following statement inserts this emoji:

```
&#x1F525;
```

5 Click **Refresh** (⟳).

The web page refreshes.

A The emoji appears.

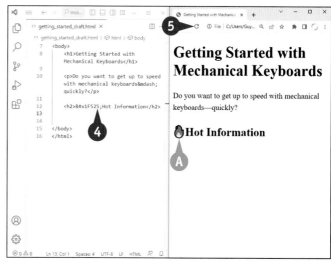

Using Custom Fonts on Web Pages

When you need to move beyond the fonts available in the browser, you can use CSS's capability to include custom fonts from external sources. If you have permission to distribute the fonts, you can host them on your web server; if not, you can have the browser download the fonts from a font library. Either way, you should define fallback fonts that specify which fonts to use if the custom fonts are not available. You can specify a stack of fallback fonts to use; the browser works its way down the stack until it finds a font that is available.

Provide Custom Fonts on Your Web Server

If you have developed fonts of your own or if you have downloaded fonts that you have permission to distribute, you can host the fonts on your web server. To help keep your files orderly, create a folder for the fonts and store them there rather than putting them in the same folder as your web pages.

Next, declare the font. If you are working in an external CSS file linked to a web page that will use the fonts, you can put the declaration anywhere; for simplicity, put the declaration along with your other declarations. If you are working in an HTML file rather than an external CSS file, put the declaration in the head section.

Declare the font using an @font-face rule, using the src attribute to provide the URL path to the font file within single quotes and parentheses. Here is an example for a custom font-family called MyFont stored in the file named myfont.ttf in the /fonts/ folder.

```
@font-face {
    font-family: 'MyFont';
    src: url('/fonts/myfont.ttf');
}
```

Next, apply the font as needed to styles. The following example uses MyFont as the preferred font for the body element, falling back to Helvetica Neue if MyFont is missing and then falling back to the system sans-serif font if Helvetica Neue is not available.

```
body {
    font-family: 'MyFont', 'Helvetica Neue', sans-serif;
}
```

Using Fonts from a Font Library

If you have neither fonts of your own nor permission to distribute other people's fonts, you can set your web pages to download fonts from a font library. A wide variety of font libraries are available on the Internet. Some font libraries are free, such as Google Fonts, fonts.google.com; other font libraries have paid subscriptions, such as Adobe Fonts, fonts.adobe.com, shown in the nearby illustration.

Browse your chosen library to find the font you want to use, and then get the embed code for the font. For example, on Google Fonts, click a font to reach its page, and then add each font to the Selected Families list (A). You can then click **<link>** (B, ◯ changes to ◉), select the link code (C), and paste it into your HTML document.

Once you have linked the HTML document to the font's source, you can start using the font in style definitions. When a browser requests the web page, the link causes the browser to download the font from the font library and use it to display the page.

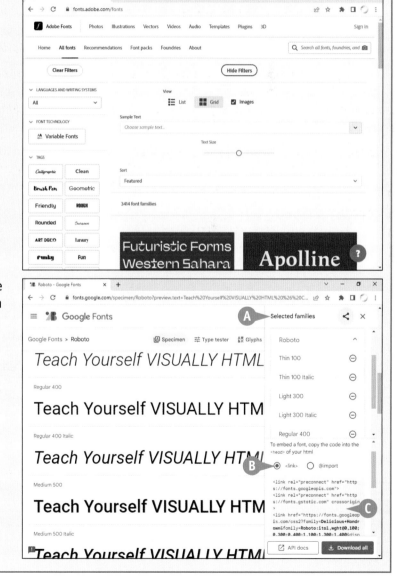

Sizing and Positioning with CSS

In this chapter, you learn how to use CSS to size and position elements in your web pages. You work with elements, pseudo-classes, and pseudo-elements; use the :important declaration to override CSS; and control padding, borders, and margins. You fix elements in place, float elements alongside other elements, and create CSS Flexboxes to allocate space dynamically.

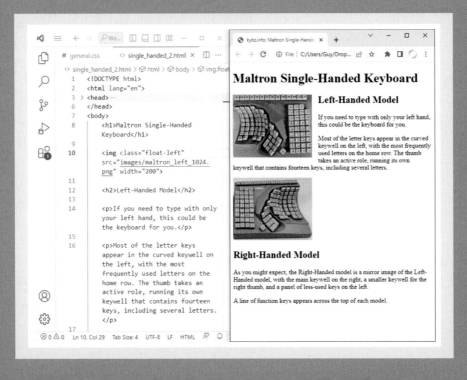

Understanding Pseudo-Classes

In Chapter 7, you learned to use CSS classes, selectors that enable you to apply styles to items you mark as belonging to a particular class. For example, if you define a style called .dramatic, you can apply it to different elements by using class statements, such as <p class="dramatic"> and <h3 class="dramatic">.

CSS also provides *pseudo-classes*, predefined special selectors that enable you to apply styles to elements depending on their current state or their relationship to other elements. This section shows you the essentials of pseudo-classes. The next section, "Apply Contextual Formatting with Pseudo-Classes," provides examples of using pseudo-classes.

What Are Pseudo-Classes, and When Do You Use Them?

Pseudo-classes are an ingenious way to apply formatting to specific states or specific attributes of HTML elements that you cannot identify using regular selectors. A pseudo-class selects elements that are in the state specified by the class. For example, the :hover pseudo-class selects the element over which the pointer is hovering, whereas the :only-child pseudo-class selects elements that are the only child of the parent element that contains them.

The CSS specification defines more than 30 pseudo-classes. You can use these pseudo-classes freely, but you cannot define pseudo-classes of your own.

Table 9-1 lists the pseudo-classes current as of this writing, but you should also check to see if further pseudo-classes have been added by the time you read this.

How to Use Pseudo-Classes

To use a pseudo-class, declare a style for it in the external CSS file linked to the HTML document or in the internal style sheet in the head section of the HTML document itself. The following example declares the :hover pseudo-class for the h1 element:

```
h1:hover {
    background-color: blueviolet;
    color: antiquewhite;
}
```

You then use the element as normal in an HTML document. For example, you might create some h1 elements like this:

```
<h1>First Heading 1</h1>
<p>First body paragraph.</p>
<h1>Second Heading 1</h1>
<p>Second body paragraph.</p>
```

First Heading 1

First body paragraph.

Second Heading 1

Second body paragraph.

When you move the pointer over one of the h1 elements, the background color changes to blueviolet, and the font color changes to antiquewhite, as shown in the nearby illustration. Note the difference from the second h1 element, which retains the default background color and font color.

Table 9-1: Pseudo-Classes in CSS

Pseudo-Class	What It Selects
`:active`	An element that is being activated, such as by clicking
`:any-link`	Any link element, including visited and unvisited links
`:checked`	A radio button or check box element that is checked
`:default`	The default option in a drop-down list
`:disabled`	A disabled element
`:empty`	An element that has no children
`:enabled`	An enabled element
`:first-child`	The first child of a parent element
`:first-of-type`	The first element of its type within a parent element
`:focus`	An element that has focus
`:hover`	An element the pointer is hovering over
`:indeterminate`	A check box element that is neither checked nor unchecked
`:in-range`	An input element with a value within a specified range
`:invalid`	An input element with an invalid value
`:last-child`	The last child of a parent element
`:last-of-type`	The last element of its type within a parent element
`:link`	An unvisited link element
`:not()`	Elements that do not match a specific selector
`:nth-child()`	Elements that are the *n*th child of their parent element
`:nth-last-child()`	Elements that are the *n*th child from the end of their parent element
`:nth-last-of-type()`	Elements that are the *n*th of their type from the end of their parent element
`:nth-of-type()`	Elements that are the *n*th of their type within a parent element
`:only-child`	An element that is the only child of its parent
`:only-of-type`	An element that is the only one of its type within a parent element
`:optional`	An input element that is optional rather than required
`:out-of-range`	An input element with a value outside the specified range
`:read-only`	An input element that is read-only
`:read-write`	An input element that is read-write
`:required`	An input element that is required
`:root`	The `html` element, the root element of a document
`:target`	The target element of the current URL
`:valid`	An input element with a valid value
`:visited`	A visited link element

In the previous section, "Understanding Pseudo-Classes," you learned what pseudo-classes are: smart selectors that enable you to select elements that you would otherwise not be able to target.

This section shows you how to use pseudo-classes to apply contextual formatting in HTML documents. The examples use the `:first-child` pseudo-class to apply formatting to the first list item in an unordered list and the `:nth-child` pseudo-class to apply formatting to subsequent list items in unordered lists.

Apply Contextual Formatting with Pseudo-Classes

1 In Visual Studio Code, open the external CSS file you want to work on.

Note: You can also use pseudo-classes in an internal style sheet. This example uses an external CSS file.

2 Also in Visual Studio Code, open an HTML file linked to the external CSS file.

3 Open the HTML file in a browser window.

4 Click to place the insertion point where you want to define the style for the pseudo-class.

5 Type the name of the element to affect, followed by the pseudo-class name and **{**. The following example applies the `:first-child` pseudo-class to the `ul li` element, the list item in an unordered list:

```
ul li:first-child {
```

Note: `ul li` is a complex selector. See the following section, "Understanding CSS Combinators."

Visual Studio Code enters the matching closing }.

6 Press **Enter** to create a blank line, and then enter the first attribute.

7 On subsequent lines, enter other attributes, as needed.

8 Click **Refresh** (⟳).

The web page refreshes.

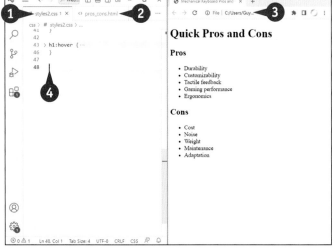

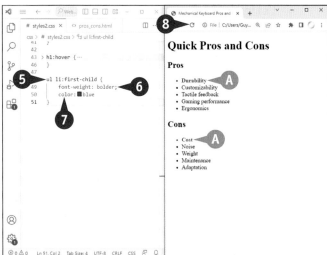

Ⓐ The first child item in each unordered list takes on the pseudo-class formatting.

9 In the CSS file, type the name of the element to affect, followed by the pseudo-class name and **{**. The following example applies the :nth-child pseudo-class to the ul li element, specifying the 2 item, the second child:

```
ul li:nth-child(2) {
```

Visual Studio Code enters the matching closing }.

10 Press Enter to create a blank line, and then enter the first attribute.

11 On subsequent lines, enter other attributes, as needed.

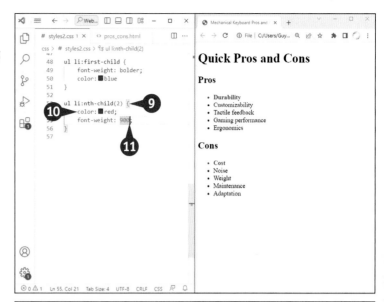

12 Create any other pseudo-class styles needed. The following example shows a style for the third list item in each unordered list:

```
ul li:nth-child(3) {
    color:darkgoldenrod;
    font-weight:900;
}
```

13 Click **Refresh** (C).

The web page refreshes.

B The items specified by the pseudo-classes take on the formatting.

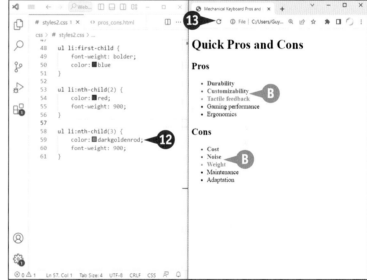

Understanding CSS Combinators

As you have seen so far in this book, CSS enables you to apply a style to an element by using a simple selector. For example, you can use the h1 selector to apply styles to all the h1 elements in an HTML document. But CSS also lets you apply styles by using multiple simple selectors linked together with four special characters called *combinators*.

In this section, you meet the four combinators and learn how they work. In the next section, "Target Elements Using CSS Combinators," you start using the combinators to create complex selectors.

Understanding the Four Combinators

CSS provides four combinators, special characters that you use to link together simple selectors to create complex selectors. Table 9-2 explains the combinators. The following subsections provide examples of putting the combinators to use.

<table>
<tr><td colspan="3" align="center">Table 9-2: CSS Combinator Characters</td></tr>
<tr><th>Combinator Character</th><th>Name</th><th>Example</th></tr>
<tr><td>[a space]</td><td>Descendant selector</td><td>ul li selects the li elements that are the descendant of ul elements.</td></tr>
<tr><td>></td><td>Child selector</td><td>div > h2 selects the h2 elements that are children of the div element.</td></tr>
<tr><td>+</td><td>Adjacent sibling selector</td><td>h1 + p selects each p element that immediately follows an h1 element.</td></tr>
<tr><td>~</td><td>General sibling selector</td><td>h2 + p selects each p element that follows an h2 element, whether the p element is immediately after the h2 element or not.</td></tr>
</table>

Using the Descendant Selector

When you need to select an element that is the descendant of another element, use the descendant selector, a space. For example, say you have an ordered list that contains a nested unordered list, like this:

```
<ol>
    <li>Get a keycap puller.
        <ul>
            <li>Many online stores
sell keycap pullers</li>
            <li>Alternatively, use
two small screwdrivers.</li>
        </ul>
    </li>
    <li>Insert the puller under
the keycap.</li>
    <li>Pull upward gently.</li>
</ol>
```

Here, the unordered list is the descendant of the ordered list, so you can target the unordered list by using the descendant selector to link the ol element and the ul element, like this:

```
ol ul {
    color:aquamarine;
}
```

Using the Child Selector

When you need to select all elements that are immediate children of a parent element, use the child selector, >. For example, suppose you have a div element that contains h2 elements, like this:

```
<div>
    <h2>Actuation Force</h2>
    <p>The distance to where the
keystroke is registered.</p>
    <h2>Chattering</h2>
    <p>When one keypress registers
as multiple keypresses.</p>
</div>
```

You could use the child selector to target the h2 elements like this:

```
div > h2 {
    color: blue;
}
```

There is some overlap between the child selector and the descendant selector. The difference between the two is that the child selector selects only the immediate children of an element, whereas the descendant selector selects all the descendants — children, grandchildren, great-grandchildren, and so on.

Using the Adjacent Sibling Selector

When you need to target each element of a particular type that immediately follows another specific element, use the adjacent sibling selector, +. For example, suppose your HTML document contains h2 elements followed by p elements, like this:

```
<h2>Chattering</h2>
<p>When one keypress registers as
multiple keypresses.</p>
<p>Chattering is generally
problematic.</p>
<h2>Click</h2>
```

```
<p>The noise made when the key
switch is activated.</p>
<h2>Clack</h2>
<p>The noise made when the switch
bottoms out.</p>
```

You could use the adjacent sibling selector to target the first p element after each h2 element like this:

```
h2 + p {
    font-style: italic;
}
```

Here, only the first p element after each h2 element receives the italic formatting. Subsequent p elements do not.

Using the General Sibling Selector

When you need to target each element of a particular type that follows another specific element, use the general sibling selector, ~. For example, if your HTML document contains the example shown in the previous subsection, you could apply italic formatting to each p element that falls after an h2 element, like this:

```
h2 ~ p {
    font-style: italic;
}
```

Target Elements Using CSS Combinators

In the previous section, "Understanding CSS Combinators," you met the four CSS combinators: the descendant selector, the child selector, the adjacent sibling selector, and the general sibling selector. These combinators enable you to target elements based on their relationship to other elements — for example, to target each h2 element that is the immediate child of a div element.

In this section, you put the CSS combinators into use to target particular elements.

Target Elements Using CSS Combinators

Open the CSS File and HTML File

1 In Visual Studio Code, open the external CSS file you want to work on.

2 Also in Visual Studio Code, open an HTML file to which you have linked the external CSS file.

3 Open the HTML file in a browser window.

4 In Visual Studio Code, click in the CSS file to place the insertion point where you want to define the first style.

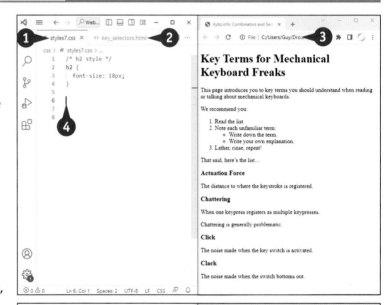

Target an Element with a Child Selector

1 Type the parent element name, a space, the child element name, another space, and **{** — for example:

```
ol ul {
```

A Visual Studio Code inserts the matching closing brace, **}**.

2 Press Enter to create a blank line (not shown).

3 On the blank line, type the style formatting.

4 Click **Refresh** (⟳).

The web page refreshes.

B The ul child element of the ol element takes on the formatting.

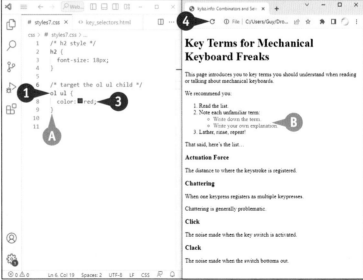

Target an Element with an Adjacent Sibling Selector

1 Type the first element name, the adjacent sibling selector, **+**; the second element name; a space; and **{** — for example:

```
h2 + p {
```

C Visual Studio Code inserts the matching closing brace, **}**.

2 Press **Enter** to create a blank line (not shown).

3 On the blank line, type the style formatting.

4 Click **Refresh** (↻).

The web page refreshes.

D The first p element after each h2 element takes on the formatting.

E Subsequent p elements are not affected.

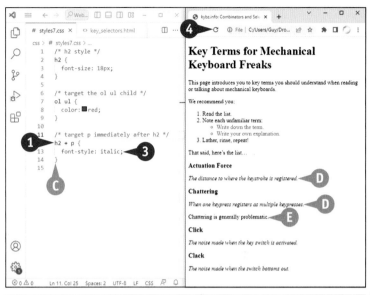

Target an Element with a General Sibling Selector

1 Go back to the previous subsection's example, select +, and type ~ over it:

```
h2 ~ p {
```

2 Click **Refresh** (↻).

The web page refreshes.

F Each p element after each h2 element takes on the formatting.

TIP

Can I combine combinators for complex selections?

Yes, you can combine multiple combinators into a single selector. For example, if you want to select all the li elements that are descendants of an ol element *and* that follow an h2 element, you could use the following selector, specifying the style as usual between the braces, {}:

```
h3 ~ ol li {}
```

Understanding Pseudo-Elements

As well as the elements with which you have now worked extensively, CSS provides *pseudo-elements*, selectors that enable you to style specific parts of an HTML element. For example, you can use the `::first-letter` pseudo-element to select the first letter of a block element, such as a heading or a paragraph.

As of this writing, CSS defines 14 standard pseudo-elements. Not all browsers fully implement all these pseudo-elements, so when you use pseudo-elements in your HTML documents, you should test those documents on all the browsers you want your website to support.

What Is the Point of Pseudo-Elements?

The pseudo-elements enable you to target parts of an HTML document that you could not otherwise target and apply formatting to those parts.

The pseudo-elements are predefined in the CSS specifications. You cannot create pseudo-elements of your own. You may be able to achieve a similar effect by creating a custom attribute for an HTML element and then using a CSS attribute selector to target that attribute. This topic is beyond the scope of this book.

Which Pseudo-Elements Are Available?

Table 9-3 explains the 14 pseudo-elements available as of this writing.

Table 9-3: CSS Pseudo-Elements	
Pseudo-Element	**What It Does**
`::after`	Inserts content after an element
`::backdrop`	Applies styles to the background behind a modal or dialog box
`::before`	Inserts content before an element
`::cue`	Applies styles to the text content of a cue element in a video or audio element
`::file-selector-button`	Applies styles to the file-selector button, the button that opens the file-selection dialog box for uploading a file
`::first-letter`	Selects the first letter of the first line of text in an element
`::first-line`	Selects the first line of text in an element
`::grammar-error`	Applies styles to text identified as having a grammatical error by the `spellcheck` attribute
`::marker`	Applies styles to the list item marker in a list
`::part`	Selects a specific part of a Shadow DOM element
`::placeholder`	Applies styles to the placeholder text in an `input` or `textarea` element
`::selection`	Selects the portion of an element that is selected by a user
`::spelling-error`	Applies styles to text identified as having a spelling error by the `spellcheck` attribute
`::target-text`	Applies styles to text to which the window has been scrolled

Examples of Using Pseudo-Elements

The `::after` pseudo-element enables you to display a specified element after a particular element. The following example uses the `::after` element to display a horizontal black line after each h2 element. The black line has no content, is 3 pixels wide, spans 75 percent of the window width, and is centered 10 pixels below the h2 element.

```css
h2::after {
  content: "";
  display: block;
  height: 3px;
  width: 75%;
  background-color: black;
  margin: 10px auto 0;
}
```

The `selection` pseudo-element lets you apply styles to the portion of an element that the user has selected. For example, if the user selects some of the text in a p element, the following CSS applies formatting to the selection:

```css
::selection {
    background-color: aquamarine;
    color: blue;
}
```

Check That the Pseudo-Elements Work on the Browsers Important to You

Generally speaking, all current browsers support these five pseudo-elements: `::after`, `::before`, `::first-letter`, `::first-line`, and `::selection`.

Not all browsers support the remaining nine pseudo-elements. Support varies depending not only on the browser version but also the platform on which it is running. For example, Google Chrome does not support the `::cue` pseudo-element at all and does not fully support the `::marker` pseudo-element, whereas Mozilla Firefox does not support the `::backdrop` pseudo-element.

Because of this limited support, be sure to test your HTML documents that use pseudo-elements on all the browsers for which you want your website to work. If possible, test these documents with screen readers as well, because pseudo-elements can cause problems for some screen readers.

Apply CSS to Pseudo-Elements

In the previous section, "Understanding Pseudo-Elements," you learned what the pseudo-elements in CSS are and how they work. In this section, you put two of the pseudo-elements to use. The `::first-letter` pseudo-element enables you to apply styles to the first character in a particular element, whereas the `::first-line` pseudo-element lets you apply styles to the first line of an element.

The key difference between pseudo-elements and pseudo-classes is that pseudo-elements target a specific part of an element, whereas pseudo-classes target an element when it is in a specific state, such as when the pointer is hovering over it.

Apply CSS to Pseudo-Elements

1. In Visual Studio Code, open the external CSS file you want to work on.

2. Also in Visual Studio Code, open an HTML file to which you have linked the external CSS file.

3. Open the HTML file in a browser window.

4. In the style sheet, click to place the insertion point where you want to add the pseudo-element.

Add the `::first-letter` Pseudo-Element

1. Type the element you want to affect, followed by **::first-letter**, a space, and **{** — for example:

    p::first-letter {

   Visual Studio Code inserts the matching closing brace, }.

2. Press Enter to create a blank line (not shown).

3. On the blank line, enter the first attribute of the formatting you want to apply.

4. On subsequent lines, enter other formatting, as needed.

5. Click **Refresh** (↻).

   The web page refreshes.

Ⓐ The first character of each instance of the element takes on the formatting.

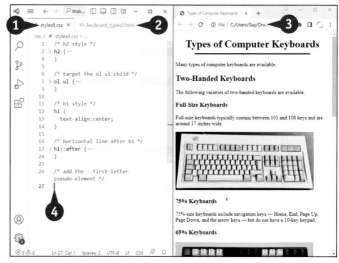

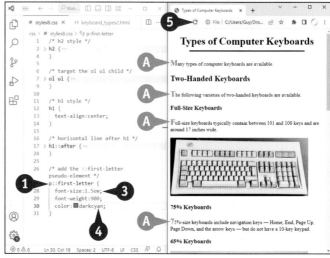

Add the ::first-line Pseudo-Element

1 In the CSS file, type the element you want to affect, followed by **::first-line**, a space, and **{** — for example:

```
p::first-line {
```

Visual Studio Code inserts the matching closing brace, **}**.

2 Press Enter to create a blank line (not shown).

3 On the blank line, enter the first attribute of the formatting you want to apply.

4 On subsequent lines, enter other formatting, as needed.

5 Click **Refresh** (C).

The web page refreshes.

B The first line of each instance of the element takes on the formatting.

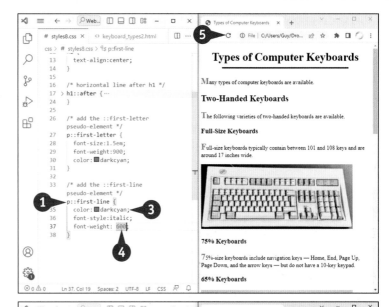

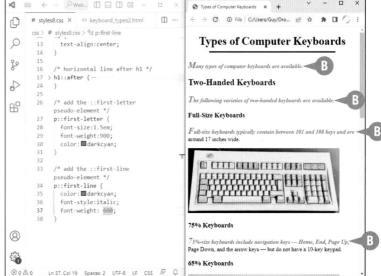

What is the best way to use pseudo-elements in my HTML documents?

Use pseudo-elements to add decoration rather than content to your HTML documents. For example, you might use pseudo-elements to apply decorative shapes after elements such as headings. While you *can* use pseudo-elements to add content to documents, using actual HTML elements to add content and then applying styles as needed to those elements is usually better. Avoid overloading a page with pseudo-elements, because they may make the page display more slowly on visitors' computers.

Override CSS by Using the `!important` Declaration

When you apply multiple CSS properties to the same element, some properties may override other properties. To help you control which properties get applied, CSS provides a declaration called `!important` that you can use to specify a CSS property that you want to assign higher priority. Marking a property as `!important` makes it override any other style rules that apply to the same property.

This section uses a straightforward example to illustrate the use of the `!important` declaration. In your web development, you will likely encounter subtler CSS problems that the `!important` declaration can solve.

Override CSS by Using the `!important` Declaration

1 In Visual Studio Code, open the external CSS file you want to work on.

2 Also in Visual Studio Code, open an HTML file to which you have linked the external CSS file.

Ⓐ The sample HTML file contains a `dl` element, a definition list.

Ⓑ Each `dt` element contains a definition term.

Ⓒ Each `dd` element contains a definition description.

3 Open the HTML file in a browser window.

Ⓓ The definition list appears.

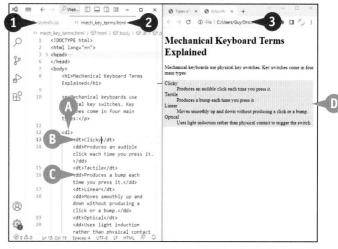

4 Click the CSS file's tab.

The CSS file appears.

5 Type a style definition for the element to which you will apply multiple styles. This example uses the `dt` element and applies red color and 900 weight:

```
dt {
    color: red;
    font-weight:900;
}
```

6 Click **Refresh** (🔄).

The web page refreshes.

Ⓔ The definition terms take on the red boldface.

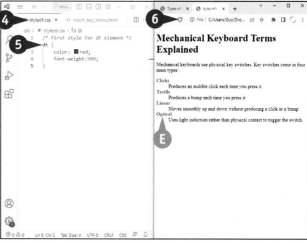

7 Click in the CSS file again.

The CSS file becomes active.

8 Type a second style definition for the same element, using visibly different formatting. This example applies blue color and 400 weight to the dt element:

```
dt {
    color: blue;
    font-weight:400;
}
```

9 Click **Refresh** (↻).

The web page refreshes.

F The definition terms take on the blue formatting and lighter weight.

10 Click to place the insertion point just before the ; ending the style property you want to make important (not shown).

In this example, you would click between red and ;.

11 Type **!important**, as in this example:

```
dt {
    color: red !important;
    font-weight:900;
}
```

12 Click **Refresh** (↻).

The web page refreshes.

G The definition terms take on the red color because it is marked !important, but their weight remains 400.

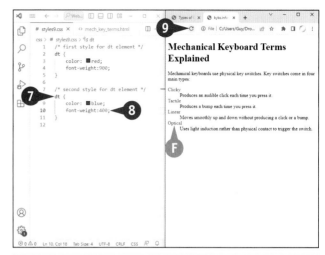

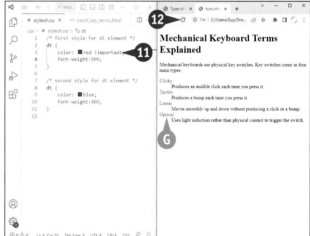

TIP

When a style sheet defines the same style twice, which definition does the browser use?

When there are multiple definitions of the same style in the same style sheet file, the browser applies the style that it encounters last when reading the style sheet file from start to finish. In this section's example, the first dt style applies red and 900 weight, while the second dt style applies blue and 400 weight; so the browser uses blue and 400 weight.

Where there are multiple style sources, the style cascade applies as usual: Inline styles override internal styles, which in turn override external styles.

Understanding the CSS Box Model

CSS uses a concept called a *box model* to describe how to render HTML elements on a web page. The CSS box model consists of four parts: the content on the inside, the padding around it, the border around the padding, and the margin outside the border.

This section explains the CSS box model, using brief examples. The following three sections show you how to use the box model, using hands-on examples.

Visualize the CSS Box Model

The CSS box model consists of four main parts, as shown in the nearby illustration:

- **Margin** (A). The *margin* is the space between the box's border and the next element above the box, below it, or to its left or right.

- **Border** (B). The *border* is the line around the box. You can format the border as needed — for example, you can set the line thickness and color. You can hide the border by setting the `border` property to `none`.

- **Padding** (C). The *padding* is the space between the inside of the border and the outside of the content.

- **Content** (D). The *content* appears inside the padding. The content may be text, an image, or another object.

Understanding the Three Ways of Setting Margins, Borders, and Padding

CSS enables you to set each of the three outer elements of the CSS box — the margins, the borders, and the padding — in three different ways:

- Set a single measurement for all sides by using the `margin` property, the `border` property, or the `padding` property.

- Set each side separately by using the individual properties. For example, to set the margin, you would use the `margin-top` property, the `margin-right` property, the `margin-bottom` property, and the `margin-left` property.

- Set each side with a single statement by using shorthand properties.

The following subsections show you how to use each of these methods.

Set a Single Measurement for All Sides

When you want to use the same measurement for each side's margin, border, or padding, you can use the `margin` property, the `border` property, or the `padding` property. For example, the following style sets a three-pixel solid blue border all round the box:

```
.box {
    border: 3px solid blue;
}
```

Set a Measurement for Each Side Separately

When you want to use different settings for different sides of a CSS box, you can use the properties for the individual sides. The properties are largely self-explanatory, as you can see in the nearby illustration.

- Margin properties: `margin-top`, `margin-right`, `margin-bottom`, `margin-left`

- Border properties: `border-top`, `border-right`, `border-bottom`, `border-left`

- Padding properties: `padding-top`, `padding-right`, `padding-bottom`, `padding-left`

The following example uses the four margin properties to set top and bottom margins of 20 pixels and left and right margins of 10 pixels:

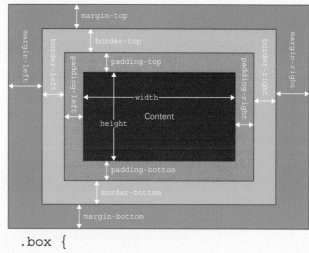

```
.box {
    margin-top: 20px;
    margin-right: 10px;
    margin-bottom: 20px;
    margin-left: 10 px;
}
```

Set Margins, Borders, and Padding Using Shorthand Properties

The third way of setting margins, borders, and padding is by using shorthand properties. These properties enable you to set a specific measurement for each size by using only a single property — the `margin` property, the `border` property, or the `padding` property.

The easiest way to use these properties is to provide the value for each side, separated by a space. You start at the top and go clockwise around the box: top first, right second, bottom third, and left fourth. The following example sets padding of 20 pixels on the top, 10 pixels on the right, 20 pixels on the bottom, and 10 pixels on the left:

```
padding: 20px 10px 20px 10px;
```

If you want the top to have the same value as the bottom and want the left to have the same value as the right, you can use two values. The following example sets 20 pixels of padding on the top and bottom and 10 pixels of padding on the left and right:

```
padding: 20px 10px;
```

If you want the top and the bottom to have different values from each other but the left and the right to have the same value as each other, you can use three values. The following example sets 20 pixels of padding on the top, 5 pixels of padding on the left and right, and 10 pixels of padding on the bottom:

```
padding: 20px 5px 10px;
```

You should understand the two-value and three-value usages, but your code will be easiest to read if you provide four values each time.

Understanding Ways of Sizing Elements

To make elements appear the way you want them on your web pages, you will often need to specify their sizes. CSS enables you to specify the size by using the `width` property to set the width and using the `height` property to set the height. You can set `width` and `height` to specific values, such as a number of pixels, or to relative values, such as a percentage of the container width.

This section explains the essentials you need to know about sizing elements. The following section, "Specify the Size for an Element," provides hands-on examples of setting sizes.

Choose Whether to Size the Content Box or the Border Box

The first key to sizing elements successfully is to be clear about what you are sizing. Normally, this is the content area, whose height you can set using the `height` property and whose width you can set using the `width` property. These properties do not include the padding outside the content area, the borders outside the padding, or the margins outside the borders.

If you want to include the padding, borders, and margin when sizing an element, you can use the `box-sizing` property, which lets you specify which box size you are setting. Use `box-sizing: border-box` to set the size of the border box, including the border and the padding but not any margins; or use `box-sizing: content-box` to set the size of the content box but be explicit about it. The nearby illustration illustrates `box-sizing: content-box` and `box-sizing: border-box`.

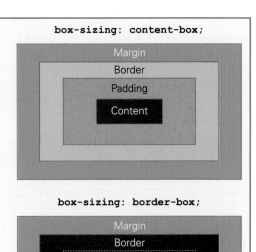

Set a Fixed Size or a Percentage of the Parent Container

The most straightforward way to specify an element's size is by setting its `width` property and its `height` property to the appropriate values, such as pixels or a proportion of the *viewport*, the area of the browser available to display content. You can set these properties to various units, which Table 9-4 explains.

Table 9-4:   Units for Sizing Elements

Unit	Abbreviation	Explanation
Pixels	px	A fixed unit of measurement.
Percentage	%	The measurement is relative to the size of the parent element — for example, `width: 50%;` gives a width 50 percent of the width of the parent element.
Viewport units	vw, vh	Units relative to the size of the viewport, where `vw` is 1/100th of the viewport width and `vh` is 1/100th of the viewport height. For example, setting `height: 50vh;` makes the element half the height of the viewport.
Current elements	em	Units relative to the font size of the current element. For example, if the current element's font size is 20px, 1em equals 20 pixels, and 1.25em equals 25 pixels.
Root elements	rem	Units relative to the font size of the root element, which is usually the `html` element. For example, if the font size of the root element is 16px, 1rem equals 16px, and 1.5rem equals 24px.
Inches, centimeters, points	in, cm, pt	You can use absolute units, such as inches and centimeters, but these are usually much less useful in web design than in the physical world.

Specify Maximum or Minimum Width or Height for an Element

When you want to make sure that the layout of an element remains consistent on viewports of different sizes, you can specify the maximum width and minimum width for that element by setting the `max-width` property and the `min-width` property. Similarly, you can specify the maximum height and minimum height by setting the `max-height` property and the `min-height` property.

The following example sets the maximum width and minimum width in pixels for a `div` element:

```
div {
    max-width: 600px;
    min-width: 250px;
}
```

This `div` element will have a minimum width of 250 pixels and a maximum width of 600 pixels.

You may also want to set the maximum width and minimum width as a percentage of the parent element's width, as in the following example:

```
div {
    max-width: 90%;
    min-width: 40%;
}
```

This `div` element's width will be at least 40 percent of the width of the parent element and at most 90 percent of the width.

Specify the Size for an Element

In the previous section, "Understanding Ways of Sizing Elements," you learned the ways of specifying the sizes of elements. In this section, you put several of those ways into action.

CSS enables you to specify fixed sizes for elements, such as a width and a height measured in pixels or other absolute units. But usually it is better to use relative units — such as ems, rems, or percentages — to allow your web pages to adapt to different screen sizes.

Specify the Size for an Element

1 In Visual Studio Code, open the external CSS file you want to work on.

2 Also in Visual Studio Code, open an HTML file to which you have linked the external CSS file.

Note: This example uses a boxed `div` element to show the border positions clearly.

3 Open the HTML file in a browser window.

4 Click in the CSS file and type **box-sizing: content-box;**.

5 On the next line, specify the width, such as **width: 90%;**.

6 Click **Refresh** (↻).

The web page refreshes.

A The content box takes up 90% of the available width. The padding and border take up further space.

7 Change the `box-sizing` property statement to **box-sizing: border-box;**.

8 Click **Refresh** (↻).

The web page refreshes.

B The border box takes up 90% of the available width, leaving more space.

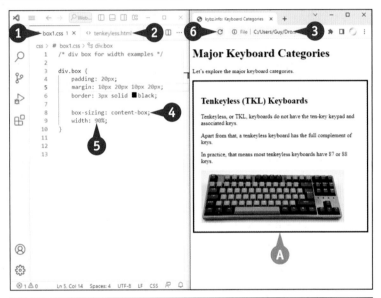

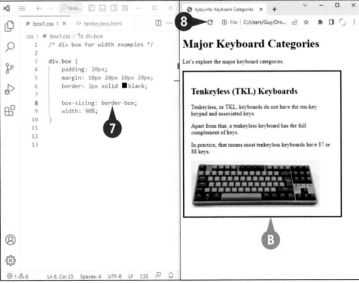

9 Select the `width` property and type the `max-width` property over it, assigning a value in pixels — for example:

`max-width: 600px;`

10 Press Enter to create a blank line, and then type the `min-width` property, again assigning a value in pixels — for example:

`min-width: 250px;`

11 Click **Refresh** (C).

The web page refreshes.

C The border box takes up most of the width.

12 Click **Maximize** (□).

The window expands to fill the screen.

D The border box expands only to its maximum width, 600 pixels, rather than taking up the full width of the screen.

Note: Drag the browser window to a narrow width. Observe how the border box decreases in width until it reaches its minimum width, 250 pixels, and then stays at that width.

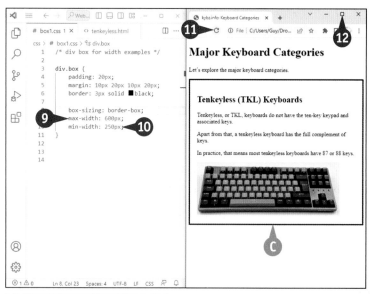

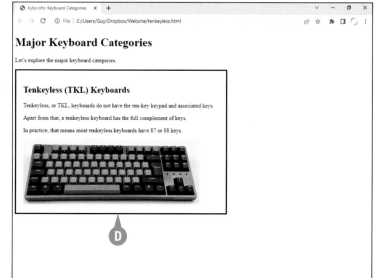

Is using `box-sizing:border` a good idea?

Many people find border box sizing helpful because it reduces the number of items you have to factor in to your calculations — when using `box-sizing: border;`, you need add only the margin, if any, rather than having to add padding, border thickness, and any margin to the content area's width and height. But if you prefer to work from the content area's dimensions, feel free to do so.

How can I adjust element size and layout based on screen width?

Use media queries. See the section "Add Media Queries to a Page" in Chapter 10 for details.

Specify Padding and Borders for an Element

As you learned in the section "Understanding the CSS Box Model," earlier in this chapter, *padding* is the space — if any — between the outside of the content and the border around the outside of the box. Many elements benefit from having at least a little padding to separate the border from the content. You can set the same padding for each side of the content box or set separate values for the top padding, right padding, bottom padding, and left padding. Similarly, you can configure a single border value all around or set separate borders for the four sides.

Specify Padding and Borders for an Element

1 In Visual Studio Code, open the external CSS file you want to work on.

2 Also in Visual Studio Code, open an HTML file to which you have linked the external CSS file.

3 Open the HTML file in a browser window.

Ⓐ These steps demonstrate formatting the "75-Percent Keyboards" section.

Ⓑ In the HTML file, the section is a `div` element assigned the `box2` class.

4 Click the CSS file's tab.

The CSS file appears.

5 Type a name targeting the element you will format, followed by a space and an opening brace, `{`. In the example, you would type **div.box2 {**.

Visual Studio Code enters the matching closing brace, `}`.

6 Press Enter to create a blank line (not shown).

7 On the blank line, type **border:** and the details of the border you want. The example creates a solid blue border three pixels wide.

```
border: 3px solid blue;
```

8 Click **Refresh** (🔄).

The web page refreshes.

Ⓒ The border appears.

The border is too close to the contents on the left side and at the bottom.

9 In the CSS file, press `Enter` to create a new line, type **padding:**, and specify the padding. This example uses 10 pixels at the top and bottom and 20 pixels left and right:

```
padding: 10px 20px 10px
20px;
```

10 Click **Refresh** (↻).

The web page refreshes.

D The padding appears, adding space. This is especially noticeable between the left border and bottom border and the content.

11 Try adjusting the borders. For example, you might use the individual border properties to set borders of different widths and colors:

```
border-top: 4px solid
black;
border-right: 2px solid
red;
border-bottom: 4px solid
green;
border-left: 2px solid
blue;
```

12 Click **Refresh** (↻).

The web page refreshes.

E The customized borders appear.

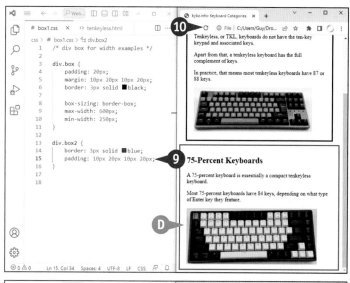

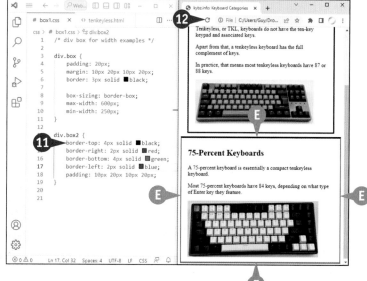

TIP

How do I create borders with rounded corners?

Add the `border-radius` property to the style definition. For example, use `border-radius: 20px;` to specify rounded corners that curve with a 20-pixel radius.

Set Margins to Control Element Spacing

As explained in the section "Understanding the CSS Box Model," earlier in this chapter, the *margin* is the space outside the border of a CSS box, the space between the border and the next element. You can set margins to control the amount of space around each element and make sure that elements do not touch each other — unless you want them to.

CSS enables you to overlap elements by specifying negative margins. This capability can be helpful for creating design effects. If you specify negative margins, be sure to verify the results are what you intend.

Set Margins to Control Element Spacing

1 In Visual Studio Code, open the external CSS file you want to work on.

2 Also in Visual Studio Code, open an HTML file to which you have linked the external CSS file.

3 Open the HTML file in a browser window.

Ⓐ These steps demonstrate formatting the boxed sections of the page.

Ⓑ In the HTML file, each section is a div element assigned the box2 class.

4 Click the CSS file's tab.

The CSS file appears.

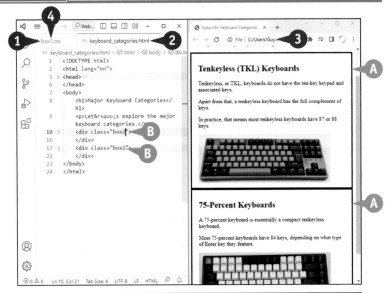

5 Click to place the insertion point in the style for the element you will format. In the example, it is the div. box2 style.

6 Press Enter to create a blank line (not shown).

7 Type **margin:** followed by the values for the four margins — for example:

```
margin: 10px 20px 10px 20px;
```

Note: Remember that you specify the settings in the order top–right–bottom–left when using single properties.

8 Click **Refresh** (C).

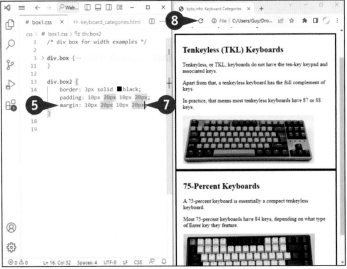

The web page refreshes.

C More space appears to the left and right of the boxes.

D Space appears between the two boxes.

9 Select the `margin` statement you created in step **7**.

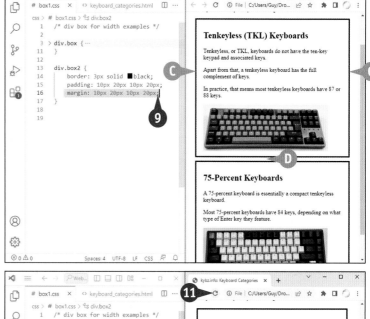

10 Type over the `margin` statement, entering four statements that use the specific properties for setting individual margins:

```
margin-top: 20px;
margin-bottom: 20px;
margin-left: 25px;
margin-right: 25px;
```

Note: Experiment with different margin measurements, as needed.

11 Click **Refresh** ().

The web page refreshes.

The margins take on the values you specified.

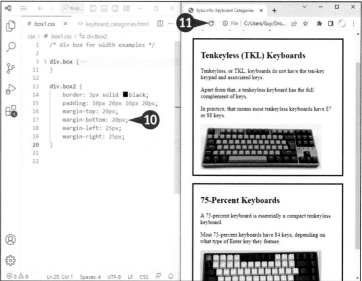

TIP

How do I use a negative margin to make elements overlap?
Set a negative value for the margin on the side of the element that you want to move toward the other element. For example, if you wanted to make the two boxes in this section overlap, rather than separating them, you could specify a negative `margin-top` value for the lower box. This would have the effect of moving the lower box up toward, or over, the upper box.

Understanding CSS Positioning Essentials

To make your web pages appear the way you want them to, you will need to specify positioning and layout for the objects they contain. CSS enables you to control the positioning and layout of elements on a web page in four different ways. First, you can simply let the browser display the elements in the order in which they appear in the HTML document. Second, you can position elements relative to their normal position in the document flow. Third, you can specify absolute positioning relative to a parent element. Fourth, you can specify a fixed position relative to the viewport.

Static Positioning: Letting the Browser Position Elements

Static positioning is the default type of positioning in CSS. *Static positioning* causes elements to be displayed in the order in which they appear in the HTML document. You would normally use static positioning for elements that need no special positioning on the page. For example, headings, text paragraphs, and lists typically use static positioning, because you want them to appear in the web page in the same order in which they appear in the HTML document.

You can specify static positioning for the element by including the `position` property and setting it to `static`. But because `position: static` is the default setting, you do not need to include the

property in your code unless you need to override a `position` property you have already declared with a different value.

For example, you might use static positioning for a `div` element like this:

```
div {
    position: static;
    height: 200px;
    width: 300px;
}
```

Here, the `position: static;` statement is likely unnecessary, but it makes your code more explicit. The `div` element has a height of 200 pixels and a width of 300 pixels.

Relative Positioning

By using relative positioning, you can position an element relative to its default position in the HTML document. Relative positioning moves the element from its normal position, but the browser still reserves the space for it in its normal position, so other elements do not move into that space.

Normally, you would use relative positioning to make relatively small adjustments to an element's position — for example, to make its relationship to other elements easier to grasp visually. While you *can* use relative positioning to make larger adjustments to an element's position, doing so may leave gaps in your web pages.

To apply relative positioning, you set the element's `position` property to `relative`. You can then set the element's `top`, `right`, `bottom`, and `left` properties to specify how far to move the object from its normal position. The following example moves the `.box` element 30 pixels down and 20 pixels to the left from its normal position:

```
.box {
    position: relative;
    top: 30px;
    left: 20px;
}
```

Absolute Positioning

Absolute positioning enables you to position an HTML element relative to its nearest positioned ancestor or — if there is no such ancestor — relative to what is called the initial containing block. The *initial containing block* is the box that contains all the web page's content.

To apply absolute positioning, you set the element's position property to absolute. Once you have done that, you can set the element's top, right, bottom, and left properties to set the distance between the element and either its nearest positioned ancestor or — if there is none — the initial containing block.

For example, assuming there is no nearest positioned ancestor, the following code positions the div element with the upright class in the upper-right corner of the initial containing block:

```
.upright {
    position: absolute;
    top: 0;
    right: 0;
}
```

Fixed Positioning

Your fourth choice for positioning with CSS is fixed positioning relative to the viewport rather than to the document itself. Fixed positioning relative to the viewport makes the element stay in the same position in the viewport even when the user scrolls the page. This behavior makes fixed positioning useful for elements you need to keep displayed in the browser window all the time.

To apply fixed positioning, you set the element's position property to fixed. Once you have done that, you can set the element's top, right, bottom, and left properties to specify the distance between the element and the edges of the viewport.

The following example positions the div element with the keep class in the lower-left corner of the screen, providing 10 pixels of padding:

```
.keep {
    position: fixed;
    left: 0;
    bottom: 0;
    padding: 10px;
}
```

Create Block Quotes

If your web pages contain text drawn from other sources, you may want to format sections of text as block quotes to distinguish them visually from regular text. You can do this by using HTML's `blockquote` element to create a barebones block quote and then apply styles via CSS to achieve the visual look you want.

Most web browsers use indentation to set off the `blockquote` element visually. Some use other styles as well, such as displaying a different background color for the block quote or adding a border to it.

Create Block Quotes

1 In Visual Studio Code, open the external CSS file you want to work on.

2 Also in Visual Studio Code, open an HTML file to which you have linked the external CSS file.

3 Open the HTML file in a browser window.

Ⓐ The example quote is formatted as a paragraph.

Ⓑ The quote appears as a standard paragraph in the web page.

4 Replace the opening `<p>` tag with the opening `<blockquote>` tag.

5 Replace the closing `</p>` tag with the closing `</blockquote>` tag.

6 Replace the opening `<p>` tag on the citation line with the opening `<cite>` tag.

7 Replace the closing `</p>` tag with the closing `</cite>` tag.

8 Click **Refresh** (⟳).

The web page refreshes.

Ⓒ The `blockquote` element appears indented but without other formatting.

Ⓓ The citation appear in italics but without an indent.

9 Click the CSS file's tab.

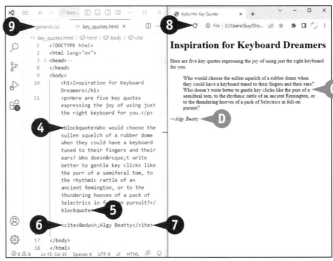

The CSS file appears.

10 Type **blockquote**, a space, and the opening brace, **{**.

Visual Studio Code enters the matching closing brace, }.

11 Press Enter to create a blank line (not shown).

12 Enter the formatting for the quote. The following example applies an off-white background, a light-gray bar on the left, plus margins and padding:

```
blockquote {
    background-color: #f9f9f9;
    border-left: 10px solid #ccc;
    margin: 1.5em 10px;
    padding: 0.5em 10px;
}
```

13 Click **Refresh** (C).

The web page refreshes.

The formatting appears.

14 On a new line in the CSS file, type **cite**, a space, and the opening brace, **{**.

Visual Studio Code enters the matching closing brace, }.

15 Press Enter to create a blank line (not shown).

16 Enter the formatting for the citation. This example simply adds indentation:

```
cite {
    margin-left: 3em;
}
```

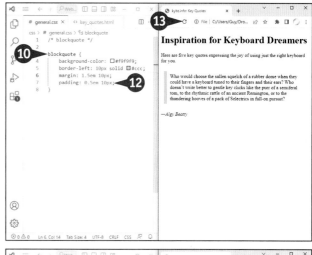

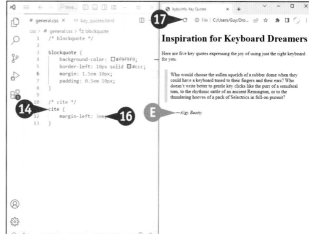

17 Click **Refresh** (C).

The web page refreshes.

E The citation takes on the formatting.

TIP

Is there an advantage to using the blockquote element rather than just applying indentation to set off a quote?

Yes — using the blockquote element has a semantic purpose as well as a visual purpose, as the element tells search engines and assistive technologies that the material is a quote. This extra information can increase accessibility and may improve SEO scores.

Fix an Element in Place in the Viewport

As you learned in the section "Understanding CSS Positioning Essentials," earlier in this chapter, you can fix an element in place in the viewport — the area of the browser that displays the web page — by setting the element's `position` property to `fixed`. A fixed element remains visible in the viewport even when the user scrolls the web page.

You might want to fix an element in place to display essential information, such as a warning or a disclaimer; to display navigation menus, so that visitors can find their way around easily; or to display advertisements prominently.

Fix an Element in Place in the Viewport

1 In Visual Studio Code, open the external CSS file you want to work on.

2 Also in Visual Studio Code, open an HTML file to which you have linked the external CSS file.

Note: Open an HTML file long enough to let you scroll up and down at whatever window size you are using.

3 Open the HTML file in a browser window.

4 In the HTML file, click where you want to add the fixed element.

5 Type **<div class="**, the name you will give the class, and **"> —** for example:

`<div class="disclaimer">`

6 Press Enter twice to create a blank line, and then type the closing **</div>** tag.

7 In between, type the information you want to display — for example:

`DISCLAIMER: This information is provided as-is and without guarantee.`

8 Click the CSS file's tab.

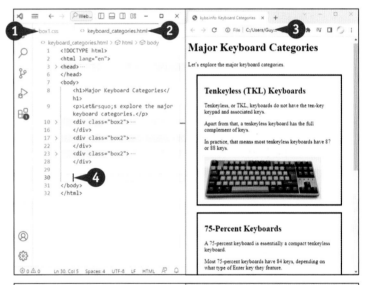

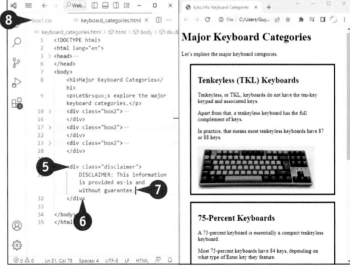

The CSS file appears.

9 On a blank line, type the name for the class style followed by a space and an opening brace, **{** — for example:

```
div.disclaimer {
```

Visual Studio Code inserts the matching closing brace, **}**.

10 Press Enter to create a blank line (not shown).

11 On the blank line, type **position: fixed;**.

12 On subsequent lines, specify the style formatting — for example:

```
div.disclaimer {
    position: fixed;
    bottom: 0;
    right: 0;
    padding: 10px;
    background-color: navy;
    color: white;
}
```

13 Click **Refresh** (⟳).

The web page refreshes.

Ⓐ The fixed element appears.

14 Scroll down.

Ⓑ The fixed element remains in place in the viewport even though the page scrolls.

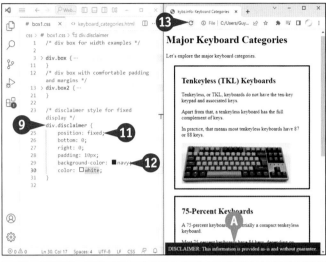

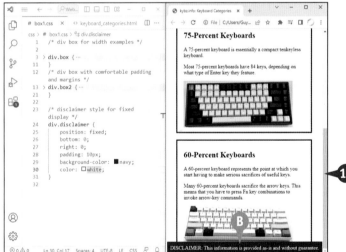

TIP

What do I need to be careful about when fixing elements?
The most important consideration is making sure that the elements appear in the viewport and that they appear the way you want them to. Be prepared to test your pages with a variety of devices and browsers to make sure that elements are visible and appear correctly, without overlapping each other.

For fixed elements, use relative measurements — such as ems, rems, or percentages — rather than pixel values to make sure that elements are positioned correctly on different devices and screen sizes.

Float an Element Beside Another Element

CSS enables you to make one element float to the left or right of another element. For example, you might want to make an image float to the right of a paragraph of text related to the image.

To make an element float, you set its `float` property to `left` or `right`; you can also set `float: inherit;` to have the element inherit its flotation from its parent. When you make an element float, you can set the `clear` property on subsequent elements to keep them clear of the floating element on one side or both.

Float an Element Beside Another Element

1 In Visual Studio Code, open the external CSS file you want to work on.

2 Also in Visual Studio Code, open an HTML file to which you have linked the external CSS file.

3 Open the HTML file in a browser window.

4 In the CSS file, click to place the insertion point on a blank line.

Note: This example creates class styles for floating elements, enabling you to apply the classes to different elements, as needed.

5 Type the class name you will use for floating an element to the left, followed by a space and an opening brace, **{** — for example:

```
.float-left {
```

Visual Studio Code enters the matching closing brace, **}**.

6 Press Enter to create a blank line, and then type **float: left;**.

7 Press Enter and add other properties, as needed — for example:

```
padding-right: 1rem;
}
```

8 Repeat steps **5** to **7** to create a class style for floating an element to the right — for example:

```
.float-right {
    float: right;
    padding-left: 1rem;
}
```

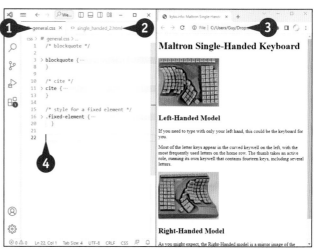

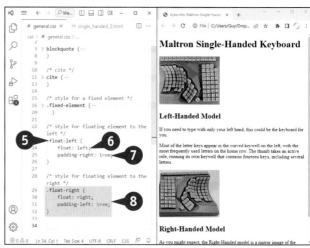

9 Click the HTML file's tab.

The HTML file appears.

10 Locate the content that you will float.

Note: If the content you will float does not yet exist, create it.

11 Click in the opening tag for an element you will float left, and type **class="**, the class name, and **"** — for example:

```
class="float-left"
```

12 Click **Refresh** (C).

The web page refreshes.

A The image floats to the left of the heading and paragraph.

13 In the HTML file, click in the opening tag for an element you will float right, and type **class="**, the class name, and **"** — for example:

```
class="float-right"
```

14 Click **Refresh** (C).

The web page refreshes.

B The image floats to the right of the heading and paragraph.

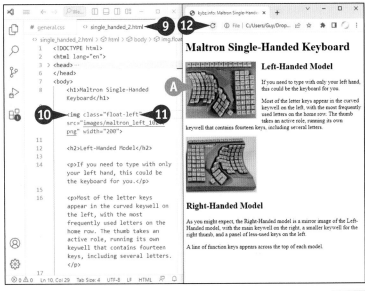

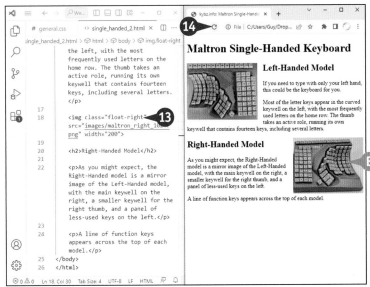

TIP

How do I use the `clear` property?

Use the `clear` property when you need to tell the browser to move an element below any floating elements that precede it. Enter `clear: left;` to move the element below any floated element that precedes it on the left; similarly, enter `clear: right;` to move the element below any floated element that precedes it on the right; and enter `clear: both;` to sink the element below floated elements on two sides. You can also use `clear: inherit;` to inherit the `clear` setting from the element's parent element. You can use `clear: none;` to specify no clearance; but since this is the default, you need not enter it.

Understanding the `display` Property

CSS provides a property called `display` that enables you to control how an element is displayed in a browser window. For example, you can use the `display` property to make the browser display an element as a block that takes up the full window width or as a grid container in which you can lay out child elements. You can also use the `display` property to hide an element completely.

This section gives you an overview of the `display` property. The following section provides quick examples of using the `display` property.

Grasp the Use of the `display` Property

The `display` property lets you instruct the browser how to display a particular element. You add the `display` property to the element's style and assign the appropriate value, as shown in Table 9-5.

Table 9-5:	Values for the `display` Property
Value	**How the Element Is Displayed**
`none`	Not at all
`block`	As a block-level element, occupying the full width available in the container and pushing subsequent elements onto a new line
`inline`	Inline, so other elements can appear on the same line
`inline-block`	As an inline block whose height and width you can set
`flex`	As a flexible container in which you can arrange child elements as needed
`grid`	As a grid container in which you can lay out child elements on a grid
`table`	As a table
`table-row`	As a table row
`table-cell`	As a table cell
`list-item`	As a list item
`inherit`	Using the same `display` value as its parent object
`initial`	Using the browser's default style for the element
`unset`	Using the same `display` value as its parent object; if there is no parent, using the default style for the element

For example, you can use the following code in your style sheet to display a `div` element as a block:

```
div {
    display: block;
}
```

Control the Display of an Element

In the previous section, "Understanding the `display` Property," you learned about the `display` property and the settings it offers for controlling how elements appear in your web pages. In this section, you put two of those settings to use so that you can see the effects they produce. First, you set an element's `display` property to `none` to make the browser hide the object. Second, you set the `display` property of a nonblock element to `block` to force the browser to display the element as a block, giving the element greater prominence.

Control the Display of an Element

1 In Visual Studio Code, open the external CSS file.

2 Also in Visual Studio Code, open an HTML file to which you have linked the external CSS file.

3 Open the HTML file in a browser window.

A An image appears.

B A link appears as an inline element.

4 Type a class style for hiding elements by specifying `display: none;`:

```
.hide {
    display: none;
}
```

5 Type a class style for forcing an element to display as a block by specifying `display: block;`:

```
.force-block {
    display: block;
}
```

6 Click the HTML file's tab.

7 In the opening tag for the element you want to hide, type **class="hide"**.

8 In the opening tag for the element you want to display as a block, type **class="force-block"**.

9 Click **Refresh** (⟳).

The web page refreshes.

The browser suppresses the display of the image.

C The link appears as a block element, on its own line.

Create a Flexbox Layout

CSS provides a layout model called Flexbox for creating flexible and responsive layouts in web pages. You can use Flexbox to lay out items in a container without knowing how large the container is, which helps you to create dynamic layouts that can adjust to different screen sizes and device types.

Most current web browsers fully support Flexbox, so you can use it with a high degree of confidence that your layouts will work. That said, testing using various browsers and devices remains a wise move.

Create a Container Element for Your Flexbox

To start creating a Flexbox layout, open the HTML document in which you want to create the layout, or start a new HTML document, as needed. At the point in the HTML document where you want to create the layout, add an element to act as the container.

For example, you might create a div element and assign to it a class called my_flex that would allow you to format each of your containers from an external CSS file. Your div element might look like the following example:

```
<div class="my_flex">
</div>
```

Set the Class Style's display Property to flex

Next, in the external CSS file attached to the HTML document, create a style for the class, specifying display: flex; to make the container flexible. Your style definition might look like this:

```
.my_flex {
    display: flex;
}
```

Add Content to Your Container Element

Next, go back to your HTML document and add to your container element the content elements you want to appear in the Flexbox. These elements work as usual, even though the Flexbox will rearrange their layout as needed for different browsers and devices.

For example, you might add six div elements to your container element, making it look like the following example, which does not show the elements inside each of those six div elements:

```
<div class="my_flex">
    <div>Section 1</div>
    <div>Section 2</div>
    <div>Section 3</div>
    <div>Section 4</div>
    <div>Section 5</div>
    <div>Section 6</div>
</div>
```

Set Flexbox Properties

After adding content to your container element, return to your external CSS file and set Flexbox properties to control how the container aligns the elements it contains.

Table 9-6 explains the properties you can set for a Flexbox.

Table 9-6: Flexbox Properties	
Property	**Explanation**
`display`	Specifies the display box type. Set it to `flex` to enable the flex container.
`flex-direction`	Specifies the direction of the flex container's main axis. You can set it to `row`, `row-reverse`, `column`, or `column-reverse`.
`flex-wrap`	Specifies whether flex items should wrap onto multiple lines. You can set it to `wrap`, `wrap-reverse`, or `nowrap`.
`flex-flow`	A shorthand property that combines the `flex-direction` property and the `flex-wrap` property.
`justify-content`	Specifies how to align flex items along the main axis of the flex container. You can set it to `flex-start`, `flex-end`, `center`, `space-between`, `space-around`, or `space-evenly`.
`align-items`	Specifies how to align flex items along the cross axis of the flex container. You can set it to `flex-start`, `flex-end`, `center`, `baseline`, or `stretch`.
`align-content`	Specifies how to align multiple lines of flex items along the cross axis of the flex container. You can set it to `flex-start`, `flex-end`, `center`, `space-between`, `space-around`, or `stretch`.
`order`	Specifies the order in which to display flex items. The default value is `0`. You can enter positive values or negative values to change the order.
`flex-grow`	Specifies how much a flex item should grow relative to other flex items in the same container. The default value is `0`, which prevents the item from growing.
`flex-shrink`	Specifies how much a flex item should shrink relative to other flex items in the same container. The default value is `1`, which allows the item to shrink if necessary.
`flex-basis`	Specifies the initial size of a flex item before the browser distributes any remaining space. The default value, `auto`, bases the item's size on its content.
`flex`	A shorthand property that combines the `flex-grow` property, the `flex-shrink` property, and the `flex-basis` property.
`align-self`	Aligns a single flex time across the cross axis of the flex container, overriding the `align-items` property. You can set this property to `auto`, `flex-start`, `flex-end`, `center`, `baseline`, or `stretch`.

For example, you might use the following style to specify a flex layout, center the items horizontally, center the items vertically, lay out the items in a row, and wrap the items to the next line if needed:

```
.my_flex {
  display: flex;
  justify-content: center;
  align-items: center;
  flex-direction: row;
  flex-wrap: wrap;
}
```

CHAPTER 10

Creating Responsive and Appealing Pages

In this chapter, you learn how to create responsive and appealing web pages. To make pages responsive, you can use techniques such as applying relative sizing, specifying flexible positioning, and adding media queries. To make pages appealing, you can apply gradients and transitions, use sprites, and create keyframe animations.

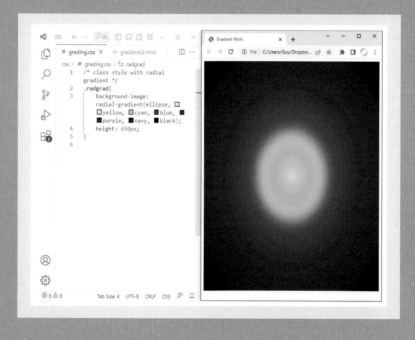

Understanding the Tools for Creating Responsive Pages

CSS provides a suite of tools for creating responsive web pages, web pages designed to adapt successfully to different screen sizes and devices. You can use relative sizing to let elements adapt to the space available. You can specify flexible positioning to allow the browser to rearrange elements within constraints. You can detect device capabilities using media queries, increase tap target size, and configure the viewport. You should also test your pages on various devices and screens.

This section gives you an overview of these tools and techniques and points you to the sections later in the chapter that discuss them.

Relative Sizing

CSS enables you to specify either fixed sizing or relative sizing. Fixed sizing typically uses pixels, although other units are available. For example, you might set a `div` element's `width` property to `500px`, making the browser display the element at 500 pixels wide. The fixed value does not change for different screens, so what looks good on a desktop or laptop screen may be unreadable on a phone screen.

Relative sizing uses either percentages of the available space or relative units, such as ems and rems. Ems are units for font sizing based on the parent element, while rems are units for font sizing based on the root element. For example, if the root element uses a 16-point font, you could specify `2rem` to apply 32-point font to an element.

See the following section, "Apply Relative Sizing," for more information on relative sizing.

Flexible Positioning

CSS enables you to use various techniques to position elements flexibly on your pages. You can float an element to the left or right of another element. You can specify relative positioning or absolute positioning for an element. You can also create Flexbox layouts that permit the browser to rearrange elements within constraints you specify.

Look back to Chapter 9 for coverage of these topics.

Media Queries

CSS includes a feature called *media queries* that enables you to find out what type of device and what type of display a web page is being displayed on. "Media queries" sounds like journalists hunting a story, but in this case, the protagonist is you — or rather, your website — querying the visitor's browser about what type of medium it is using to display the page. You can use this information to specify different styles for different screen types, helping optimize the web page for all devices.

See the section "Add Media Queries to a Page," later in this chapter, for more information on using media queries.

Tap Targets

If you have ever struggled to tap a microscopic button on a web page on your phone's screen, such as the Close (⊠) button that supposedly closes an unwanted ad, you will grasp the importance of tap targets at once. A *tap target* is the clickable area of an element, such as a button or a link, on a web page. You can adjust the size of tap targets on your web pages to suit the device the visitor is using. For example, you would normally increase the size of tap targets when you know the visitor is using a touch screen, to make tapping the targets easier.

See the section "Set Tap Targets for Touch Screens," later in this chapter, for more information on tap targets and how to set them.

Viewport Size and Behavior

The *viewport* is the area of a web page visible in the browser on a visitor's device — one "screenful" of web page or one "windowful" of web page, if you like. The viewport varies in both size and orientation depending on the device the visitor is using. For example, a smartphone's viewport might be small and portrait orientation, taller than it is wide; a laptop's or desktop's viewport would typically be larger and landscape — wider than it is tall — though it might also be portrait or square, depending on how the user has sized the window.

CSS enables you to configure the viewport by setting the `viewport` meta tag in the `head` section of an HTML document. See the section "Set the Viewport Size," later in this chapter, for more information on setting the viewport size.

Check Your Web Pages on Various Devices and Screens

Most likely, some visitors to your website will use smartphones, while others will use tablets, laptop computers, or desktop computers. These devices will have screen sizes ranging from small to huge and resolutions ranging from modest to extremely high; some will use portrait orientation and others landscape orientation, with the occasional square screen to keep you guessing.

To make sure that your web pages display successfully on different screen sizes and devices, you must test them on different screen sizes, using either hardware devices or software simulators.

See the section "Check Your Pages on Various Devices and Screens," later in this chapter, for more on this topic.

Apply Relative Sizing

To make your web pages responsive, use relative sizing rather than fixed sizing to specify the size of elements on the pages. Relative sizing uses proportionate units, such as percentages or rems, rather than fixed pixel values. Relative sizing lets the page scale smoothly to adapt to different devices and screen sizes.

To size an element by percentage, you specify the percentage — either of the viewport or of the element's parent element — the element should occupy. For example, you might set a container element's width to 75% to make it occupy three-quarters of the viewport's width.

Grasp the Advantages of Relative Sizing over Fixed Sizing

Relative sizing for web pages has four main advantages over fixed sizing:

- **Relative sizing adds flexibility.** By using relative sizing, you can create web pages that adjust to different screen sizes and devices. This flexibility enables visitors to view your web pages as you intend them to appear, no matter which devices they are using.

- **Relative sizing implements responsive design.** Relative sizing lets you create responsive web pages whose content and layout adjust dynamically to suit the screen size and orientation of each visiting device.

- **Relative sizing improves accessibility.** Visitors can customize the display of the web pages to sidestep accessibility issues. For example, a visitor with vision problems can increase the font size to make a page easier to read.

- **Relative sizing increases consistency.** By using relative sizing, you can make sure your pages deliver a consistent look and experience across a range of devices and screen sizes. This consistency makes for a better user experience and can increase visitor engagement.

Understanding the Measurements for Applying Relative Sizing

CSS provides five main measurements for applying relative sizing:

- **em.** In digital typography, one *em* is the font size of an element's parent element. For example, if the parent unit uses 16-pixel font, 1em equals 16px. The term derives from traditional printing, where one em is the width of a capital M in a particular font; an em dash, —, is a dash the width of a capital M in that font, and an em space is a space the width of a capital M.

- **rem.** The rem is a "root em," an em based on the document's root element rather than the parent element of the element you are formatting. The root element is the `html` element in the document unless this element is missing or — more likely — malformed, such as not being closed properly. If there is no valid `html` element, the browser treats the `body` element as the root element. If the `body` element is also missing or malformed, rem sizing will not work properly.

- **%.** Percent sizing enables you to base an element's size on the size of its parent element. For example, if the parent element is 600 pixels wide, specifying `width: 50%;` makes the element 300 pixels wide.

- **vw and vh.** The `vw` unit is based on the width of the viewport, while the `vh` unit is based on the viewport's height. The full width is `100vw`, and the full height is `100vh`, so a setting of `50vw` is half the viewport's width, and `50vh` is half the viewport's height.

Examples of Applying Relative Sizing

To apply relative sizing to your documents, use em sizing or rem sizing for fonts.

If you want to size based on the root element, use rem sizing. Start by setting the `font-size` property of the `html` element in your CSS file. The following example sets 16-pixel font for the `html` element:

```
html {
    font-size: 16px;
}
```

Once you have done this, you can base the font size of other elements on it. The following example sets `1.5rem` for the h2 element, giving a 24-pixel font:

```
h2 {
    font-size: 1.5rem;
}
```

If you want the font size of elements to be relative to the size of their parents, use em sizing. The following example defines a `.parent` class with a 20px font size and a `.child` class with `0.8em` font sizing, giving a 16-pixel font:

```
.parent {
    font-size: 20px;
}
```

```
.child {
    font-size: 0.8em;
}
```

To size elements based on the viewport's dimensions, use `vw` and `vh` units. The following example sets a `div` element to half the viewport's width and three-quarters of its height:

```
div {
    width: 50vw;
    height: 75vh;
}
```

To size an element based on its parent element's dimensions, use % measurements. The following example sets the `div` element to half the parent element's width:

```
div {
    width: 50%;
}
```

Add Media Queries to a Page

CSS media queries enable you to learn the screen size, resolution, and color depth of the display used by the device requesting a web page. You may also be able to learn about the device's input method — for example, a pointing device or a touch screen. You can use the information returned by media queries to implement rules specifying how the web page should appear at different screen sizes or on different devices. Media queries let you create web pages that adapt and respond to the visitor's device and provide a good viewing experience on it.

Understanding the Syntax for Media Queries

The general syntax for a media query looks like this:

```
@media mediatype and (media feature) {
    CSS style to apply
}
```

Here are the components of the syntax:

- `@media`. This is the key term you use to start a media query.

- *mediatype*. This parameter specifies the type of media the query affects. Use `screen` for device screens, `speech` for screen readers, or `print` for printed documents.

- *media feature*. This parameter states the condition to test. Table 10-1 explains the most widely useful media features.

- *CSS style to apply*. This parameter specifies the CSS style to apply when the media query returns True.

Table 10-1:	Media Features for Media Queries
Media Feature	**Explanation**
width	The viewport's width, in pixels
height	The viewport's height, in pixels
min-width	The viewport's minimum width, in pixels
max-width	The viewport's maximum width, in pixels
min-height	The viewport's minimum height, in pixels
max-height	The viewport's maximum height, in pixels
aspect-ratio	The viewport's aspect ratio, the ratio of its width to its height
min-aspect-ratio	The viewport's minimum aspect ratio
max-aspect-ratio	The viewport's maximum aspect ratio
orientation	The viewport's orientation, either `landscape` or `portrait`
color	The color depth per channel, such as 8 or 16
color-index	The number of colors the device's screen can display

Media Feature	Explanation
resolution	The screen's pixel density
scan	The screen's scan process, either interlace or progressive
grid	Whether the screen has a grid-based display
pointer	The approximate accuracy of the device's pointing method, such as fine, coarse, or none
any-pointer	Whether the device has any input mechanism available
hover	Whether the primary input mechanism supports hover interactions
any-hover	Whether any input mechanism supports hover interactions

Media Queries Example: Change Font Formatting for Smaller Screens

You can use media queries to change an element's font formatting to make the element more readable on smaller screens. This example shows a change to the font size, but you could also make other changes, such as using a heavier font weight or a color that will stand out more against the background.

Your CSS file might contain styles such as the following for the h1 element and h2 element on standard, decent-size screens:

```
/* h1 style for standard screens */
h1 {
    font-size: 30px;
}

/* h2 style for standard screens */
h2 {
    font-size: 24px;
}
```

You could use a media query to check for screens with a maximum width of 600 pixels and change to a larger font size:

```
/* h1 and h2 styles for smaller screens */
@media only screen and (max-width: 600px) {
    h1 {
        font-size: 36px;
    }
    h2 {
        font-size: 28px
    }
}
```

Set Tap Targets for Touch Screens

CSS enables you to specify the size of tap targets, the clickable areas of elements such as button or links. To make your pages responsive, you can adjust the size of tap targets to suit the screen size and type of device a visitor is using. For example, if the visitor is using a smartphone with a touch screen, you would normally increase the size of the tap targets to make them easier to tap without finicky fingering. You might also make your tap targets easier to see and add a hover effect to show when they are being tapped.

See the Benefit of Formatting Tap Targets

By formatting tap targets, you can make them much easier to use on smaller screens and easier to use when using touch screens rather than mice or other hardware pointing devices.

For example, say you have a form that includes the controls shown in the next illustration: several buttons and a link. This spacing is fine for a desktop or laptop computer with a mouse or trackpad, but the buttons are uncomfortably small for touch-screen use.

Chapter 11 discusses forms and their controls in detail.

Apply a Minimum Size to the Tap Targets

As a first move, you could apply a minimum size to the tap targets. The World Wide Web Consortium (W3C) recommends a minimum size of 44×44 pixels for tap targets for touch devices.

The following CSS code applies this minimum size:

```
/* Set a minimum size of 44x44 pixels
for all tap targets */
a, button, input[type="button"],
input[type="submit"] {
    min-width: 44px;
    min-height: 44px;
}
```

This illustration shows the result of applying the minimum size.

Add Padding to Bulk Up the Tap Targets

Next, you might bulk up the tap targets by adding some padding to them. The following CSS code provides an example:

```
/* Add padding to bulk up the tap
targets */
a, button, input[type="button"],
input[type="submit"] {
    padding: 20px;
}
```

This illustration shows the result of applying the padding.

Add Margin Space Between the Tap Targets

The tap targets are now a decent size, but the link is perhaps awkwardly close to the bottom of the buttons. To place clear air between them, you could add margin space below the tap targets, as in the following CSS code:

```
/* Add margin to provide vertical
separation */
a, button, input[type="button"],
input[type="submit"] {
    margin-bottom: 20px;
}
```

This illustration shows the effect of adding this margin space.

Format the Border of the Tap Targets

The buttons, such as the Submit button and Reset button, automatically receive a border in most browsers, but the hyperlinks do not. To make all the controls easier to see on a small screen, you could apply a heavier border, as in the following CSS code:

```
/* Format the border of the tap
targets */
a, button, input[type="button"],
input[type="submit"] {
    border: 2px solid black;
}
```

This illustration shows the borders. The tap target for the hyperlink is now clearly visible.

Format the Background of the Tap Targets

You might also format the background of the tap targets to increase contrast, as in the following CSS code:

```
/* Give the tap targets a white
background */
a, button, input[type="button"],
input[type="submit"] {
    background-color: white;
}
```

This illustration shows the tap targets with the white background.

Change the Tap Target Color on Hover

You could also change the color of tap targets when the visitor hovers the pointer over them or touches them briefly on a touch screen without executing a tap. The following CSS code provides an example:

```
/* Change the tap target color on
hover */
a:hover, button:hover,
input[type="button"]:hover,
input[type="submit"]:hover {
    background-color: cyan;
}
```

This illustration shows how a tap target changes color when the pointer hovers over it.

Change the Tap Target Color on Tap

You could also change the color of tap targets when the visitor taps or clicks them. This feedback helps the visitor see that the tap or click has registered the tap or click. The following CSS code provides an example:

```
/* Change the target color when tapped
or clicked */
a:active, button:active,
input[type="button"]:active,
input[type="submit"]:active {
    background-color: black;
    color: white;
}
```

This illustration shows how a tap target changes color when the visitor taps or clicks it.

Set the Viewport Size

The viewport is the area of a web page visible in the browser on a visitor's device. CSS enables you to configure the viewport by setting the `content` property of the `viewport` meta tag in the head section of the web page. By choosing suitable settings, you can make the web page display in a suitable way for the screen on the device each visitor is using.

Table 10-2 explains the settings you can use for the `content` property of the `viewport` meta tag.

Table 10-2:	Settings for the `content` Property of the `viewport` Meta Tag
Property	**Explanation**
`width`	Specifies the viewport width. You can set a specific number of pixels or use `device-width` to use the device's width.
`height`	Specifies the viewport height. You can set a specific number of pixels or use `device-height` to use the device's height.
`initial-scale`	Specifies the initial zoom level when loading the page. For example, use `initial-scale=1` to set the zoom level to 100 percent.
`minimum-scale`	Specifies the minimum zoom level allowed for the page. For example, use `minimum-scale=0.5` to allow zooming out to 50 percent.
`maximum-scale`	Specifies the maximum zoom level allowed for the page. For example, use `maximum-scale=2` to allow zooming in to 200 percent.
`user-scalable`	Controls whether the user can zoom in or out on the page. You can set this to `yes` or `no`.
`fullscreen`	Displays the page in full-screen mode. You can set this setting to `yes` to allow full-screen mode, `no` to disallow full-screen mode, `minimal-ui` to display a minimal UI when the page enters full-screen mode, or `browser` to display the browser's UI when the page enters full-screen mode. Not all browsers support the `fullscreen` setting, and the `minimal-ui` value is deprecated; that is, it is not recommended for usage anymore.
`shrink-to-fit`	Shrinks the page's content to fit the screen width. You can specify `yes` to shrink the content or `no` to let the content overflow the screen's width.
`viewport-fit`	Controls how the viewport should fit the screen; settings include `cover`, `contain`, `auto`, and `100%`.
`target-densitydpi`	Specifies the pixel density of the target device. This setting is deprecated, so you should not use it anymore.

Property	Explanation
`viewport-initial-scale`	Specifies the viewport's initial zoom level. The default value is `1.0`, which applies 100 percent zoom — normal size.
`viewport-minimum-scale`	Specifies the viewport's minimum zoom level. The default value is `0.25`, allowing the user to zoom out to 25 percent of the normal size.
`viewport-maximum-scale`	Specifies the viewport's maximum zoom level. The default value is `5.0`, which lets the user zoom in to 500 percent of the normal size.
`viewport-user-scalable`	Controls whether the user can zoom in or out on the viewport. You can set it to `yes` to allow zooming, to `no` to disallow zooming, or to `1` to allow the user to zoom in or out only until the page reaches its original size.
`overscroll-behavior`	Specifies how the viewport behaves when the user *overscrolls* — when they try to scroll beyond the end of the content. Use `auto` to allow the browser to control the overscroll behavior. Use `contain` to prevent overscrolling outside the element so as to perhaps display parts of parent elements. Use `none` to disable overscrolling completely.

The `initial-scale` setting, `minimum-scale` setting, and `maximum-scale` setting affect the page as a whole. The `viewport-initial-scale` setting, the `viewport-minimum-scale` setting, and the `viewport-maximum-scale` setting affect only the part of the page displayed in the viewport. Normally, you would set the `initial-scale` setting to specify the default zoom level for the page and then configure settings such as `height` and `width`, rather than using `viewport-initial-scale`, `viewport-minimum-scale`, and `viewport-maximum-scale`.

For many pages, you may simply want to set the viewport's width to the device width:

```
<meta name="viewport" content="width=device-width">
```

For some pages, you may want to set the viewport's height to the device height:

```
<meta name="viewport" content="height=device-height">
```

In some cases, you may need to set a specific width and height for the viewport:

```
<meta name="viewport" content="width=500, height=700">
```

Check Your Pages on Various Devices and Screens

Visitors to your website will use different types of devices, from desktop and laptop computers down through tablets and smartphones — not to mention extended-reality devices, such as headsets. Those devices will have different screen sizes, screen resolutions, and orientations; and these variables will affect the layout, font size, and functionality of your web pages. To make sure your website can accommodate this diversity of visitors, you must check your web pages at different screen sizes and on different devices. Doing so will enable you to identify problems that arise, such as unreadably small text or broken layouts, and fix them.

Assess Your Visitors' Devices and Screen Sizes

As far as possible, try to determine which devices and screen sizes your website's visitors are using most. You may need to make an educated guess at first, but once your site is up and running, you can get a breakdown from Google Analytics.

Sign in to your Google Analytics account, and then click **Reports** () in the left navigation pane to display the Reports pane. Click the **Tech** heading to expand its content, click the **Overview** item below the Tech heading, and then look at the various histograms and readouts: Users by Platform, Users by Operating System, Users by Platform/Device Category, Users by Screen Resolution, Users by Device Model, and so on.

Test Your Web Pages on Hardware Devices

Once you have established which devices, browsers, and screen sizes your visitors prefer, assemble as full a range of test equipment as you can muster. The testing equipment need not be new and expensive — in fact, testing is a great way to extend the life of outmoded smartphones rejected by your colleagues or family, tablets with batteries that are fading but not economically replaceable, and ancient laptops or desktops.

See what you can exhume from your company's tech graveyard or your family's junk drawer. Ideally, you might want an iPhone and an Android phone for small-screen testing, an iPad and a Windows tablet for medium-screen testing, and an old laptop and some form of Mac for large-screen testing. However, you can use development tools in Chrome or Firefox to simulate devices you do not have, as discussed in the following subsection. You can also find cloud-based testing services online that offer a smorgasbord of simulators and physical devices.

Update the operating system on each device to bring it up to date or as close to up to date as possible. Update the default browsers, too, and install the other browsers your visitors favor.

Connect a second monitor to your test laptop or desktop and turn it to portrait orientation so that you can view pages easily in both landscape and portrait orientations.

You should now be ready to test your pages. When testing them on smartphones and tablets, switch the devices between portrait orientation and landscape orientation to make sure that Bluetooth works properly.

Test Your Pages Using Chrome's Development Tools

Both Google Chrome and Mozilla Firefox include development tools that enable you to emulate different screen sizes, orientations, and devices. These tools give you another way to test your web pages and are especially useful when you have only a limited selection of hardware available for testing. This section introduces you to Chrome's development tools, leaving you to explore Firefox's development tools on your own.

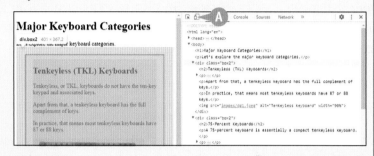

Launch Chrome on your computer as usual and open the web page you want to test. Right-click on the page to display the contextual menu, and then click **Inspect** to display the developer tools. Next, click **Toggle Device Toolbar** (A, 🔲 changes to 🔲) to display the Device toolbar; alternatively, press Control + Shift + M on Windows or Linux or ⌘ + Shift + M on the Mac to display the Device toolbar.

The Device toolbar (B) appears above the preview pane. Click the Dimensions pop-up menu button (C) to display the menu of devices. Here, you can click the device you want to emulate or click **Edit** (D) to display the Emulated Devices category in Chrome development tools settings, where you can select (✓) other existing devices to add them to the menu or click **Add custom device** to add a custom device whose settings you specify.

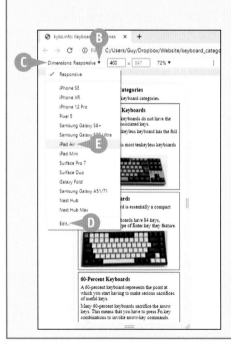

The third illustration shows the result of clicking **iPad Air** (E) on the menu: an emulation showing how the page will look on the iPad Air's screen. To add the rulers, as shown in the illustration, click **Menu** (⋮) and then click **Show rulers** on the menu. The menu also enables you to toggle the display of the device frame and media queries and add the device pixel ratio.

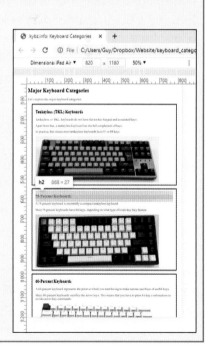

Understanding How CSS Gradients Work

Among the various tools that CSS provides for building and enhancing your web pages, gradients can be a great way to add visual interest to your designs. CSS enables you to easily create gradients, smooth transitions between two or more colors. You can create either linear gradients or radial gradients. You can use gradients for various purposes, such as providing a background on which to locate design elements such as buttons or headers.

What Are Linear Gradients?

A *gradient* is a color pattern that creates a smooth transition between multiple colors. A *linear gradient* has the colors in a straight line from one point to another. For example, the first linear gradient shows the color transitioning from red on the left to violet on the right.

You can add further colors, as needed. For example, the second linear gradient adds blue between the red and the violet.

And the third linear gradient runs the full rainbow.

Learn the Syntax and Settings for Linear Gradients

To create a linear gradient, you enter the `linear-gradient()` function as the value for the property to which you are assigning the gradient. You then use the parameters and values shown in Table 10-3 to specify the details of the linear gradient.

The following example assigns to the `background-image` property a linear gradient that runs from left to right, starting with `red` and moving through `blue` to `violet`:

```
background-image: linear-gradient(to right, red, blue, violet);
```

Table 10-3: Settings for Linear Gradients	
Setting	**Explanation**
`to`	Specify the direction. Use `to left`, `to right`, `to top`, or `to bottom`.
`angle`	Specify the angle of the gradient in degrees — for example, `45deg` or `270deg`.
`color`	Specify the colors to use. You can use named colors, such as `purple`; hexadecimal codes; or RGB values. Include the `transparent` keyword to create a gradient featuring transparency.
`color stop`	Specify the point at which each color in the gradient starts and stops. You can use either decimal values between 0 and 1, such as `0.25` for one-quarter of the element's size; or percentages, such as `25%` for that same one-quarter.

What Are Radial Gradients?

A *radial gradient* is a gradient that starts from a circle or ellipse and changes in color or intensity outward. The next illustration shows a radial gradient that starts from an ellipse using the color `darkred`, moves through `red` and `orange`, and ends with `yellow`.

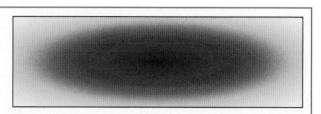

Learn the Syntax and Settings for Radial Gradients

To create a radial gradient, you enter the `radial-gradient()` function as the value for the property to which you are assigning the gradient. You then use the parameters and values explained in Table 10-4 to specify the gradient's details.

The following example assigns to the `background-image` property a radial gradient that creates the gradient shown in the previous illustration.

```
background-image: radial-gradient(ellipse at 50% 50%, darkred 0%, red
33%,orange 67%, yellow 100%);
```

Table 10-4: Settings for Radial Gradients	
Setting	**Explanation**
`at`	Specify the position of the center of the gradient. The default is the center of the element. You can use paired percentages of the element's height and width — for example, you could use `25% 75%` to specify 25 percent of the element's width, measuring from the left, and 75 percent of its height, measuring from the top. Alternatively, spell out the position, such as `bottom left`.
`shape`	Specify the shape of the gradient: `ellipse`, the default; or `circle`.
`size`	Specify the size of the gradient — the place to stop it. You can specify a CSS length value, such as `50%`; `closest-side` or `furthest-side`; or `closest-corner` or `furthest-corner`.
`color`	Specify the colors to use. You can use named colors, such as `mediumaquamarine`; hexadecimal codes; or RGB values. Include the `transparent` keyword to create a gradient featuring transparency.
`color stop`	Specify the point at which each color in the gradient starts and stops. You can use either decimal values between `0` and `1`, such as `0.75` for three-quarters of the element's size; or percentages, such as `75%`.

Apply a Linear Gradient to an Element

CSS linear gradients enable you to add a striking or attractive pattern to HTML elements. For example, you can use a linear gradient as the background image for an element, adding controls in front of the background as needed.

In this section, you first create a linear gradient running left to right and using only two colors. You then change the gradient's direction and add further colors to it.

Apply a Linear Gradient to an Element

1 In Visual Studio Code, open the external CSS file you want to work on.

2 Also in Visual Studio Code, open an HTML file to which you have linked the external CSS file.

3 Open the HTML file in a browser window.

4 In the HTML file, type the code for a `div` element, assigning it to a class with the name you will give your linear-gradient style. This example uses the name `lingrad`:

```
<div class="lingrad"></div>
```

5 Click the CSS file's tab.

The CSS file becomes active.

6 Click a blank line and type a period, the class style name you used in step **4**, a space, and an opening brace, **{** — for example:

```
.lingrad {
```

Visual Studio Code enters the matching closing brace.

7 Press **Enter** to create a blank line, and then type **background-image: linear-gradient(to right, red, blue);**.

8 Press **Enter** to create a blank line, and then type **height: 400px;**.

9 Click **Refresh** (⟳).

The web page refreshes.

Ⓐ The linear gradient appears.

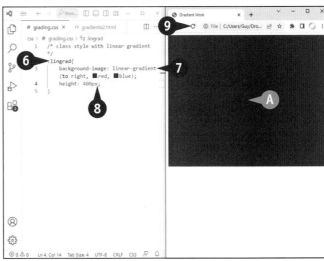

10 Select to right and type **to bottom** over it to change the direction.

11 Click after red, and type **green,**.

12 Click **Refresh** (⟳).

The web page refreshes.

Ⓑ The new version of the linear gradient appears, running from top to bottom with the colors red, green, and blue.

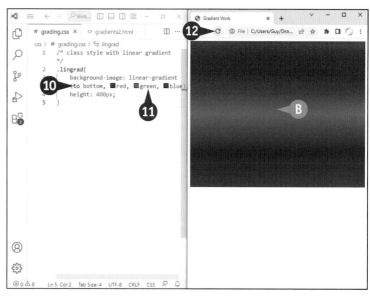

13 Select to bottom and type **225deg** over it.

14 Click after red, and type **orange, yellow,**.

15 Click **Refresh** (⟳).

The web page refreshes.

Ⓒ The new version of the linear gradient appears, running diagonally down from the upper-right corner of the screen with the colors red, orange, yellow, green, and blue.

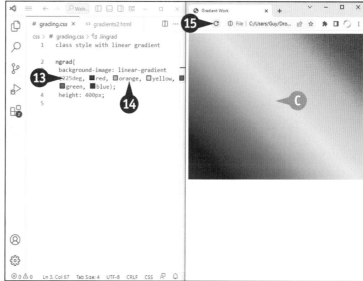

TIP

How do I create a linear gradient that repeats?
Use the repeating-linear-gradient function instead of the linear-gradient function. This function works in a similar way but repeats the gradient rather than displaying it once.

Apply a Radial Gradient to an Element

Like linear gradients, radial gradients enable to you to add eye-catching or eye-pleasing patterns to HTML elements. Radial gradients are especially useful for creating visual effects such as lighting and shadows. You can start a radial gradient either with its default ellipse shape or with a circle, positioning the shape wherever you want it within the element to which you are adding the gradient. You can choose which colors feature in the gradient, and you can specify where to stop the gradient — for example, at `closest-side` or at `furthest-side`.

Apply a Radial Gradient to an Element

1 In Visual Studio Code, open the external CSS file you want to work on.

2 Also in Visual Studio Code, open an HTML file to which you have linked the external CSS file.

3 Open the HTML file in a browser window.

4 In the HTML file, type the code for a `div` element, assigning it to a class with the name you will give your linear-gradient style. This example uses the name `radgrad`:

`<div class="radgrad"></div>`

5 Click the CSS file's tab.

The CSS file becomes active.

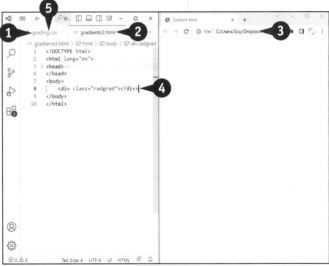

6 Click a blank line and type a period, the class style name you used in step **4**, a space, and an opening brace, **{** — for example

`.radgrad {`

Visual Studio Code enters the matching closing brace.

7 Press Enter to create a blank line, and then type **background-image: radial-gradient(circle, yellow, blue);**.

8 Press Enter to create a blank line, and then type **height: 650px;**.

9 Click **Refresh** (↻).

The web page refreshes.

A The radial gradient appears.

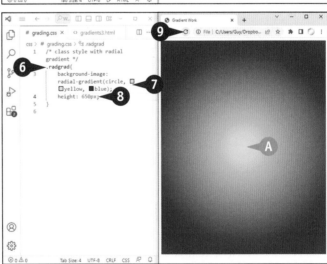

10 Select `circle` and type **ellipse** over it.

11 Edit the color sequence by adding further colors to it. The example uses the following code:

```
radial-gradient(ellipse,
yellow, cyan, blue, purple,
navy, black)
```

12 Click **Refresh** (↻).

The web page refreshes.

B The radial gradient displays the changes you made.

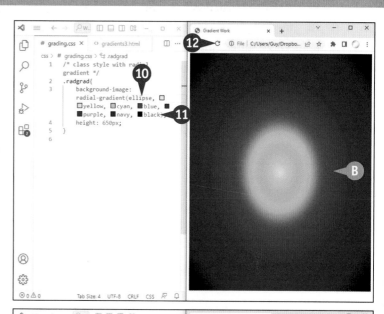

13 Click after `ellipse` and type a `size` instruction. This example uses **closest-side at 33% 66%**:

```
radial-gradient(ellipse
closest-side at 33% 66%,
yellow, cyan, blue, purple,
navy, black)
```

14 Click **Refresh** (↻).

The web page refreshes.

C The radial gradient displays the changes you made.

In the example, the gradient starts one-third of the way across the `div` element and two-thirds of the way down it and stops when it reaches the closest side of the element.

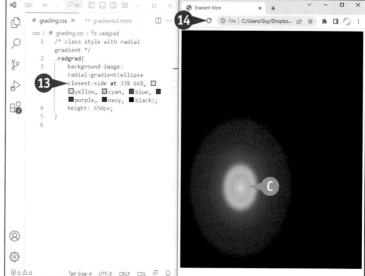

TIP

How do I create a radial gradient that repeats?
Use the `repeating-radial-gradient` function instead of the `radial-gradient` function. This function works in a similar way but repeats the gradient rather than displaying it once.

Using Sprites

A sprite is an elf or fairy, a disembodied spirit, or an upward flash of lightning. But in HTML and CSS, as in some game programming, a *sprite* is a single image that contains multiple smaller images used on your website. For example, a sprite might contain all of the custom button images that your website uses or the set of icons you use to illustrate key points. A visitor's browser requests the sprite file only once rather than requesting each individual image. You tell the browser to display only the section of the sprite file that contains the image you want to show.

What Are Sprites For, and When Should You Use Them?

Sprites have two main purposes:

- **Reduce the burden on the web server.** Using sprites reduces the number of requests to the web server, thus lightening its load and helping it remain able to respond quickly to requests.

- **Help web pages to load quickly.** Because the visitor's web browser requests and downloads only one sprite file rather than a whole suite of individual files, web pages should load more quickly.

Sprites are especially useful for icons, particularly if your website uses many icons. They are also useful for creating hover effects on navigation menus, where sliding another part of the background image into view can be faster and smoother than loading a separate image file.

Whether you should use sprites largely depends on how many icons or similar small images your website uses. Generally, if your website uses many small graphical items, such as buttons or icons, it may be worth using sprites. But if your website uses only a handful of icons altogether, creating a sprite is probably not worth the time or effort.

When deciding whether to create sprites, you should factor in the time that will be needed to update the sprite file or files after an individual icon changes. If the icon size changes as well, you will need to adjust the code for displaying the sprites as well.

Create the Individual Images

Assuming you have decided to create a sprite file, your first step is to create the individual images. Each image should be the same size so that you can arrange them into a line or a grid for the sprite file.

Assemble the Sprite File from the Individual Images

Next, assemble the sprite file by combining the individual images. You can perform this task by using an image editor, such as GIMP, discussed in Chapter 4. Alternatively, you can use a sprite-focused tool. You can find various such tools online, some free and some not. One example is TexturePacker, `www.codeandweb.com/texturepacker`, which offers a free version.

Store your sprite file either in the folder you use for your images, such as an `images` folder, or in a sprite-specific subfolder, such as `images/sprites`.

Create a CSS Class for the Sprite

Your next move is to create one CSS class for the sprite file as a whole plus one CSS class for each of the individual images you will display from the sprite file.

The CSS class for the sprite file itself sets the sprite file as the background image for the element. For example, say you have a sprite file called `sprite1.png` stored in your `images/sprites` folder. You could use CSS code such as the following to create a class called `sprite1`, assign your `sprite1.png` file to it, and set the width and height of the area you want to show at one item — one icon's worth of the sprite file, not the whole file. In this example, each icon is 75×75 pixels.

```
.sprite1 {
  background-image: url('images/sprites/sprite1.png');
  width: 75px;
  height: 75px;
}
```

For each icon in the sprite file, you would then create a separate class specifying the background position at which to display the sprite image to show that icon. For example, the first icon would typically have a `0,0` position at the top-left corner of the file:

```
.icon1 {
  background-position: 0 0;
}
```

The class for each other icon in the file would specify the appropriate offset to display the appropriate part of the image. For example, the second 75×75-pixel icon would require the sprite file to be shifted 75 pixels to the left:

```
.icon2 {
  background-position: -75px 0;
}
```

Once you reached the second row, the sprite image would need to be shifted up 75 pixels as well.

Use the Sprite Classes in Your HTML documents

After creating the sprite classes, you can use them in your HTML documents like other classes. The following example shows how you might display two `div` elements, one that uses the `icon1` class to display the first icon and a second that uses the `icon2` class to display the second icon:

```
<div class="sprite icon1"></div>
<div class="sprite icon2"></div>
```

Understanding CSS Animations

CSS provides various animations that enable you to build dynamic and interactive effects into your HTML documents. For example, you can apply transitions, effects that make changes such as fading an element in or out. Alternatively, you can apply transforms, effects that modify an element's position or appearance by making changes such as rotating the element or scaling it. You can make an animation run when a suitable event occurs, such as when the user hovers the pointer over an element.

This section explains CSS animations. The section "Create a Keyframe Animation," later in this chapter, walks you through a step-by-step example.

Grasp the Different Categories of Animations CSS Provides

CSS provides several categories of animations you can use to animate and enliven your web pages:

- **Transitions.** A *transition* is an effect that changes an element's style. For example, you can apply a fade-in transition that makes an element gradually appear over the time period you specify, such as 10 seconds.

- **Transforms.** A *transform* is an effect that changes an element's position, appearance, or both.

- **Keyframe animations.** A keyframe animation uses *keyframes*, points in the animation's timeline that define how the animated element looks. For example, you might use two keyframes, setting an element's opacity to 0 in the first keyframe to make it completely transparent and then setting the opacity to 100 in the second keyframe to make the element completely opaque. Given these two keyframes, the browser generates the frames between them automatically to create the animation.

- **Scroll animations.** A *scroll animation* plays automatically as the user scrolls up or down the page. You can use a scroll animation to slide elements into or out of view, as needed. To implement the scroll animation, you would typically use the `scroll` event in JavaScript, which is beyond the scope of this book.

- **SVG animations.** An SVG animation animates an illustration in the Scalable Vector Graphics format, which is abbreviated to SVG. For example, you might create an animation that changed the colors in an SVG graphic.

Create Transitions

To create a transition in CSS, you add the `transition` property to the property you want to animate. For example, if you want to create a transition involving color, you add the `transition` property to the `color` property. See the following section, "Apply Transitions to HTML Elements," for an example of implementing a transition.

Create Transforms

To create a transform in CSS, you add the `transform` property to the element you want to animate and then specify the function for the type of transformation you want. The following list explains four widely used transforms:

- **Rotate.** You can rotate an element either clockwise or counterclockwise by using the `rotate()` function. To rotate an element clockwise, specify a positive number of degrees; to rotate counterclockwise, specify a negative number. The following example rotates the element 180° counterclockwise:

```
.element {
    transform: rotate(-180deg);
}
```

- **Translate.** This is translation in the sense of moving an object rather than switching language. You can move an element by using the `translate()` function and specifying the horizontal distance first and the vertical distance second. Enter a negative value for the horizontal distance to move the object to the left or a positive value to move it to the right. Similarly, enter a negative value for the vertical distance to move the object up or a positive value to move it down. The following example moves the object 2 rem to the right and 3 rem down:

```
.element {
    transform: translate(2rem, 3rem);
}
```

- **Scale.** To increase or decrease the element's size, use the `scale()` function and provide a suitable factor, such as `0.5` to scale the element to half its size, as in the following example, or `2` to scale the element to double its size.

```
.element {
    transform: scale(0.5);
}
```

- **Skew.** To *skew* or tilt the element on both axes, use the `skew()` function. To skew on just the x-axis, use the `skewX()` function; to skew on only the y-axis, use the `skewY()` function. The following example skews the element in both directions by 45°:

```
.element {
    transform: skew(45dg);
}
```

Create Keyframe Animations

See the section "Create a Keyframe Animation," later in this chapter, for an example of creating a keyframe animation.

Apply Transitions to HTML Elements

Your website's content should be its main attraction, but competition for web eyeballs is tough, and you may want to sprinkle some stardust on your web pages to boost the site's pulling power. One way to enhance your web pages' visual appeal is to add transitions to HTML elements.

You can apply transitions to various elements, such as text, buttons, and images. For example, you can make an element's appearance change when a visitor hovers the pointer over it.

Understanding the Properties for Setting Up Transitions

CSS enables you to set up transitions either by using a single shorthand property or by using multiple individual properties.

The single shorthand property is called `transition` and takes up to four parameters:

`transition:` *property duration timing delay*

The following list explains what these parameters mean:

- *property.* This parameter specifies the CSS property that the transition is to affect, such as `background-color`, `height`, or `width`.

- *duration.* This parameter specifies how long the transition is to take, using either milliseconds, `ms`, or seconds, `s`.

- *timing.* This parameter specifies how the transition should run. Your options include `ease-in` to start slowly and speed up; `ease-out` to start fast and then slow down; and `ease-in-out`, to start slowly, go fast, and end slowly.

- *delay.* This parameter specifies the length of time to wait before running the transition, expressed as either milliseconds, `ms`, or seconds, `s`. For example, if you specify `1s` delay for a `hover` transition, the transition starts when the visitor has held the pointer over the element for one second.

The following example specifies the `transition` property for a `button` element. The button has white text — `color: white;` — on a dark-gray background —`background-color: darkgray;`. The `transition` property specifies `background-color` as the property to change, `1.0s` as the duration of the transition, and `ease-in-out` as the timing.

```
button {
    background-color: darkgray;
    color: white;
    transition: background-color 1.0s ease-in-out;
}
```

The following CSS code shows the transition itself, using the `:hover` pseudo-class. When a visitor parks the pointer over the button, the `background-color` property changes to `blue`, making the button look much more lively.

```
button:hover {
   background-color: blue;
}
```

Instead of using the single shorthand property, `transition`, you can use the following four individual properties:

- `transition-property`. This property specifies the CSS property to which the transition applies.

- `transition-duration`. This property specifies how long the transition is to take, using either milliseconds, `ms`, or seconds, `s`.

- `transition-timing-function`. This property specifies how to run the transition — for example, `ease-in` or `ease-out`.

- `transition-delay`. This property specifies the length of time to wait before running the transition, expressed as either milliseconds, `ms`, or seconds, `s`.

The following CSS code reimplements the earlier example, using the individual properties instead of the shorthand property.

```
button {
    background-color: darkgray;
    color: white;
    transition-property: background-color;
    transition-duration: 1.0s;
    transition-timing-function: ease-in-out;
}
```

Create a Keyframe Animation

CSS enables you to create a type of animation called a *keyframe animation* that specifies how an HTML element should change over a period of time. You control the change by identifying various keyframes at specific points in the animation. At these keyframes, you specify the style and position of the element in the animation.

For example, you might create a keyframe animation that manipulates the `opacity` property of an element, making it gradually appear over several seconds. You could define several keyframes over those two seconds, each with a different value, to control the rate of change.

Create a Keyframe Animation

1. In Visual Studio Code, open the external CSS file you want to work on.

2. Also in Visual Studio Code, open an HTML file to which you have linked the external CSS file.

3. Open the HTML file in a browser window.

4. In the HTML file, enter any preliminary text, plus the item you want to animate.

   The code in this example displays an h1 element followed by an img element that the example animates.

   ```
   <h1>Gradually Appearing Image</h1>
   <img src="images/frogpad_1024.png"
   width="90%">
   ```

5. Click the CSS file's tab.

   The CSS file appears.

6. Type a period and the name for the class, **fade-in**, followed by a space and an opening brace, **{**.

   Visual Studio Code enters the matching closing brace, **}**.

7. Press Enter to create a blank line, and then type the properties for the animation:

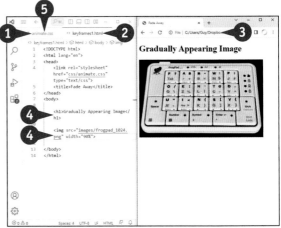

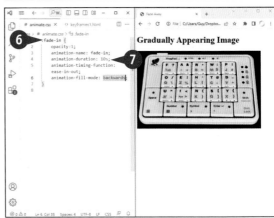

```
opacity: 1;
animation-name: fade-in;
animation-duration: 10s;
animation-timing-function: ease-in-out;
animation-fill-mode: backwards;
```

252

8 Below the `fade-in` class, type the **@keyframes** keyword followed by a space; the effect name, **fade-in**; another space; and an opening brace, **{**.

Visual Studio Code enters the matching closing brace.

9 Press Enter to create a new line, and then enter the `from` and `to` keyframe details:

```
from {
    opacity:0;
}
to {
    opacity:1;
}
```

10 Click the HTML file's tab.

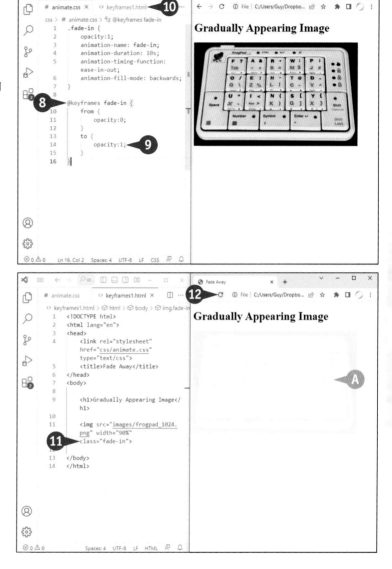

The HTML file becomes active.

11 Click before the closing > of the `<img>` tag and type **class="fade-in"**.

12 Click **Refresh** (⟳).

The web page refreshes.

Ⓐ The image appears gradually during a 10-second animation.

TIP

What does the `@keyframes` statement do?

The `@keyframes` statement defines two keyframes to control the animation. The first keyframe is the `from` keyframe, which sets the `opacity` property to 0, zero, making the image hidden at first. The second keyframe is the `to` keyframe, which sets the `opacity` property to 1, making the image fully visible.

Creating Forms

HTML enables you to create forms, web pages that provide fields in which a user can enter data before submitting the form to a server. The server processes the form, validates the data, and takes the appropriate action with the data — for example, sending it on to its destination.

Grasp Web Form Essentials

A web form is a web page that acts as an interface enabling visitors to input information and submit it. The form appears as a web page containing input controls, such as text fields in which the user can enter their name and email address, and check boxes or option buttons that the user can select to specify choices. After filling in the form, the user submits the form by clicking the Submit button. This retrieves the data from the form and submits it to a form handler, which is usually a server page containing a script for processing the data. The form can validate data as the user enters it or when the user submits the form.

Meet the Elements You Can Use in Web Forms

Table 11-1 explains the range of input elements that HTML provides for web forms. The nearby illustration shows many of the more widely used input elements.

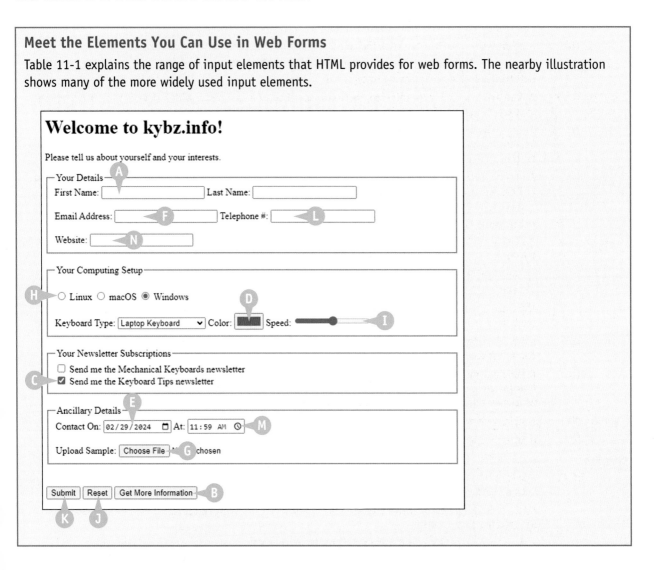

Table 11-1:   Input Elements for Web Forms

input Type	Explanation
text (A)	A single-line text input field. This is the default value for input, so if you omit the type attribute, you get a one-line text input field.
button (B)	A command button. You can control the text displayed on the button and what action occurs when the user clicks the button. For example, you might create a button called Get More Information that displayed a dialog box showing extra information.
checkbox (C)	A check box. The user can select the check box to enable an option or indicate a positive response, or deselect the check box to disable the option or indicate a negative response.
color (D)	A color picker. The user can click the color picker to display controls for selecting a color.
date (E)	A date field. Most browsers display a date picker, a mini-calendar control that enables the user to select a date visually rather than having to type it in.
datetime-local	A date and time field. For this, too, most browsers display a date picker with a time control, allowing the user to specify the date and time by clicking rather than typing.
email (F)	An input field designed to receive an email address. Most browsers support automatically validating the address when it is submitted. In iOS and Android, the onscreen keyboard displays the .com domain-picker button when an email field is selected.
file (G)	A file-picker button, such as a Choose File button. The user can click the button to display an Open dialog box or similar dialog box for selecting a file to upload.
hidden	A hidden input field. You can use a hidden field to include data when the form is submitted. Be warned that although the field is hidden in the browser, it is visible in the page's source, so anyone can view it easily.
image	An image that acts as a Submit button. You can use an image input instead of or alongside a submit button, discussed later in this table.
month	A month and year field. Most browsers display a date picker, enabling the user to select the month and year visually.
number	A numeric input field, including spin buttons for adjusting the value. You can set minimum and maximum limits on the values the field will accept — for example, a minimum of 1 and a maximum of 10.
password	A password field. This is a single-line text field in which the characters typed appeared as asterisks or circles for security against shoulder-surfing.
radio (H)	A radio button, also called an *option button*. Radio buttons appear in groups of two or more and enable the user to select one of a group of choices. Clicking one radio button selects that button and deselects whichever other radio button was previously selected.
range (I)	A slider that enables the user to select a value along a specified range. For example, a volume control.
reset (J)	A Reset button. The user can click this button to reset all the form's inputs to their default values.
search	A search box. The user can type a search term for which to search on the search engine defined in the control.
submit (K)	A Submit button. This is the button the user clicks to submit the form's data to a form handler. A submit button bears the label *Submit* by default, but you can give the button a different label if you prefer.
tel (L)	A text field designed to receive a telephone number. You can use the pattern attribute to specify an acceptable number format.
time (M)	A time field. Most browsers display a time picker, enabling the user to select the time visually.
URL (N)	A text field for a URL. Most browsers can automatically validate the URL when submitting the form.
week	A week field. Most browsers display a week picker, enabling the user to select the week and year visually.

Create a Form

When you need to give your website's visitors a way to submit information to you, create a web form. For example, you might want visitors to be able to fill out a survey, sign up for a newsletter, or submit a job application.

To start creating a form, you place a `form` element at the appropriate point in a web page, specifying either the `get` method or the `post` method if you already know which the form will use. Between the element's opening `<form>` tag and closing `</form>` tag, you enter the input controls for the form.

Create a Form

1. In Visual Studio Code, open the file in which to place the form.

2. Open the file in a browser window.

3. In Visual Studio Code, click to place the insertion point where you want to start the form.

4. Type **f** to display the expansions list.

   A. If your form will use the `get` action, click **form:get**. See the tip.

   B. If your form will use the `post` action, click **form:post**.

5. Click **form**.

   C. Visual Studio Code inserts the opening `<form>` tag, the `action` attribute with the insertion point inside double quotation marks after it, and the closing `</form>` tag:

   `<form action=""></form>`

6. Press Tab to move the insertion point to just before the `</form>` tag, and then press Enter several times to create blank lines (not shown).

7. Click to place the insertion point on the first of the blank lines.

8. Type **la** to display the expansions list.

9. Click **label**.

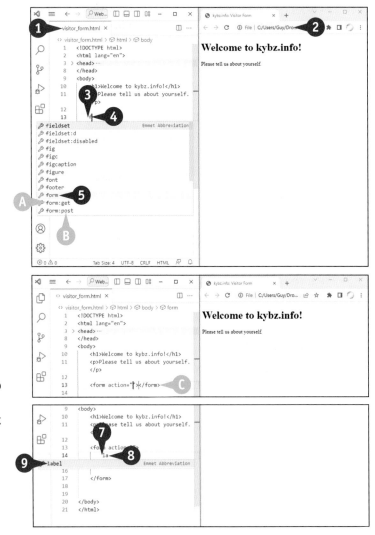

D Visual Studio Code inserts the opening `<label>` tag, the `for` attribute with the insertion point inside double quotation marks after it, and the closing `</label>` tag:

```
<label for=""></label>
```

10 Type the name you will assign to the input control you will add. In the example, the name is **first_name**.

11 Press `Tab` to move the insertion point to just before the `</label>` tag, and then type the display text for the label. In the example, this is **First Name:**.

12 Click **Refresh** (↻).

The web page refreshes.

E The label appears.

13 On the next line, type **in**, and then click **input:text** in the expansions list.

Visual Studio Code inserts the `<input>` tag, which looks like this:

```
<input type="text" name="" id="">
```

14 Assign to the `name` attribute the name from step **10** — in the example, **first_name**.

15 Assign to the `id` attribute a descriptive ID. The example uses **first_name** again.

16 Click **Refresh** (↻).

The web page refreshes.

F The text input control appears.

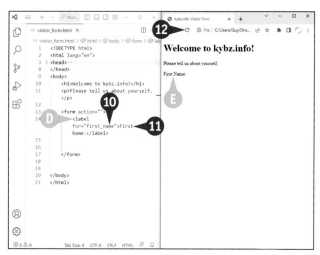

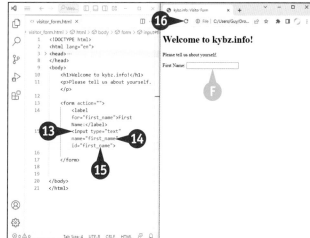

TIP

Should I choose the `get` method or the `post` method for my form?

Whether to use the `get` method or the `post` method depends on the script your website will use to gather information from the form. Ask your systems administrator which method to use. If you cannot determine which method to use, leave the method unspecified while you create the form. You can add the method when the form is otherwise finished.

For security, make the page containing the form accessible only via HTTPS, not via HTTP. Consult your systems administrator about encrypting the data submitted via the form.

Add Text Input Controls to a Form

HTML includes several input controls for getting text from the user of a form. The most straightforward of these is the `text` input, which you can use to get most any kind of text. But when you need text in a particular format, you can use an input control designed to receive that format. The `email` input type can validate an email address when the form is submitted, and the `url` input type can validate a URL. The `tel` input type is designed to receive a number in an acceptable telephone-number format you specify.

Add Text Input Controls to the Form

1 In Visual Studio Code, open the file containing the form.

2 Open the file in a browser window.

3 In Visual Studio Code, click to place the insertion point where you want to place the next input control.

A If needed, enter `<br>` to force a line break.

4 Type **la**.

The expansions list appears.

5 Click **label**.

B The `<label>` tag appears.

6 Type the name you will assign to the input control you will add. The example uses **last_name**.

7 Press Tab to move the insertion point to just before the `</label>` tag, and then type the display text for the label. The example uses **Last Name:**.

8 On the next line, type **in**, and then click **input:text** in the expansions list.

The `<input>` tag appears.

9 Assign to the `name` attribute the name from step **6** — in the example, **last_name**.

10 Assign to the `id` attribute a descriptive ID. The example uses **last_name** again.

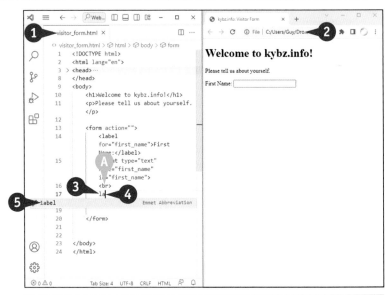

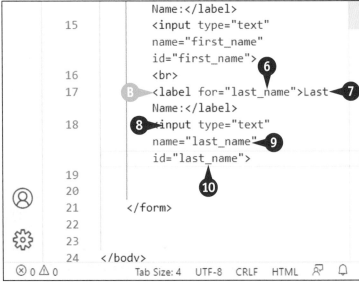

11 Click **Refresh** (⟳).

The web page refreshes.

C The Last Name text input and its label appear.

12 Type another <br> tag to force a line break.

13 Repeat steps **4** to **10** to insert another label and input field. This time, insert an email field. The example uses this code:

```
<label for="email">Email
Address:</label>
<input type="email"
name="email" id="email">
```

14 Type another <br> tag to force a line break.

15 Repeat steps **4** to **10** to insert another label and input field. This time, insert a tel field. The example uses this code:

```
<label for="telephone">
Telephone #:</label>
<input type="tel"
name="telephone" id="telephone"
pattern="[0-9]{3}-[0-9]{3}-
[0-9]{4}">
```

Note: For a different location, you might use a different pattern attribute for the phone number.

16 Click **Refresh** (⟳).

The web page refreshes.

D The email field and tel field appear.

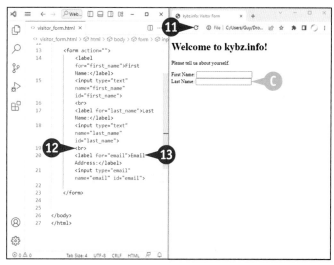

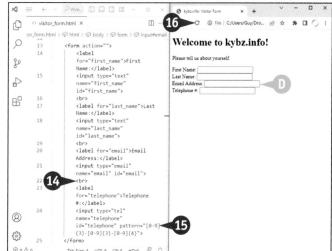

How do I use the pattern attribute for a tel input?

If you need to validate the phone number the user supplies, include the pattern attribute in the <input> tag and use a regular expression to specify the pattern. A *regular expression* is a sequence of characters that defines a search pattern. For a U.S. telephone number, you would normally use pattern="[0-9]{3}-[0-9]{3}-[0-9]{4}", which means three digits in the range 0–9, a hyphen, three more digits in the range 0–9, another hyphen, and finally four digits in the range 0–9 — for example, 415-555-1212. Not all browsers validate tel inputs, so it is wise to validate the phone number on the server after gathering the form data.

Add Radio Buttons to a Form

TML enables you to add radio buttons to a form, giving you an easy way to have the user choose one option out of a group. Radio buttons, also called *option buttons*, appear in groups of two or more and enable the user to select one of a group of choices. Clicking one radio button selects that button and deselects whichever other radio button was previously selected, if any. You can select one option button in the group by default by setting its `checked` attribute.

Add Radio Buttons to a Form

1 In Visual Studio Code, open the file containing the form.

2 Open the file in a browser window.

3 In Visual Studio Code, click to place the insertion point where you want to place the next input control.

Ⓐ If needed, enter `<br>` to force a line break.

4 Type **in**.

The expansions list appears.

5 Click **input:radio**.

Visual Studio Code inserts the `<input>` tag:

```
<input type="radio"
name="" id="">
```

6 Between the double quotation marks after `name`, type the name of the group of radio buttons — for example:

```
<input type="radio"
name="platform" id="">
```

7 Between the double quotation marks after `id`, type the name for the radio button — for example:

```
<input type="radio" name=
"platform" id="linux">
```

8 On the next line, type **l** and then click **label** on the expansion list.

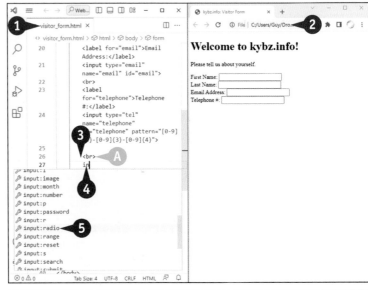

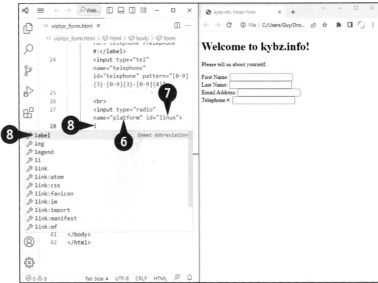

Visual Studio Code inserts a `<label>` tag, including the `for` attribute and placing the insertion point between the double quotation marks after the attribute.

9 Type the `id` you assigned in step **7**.

10 Press Tab to move the insertion point to just before the `</label>` tag, and then type the display text for the label. This example uses **Linux**.

11 Click **Refresh** (↻).

The web page refreshes.

Ⓑ The radio button appears.

12 Repeat steps **4** to **10** to add other radio buttons to the group. The example uses this code:

```
<input type="radio"
name="platform" id="macos">
<label for="macos">macOS
</label>
<input type="radio"
name="platform" id="windows"
checked="checked">
<label for="windows">Windows
</label>
```

Ⓒ If you want to select one of the radio buttons, include the `checked` property in the `<input>` tag and assign a value to it. You can assign any value, such as `checked="penguin"`, but `checked="checked"` is usually clearest.

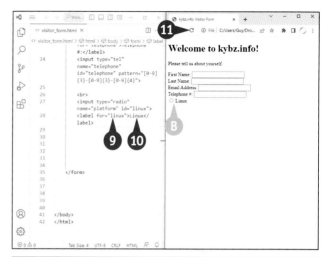

13 Click **Refresh** (↻).

The web page refreshes.

Ⓓ The radio buttons appear.

Ⓔ The radio button specified as `checked` is selected.

TIPS

Can I put multiple groups of radio buttons on a form?

Yes — as many as you need. Use the `name` attribute of the `input` element for each option button to specify the group of which it is a member. In the form's interface, make the purpose of the different groups clear and lay them out so that the user can instantly distinguish one group from another.

What happens if I set the `checked` property for more than one radio button?

HTML selects the last radio button specified as checked in your code.

Add Check Boxes to a Form

When you need to add an independent yes/no or on/off control to a form, you can insert a check box by adding an `input` control and specifying `checkbox` for the `type` attribute. The user clicks to select the check box if it is not currently selected or to deselect it if it is selected. You can select a check box by default by setting its `checked` attribute to `checked` or another value.

Add Check Boxes to a Form

1 In Visual Studio Code, open the file containing the form.

2 Open the file in a browser window.

3 In Visual Studio Code, click to place the insertion point where you want to place the first check box.

A If needed, enter `<br>` to force a line break.

4 Type **in**.

The expansions list appears.

5 Click **input:checkbox**.

Visual Studio Code inserts the `<input>` tag:

```
<input type="checkbox"
name="" id="">
```

6 Between the double quotation marks after `name`, type the name to assign the check box — for example:

```
<input type="checkbox"
name="mech" id="">
```

7 Between the double quotation marks after `id`, type the name for the radio button — for example:

```
<input type="checkbox"
name="mech" id="mech">
```

8 On the next line, type **l** and then click **label** on the expansion list.

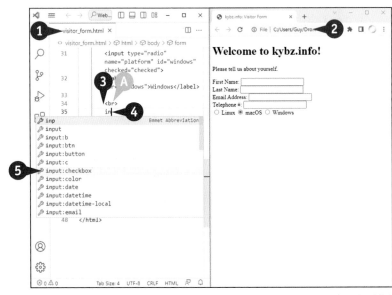

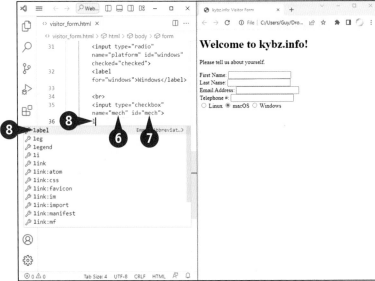

264

Visual Studio Code inserts a `<label>` tag, including the `for` attribute and placing the insertion point between the double quotation marks after the attribute.

9 Type the `id` you assigned in step **7**.

10 Press Tab to move the insertion point to just before the `</label>` tag, and then type the display text for the label. This example uses **Send me the Mechanical Keyboards newsletter**.

11 Click **Refresh** (⟳).

The web page refreshes.

B The check box and its label appear.

C Type `<br>` to insert a break, if needed.

12 Repeat steps **4** to **10** to insert further check boxes, as needed, each with a label.

D If you want to select a check box, include the `checked` attribute in the `<input>` tag and assign it a value.

Note: You can assign any value, such as `checked="yep"`, but `checked="checked"` is usually clearest.

13 Click **Refresh** (⟳).

The web page refreshes.

E The check boxes appear.

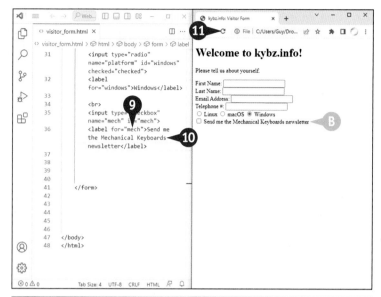

How do I assign a return value for a check box?

To assign a return value for a check box, include the `value` attribute in the `input` tag for the check box and specify the value for it. For example, if you want the check box to return the text *Newsletter 1*, you could use `<input type="checkbox" name="nl" id="nl" value="Newsletter 1">`.

Add a Drop-Down List of Options to a Form

When your form needs a user to select one option out of many possible options, you can add a drop-down list. To do so, you insert a `select` element and populate it with as many `option` elements as needed. Each `option` element appears as a separate item in the drop-down list. The user clicks the drop-down button (⌄) to display the drop-down list, on which they can click an item to select it.

Add a Drop-Down List of Options to a Form

1. In Visual Studio Code, open the file containing the form.

2. Open the file in a browser window.

3. In Visual Studio Code, click to place the insertion point where you want to place the drop-down list.

   A If needed, enter `<br>` to force a line break.

4. Type **l**.

   The expansions list appears.

5. Click **label**.

   B Visual Studio Code inserts the opening `<label>` tag.

6. Type the name you will assign to the `select` element you will add. In the example, the name is **keyboard_type**.

7. Press Tab to move the insertion point to just before the `</label>` tag, and then type the display text for the label. In the example, this is **Keyboard Type:**.

8. Click **Refresh** (↻).

   The web page refreshes.

   C The label appears.

9. On the next line, type **s**.

   The expansions list appears.

10. Click **select**.

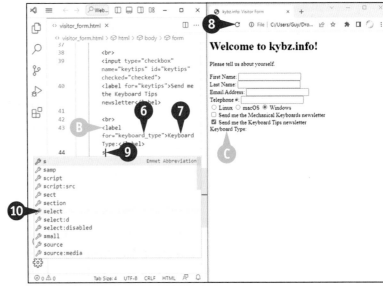

Visual Studio Code inserts the `select` element:

```
<select name="" id="">
</select>
```

11 With the insertion point between the double quotation marks after `name`, type the name for the `select` element. The example uses **keyboard_type**.

12 Press Tab to move the insertion point to between the double quotation marks after `id`, and type the value from step **6**.

13 Press Tab to move the insertion point to just before `</select>`, and then press Enter several times to create blank lines (not shown).

14 On the first blank line, type **op** and then click **option** on the expansions list.

Visual Studio Code inserts the `option` element:

```
<option value=""></option>
```

15 With the insertion point between the double quotation marks after `value`, type the return value to assign to the option. This example uses **laptop**.

16 Press Tab and type the display text for the item. This example uses **Laptop Keyboard**.

17 Repeat steps **14** to **16** to add further `option` elements to the `select` element.

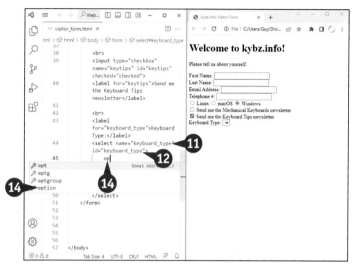

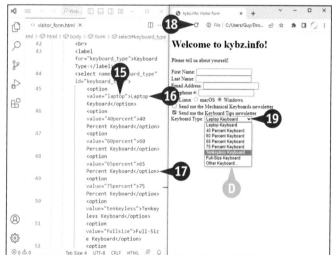

18 Click **Refresh** (⟳).

The web page refreshes.

19 Click ⌄.

Ⓓ The drop-down list opens.

TIP

What does the `name` attribute in the `select` element do?
The `name` attribute enables you to retrieve data from the `select` element when the user submits the form. If you omit the `name` attribute, you cannot retrieve any data from the `select` element.

Add Command Buttons to a Form

To be of any use, your form will need a Submit button that lets the user submit it. HTML enables you to create a Submit button easily and to add other types of buttons, as needed. For example, you may want to provide a Reset button that resets all the form's fields to their default values, allowing the user to start filling in the form afresh. You may also want to add custom buttons to display helpful information to the user.

Add Command Buttons to a Form

1 In Visual Studio Code, open the file containing the form.

2 Open the file in a browser window.

3 In Visual Studio Code, click to place the insertion point where you want to place the first command button.

Ⓐ If needed, enter <br> to force a line break. The example uses two <br> tags to add vertical space on the form.

4 Type **in**.

The expansions list appears.

5 Click **input:submit**.

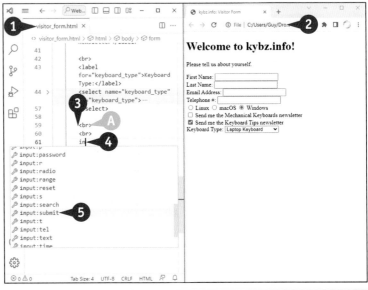

Visual Studio Code inserts the `<input>` tag, including the `type` attribute with the `submit` value and the `value` attribute with no value:

```
<input type="submit"
value="">
```

6 With the insertion point between the double quotation marks after `value`, type the display text for the Submit button — for example, **Submit** or **Submit This Form**.

7 Click **Refresh** (🔄).

The web page refreshes.

Ⓑ The Submit button appears.

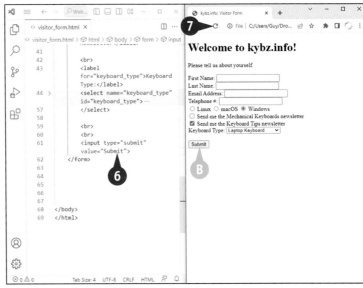

8 If your form will need a Reset button, repeat steps **4** to **7**. This time, click **input:reset** on the expansions list, and assign to the `value` attribute text such as **Reset**.

9 Click **Refresh** (⟳).

The web page refreshes.

C The Reset button appears.

10 To add a button that displays an information dialog box, repeat steps **4** to **7**. This time around, click **input:button** on the expansions list, and assign to the `value` attribute the display text for the button. This example uses **More Information**.

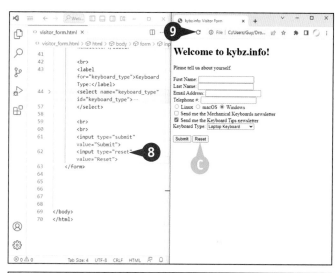

11 Click before the closing > of the `<input>` tag and add the `onclick` parameter, specifying **alert** within double quotation marks and the message to display within parentheses and single quotation marks. The example uses this statement:

```
<input type="button"
value="More Information"
onclick="alert('Please contact
our customer-service department
for help.')">
```

12 Click **Refresh** (⟳).

The web page refreshes.

13 Click the button.

The alert dialog box appears.

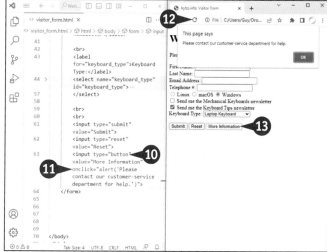

TIP

How can I split up a longer form into sections?
You can divide the form into various field sets by using the `fieldset` element. Identify the form elements you want to include in the first field set, and then enter an opening `<fieldset>` tag before the first element and a closing `</fieldset>` tag after the last element. After the opening `<fieldset>` tag, enter a `legend` element with the display text for that section of the form, such as `<legend>Your Contact Information</legend>`. Repeat this process for each other section of the form.

CHAPTER 12

Taking Your Website to the Next Level

In this chapter, you learn how search engines work and how to perform search engine optimization, SEO, on your website; how to identify and reduce accessibility issues for websites; and how to use live development tools to fix problems. You also learn about the use of staging servers and about front-end frameworks for rapid development.

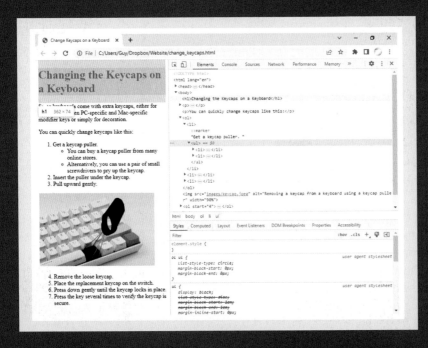

Understanding How Search Engines Work

Search engines are perhaps the most popular tool for navigating the Internet. You open a web browser window or tab to a search engine, such as Google or DuckDuckGo, and enter your query or some keywords. The search engine then returns search results for you to browse or follow.

Returning search results is the last of four steps that search engines typically perform. The first three steps are crawling the Web to gather information, indexing that information, and ranking the search results. Understanding the essentials of these three steps may help you optimize your website for search engines.

The Search Engine Discovers Information by Crawling

The search engine's first step is to use a process called *crawling* to discover information on the Internet. Automated search processes called *spiders*, *crawlers*, or *search bots* explore the Internet, starting from a list of known URLs and following links from those pages to discover other pages.

When a spider reaches a website, its first move is to locate and read a file called `robots.txt`, which provides directions for how to crawl the site. The `robots.txt` file may include a list of folders that the spider should ignore. The file may also block particular spiders to prevent the crawling from generating so much traffic as to overwhelm the web server. See the section "Guide Search Spiders with a `robots.txt` File," later in this chapter, for more information about the `robots.txt` file and how you can create one for your website.

Following the instructions in the `robots.txt` file, the spider explores the website, following both internal links — links that lead to other pages on the site — and external links, ones that lead to other websites. The spider logs the URLs it discovers, standardizing the URLs via a process called *URL normalization* that removes any unnecessary parameters, converts all characters to lowercase, and resolves any redirections in the URLs.

The spider also logs each web page's text and other content for future use, together with the page's metadata, such as the page's title, its description, and key terms. The search engine will use this information to determine the page's topic and the search terms to which it is relevant.

The Search Engine Indexes the Information Retrieved

Each spider sends back the information it has logged to the search engine, which processes the data before storing it in a database called an *index*. The index is essentially a colossal list of web pages, their contents, and associated information. The index is the database that the search engine consults to find results for searches.

The search engine organizes the index to help it return relevant search results quickly. The index creates groups of pages sorted by topic and ranks each group, assigning it various scores that express the group's relevance to specific keywords or search phrases.

In the index, the search engine also stores details of the links between pages. The search engine uses this information to assess the structure of the website and its relation to the Web as a whole and to estimate how authoritative web pages and sites are.

The Search Engine Ranks Each Page Crawled

As part of the indexing process, the search engine ranks each web page added to the database, assigning the page a value expressing its relevance to one or more particular queries. In layperson's terms, the search engine performs the ranking by assessing how many of a query's keywords and search phrases appear in the web page, how many external links point to this page, and how high the quality of those links is. For example, a page that receives links from many sites that the search engine considers high-quality and authoritative will get a higher ranking.

The search engine also attempts to determine the quality of the web page's content, algorithmically looking for original, high-quality content rather than low-quality content also available elsewhere. As part of this analysis, the search engine analyzes the usage of keywords and search phrases in the page's content, including their frequency and where they appear on the page.

Optimize Your Website for Search Engines

To get as much quality traffic as possible to your website, you will want to optimize it for search engines. This process of search engine optimization can help your website to rank higher in search engine results pages, making it more visible to web users searching for information. SEO can also help reduce your website's *bounce rate*, the percentage of visitors who land on your website but do not stay, instead "bouncing" on to another site because they have decided your site does not meet their needs.

Identify the Keywords with Which People Search for Your Product or Service

First, work to identify the keywords and search terms that people looking for your product or service will use. You can then feature these keywords and search terms prominently in your website so that the search engines' spiders will pick them up and rank your site in the results for searches.

To identify the keywords and search terms, begin by brainstorming with your colleagues to produce a base list. Involve your customer-service reps and help desk to glean keywords and search terms from customer queries and points of pain with your products or service.

Next, explore tools such as Google Keyword Planner, `https://ads.google.com/aw/keyword planner/home` and shown in the nearby illustration; SEMrush, `www.semrush.com`; and Hootsuite, `www.hootsuite.com`.

Start with Google Keyword Planner, which is free provided you have a Google Ads account; if you do not have an account, you can set one up in minutes. Google Keyword Planner enables you to search using the keywords you have identified, view new keywords, get search volume and forecasts, and read reports.

Add the Keywords to Your Website's Pages

Once you have identified the keywords your website needs, use them where appropriate in your web pages. The following are the four key areas:

- **Title tags.** Phrase your page titles to encapsulate the page's content accurately but also to include all relevant keywords.

- **Meta tags.** Make sure each page contains meta tags that accurately describe its contents. Use the appropriate search keywords and terms in the meta tags.

- **Header tags.** Structure your web pages logically with the appropriate levels of headers, using `h1` elements for major sections, `h2` elements to divide those `h1` sections, and `h3` elements to split up the `h2` subsections. Include the relevant search keywords and terms in the headers, keeping each header as brief as sensibly possible and making each header unique on its page.

- **Page content.** Use the keywords and terms where your content covers them.

Make sure each keyword or term is relevant everywhere you use it. Avoid the temptation to include hot search terms in meta tags that do not cover those topics. Well aware of webmasters trying to game the spiders, the search engines calibrate their ranking algorithms to downgrade pages whose meta tags claim coverage that the pages' content does not actually deliver.

Deliver High-Quality Content and Keep It Updated

Getting the right keywords and search terms in place is vital, but so is creating web pages that deliver high-quality content. Such content is important both for the search engines, which compare page content to keywords used to determine page quality, and for your visitors, who are presumably visiting your website for accurate information, sound advice, and compelling insights.

Once your site is up, running, and populated with strong content, do not rest on your laurels. Instead, develop and implement an update schedule to make sure your pages contain the latest information so that they do not become stale.

Optimize Technical Aspects of Your Website

You also need to optimize technical aspects of your website, making sure that it is accessible to search engines, that its code is as clean and complete as possible, and that the site is responsive to all clients.

Most likely, your website should have a `robots.txt` file to tell spiders how to crawl the site. See the next section for information.

Develop Backlinks to Your Website

Search engines use *backlinks*, links from other websites to your website, as a key factor in determining the ranking of your website among search results. This means it is important to get as many high-quality, authoritative external sites to link to your website as possible.

To develop backlinks, reach out to the websites you want to link to your site. The stronger your content, the easier developing backlinks will be. Having guests post on your site can also encourage them to link to your site.

Analyze Your Website's Performance

Analyze your website's performance by using a tool such as Google Analytics, `https://analytics.google.com`, which enables you to track your website's traffic and visitor behavior. This analysis will show you which areas of your website are performing to expectation and which need improvement.

Guide Search Spiders with a `robots.txt` File

If your website contains folders you do not want search engines' spiders to crawl, create a `robots.txt` file to tell spiders which folders to skip. The file can contain the same instructions for all spiders or different instructions for different spiders. For example, you might instruct all spiders not to crawl private folders, or you might tell particular spiders not to crawl your website at all to reduce the burden on the server. Be clear that `robots.txt` is advisory: Spiders can ignore it; and even if the spider obeys the do-not-crawl instruction, the search engine may index the pages anyway.

Understanding What a `robots.txt` File Does and Does Not Do

A `robots.txt` file provides instructions for spiders crawling your website. The file consists of one or more sets of directives. The first directive, `User-agent:`, specifies the spiders involved. The second and subsequent directives, `Disallow:`, list the folders those spiders should skip.

Table 12-1 lists widely crawling spiders with their `User-agent` names.

Table 12-1: Spiders and Their User-Agent Names	
Description	**User-agent Name**
Googlebot	`Googlebot`
Bingbot	`Bingbot`
Baidu Spider	`Baiduspider`
YandexBot	`YandexBot`
Sogou Spider	`Sogou web spider`
Yahoo! Slurp	`Slurp`
DuckDuckBot	`DuckDuckBot`
Exabot	`Exabot`
Facebot (Facebook)	`facebookexternalhit`
Alexa Crawler	`ia_archiver`
MJ12bot	`MJ12bot`
AhrefsBot	`AhrefsBot`
SemrushBot	`SemrushBot`
DotBot	`DotBot`
Applebot (Apple)	`Applebot`
Twitterbot (Twitter)	`Twitterbot`
SeznamBot	`SeznamBot`
Archive.org bot	`ia_archiver`
Discordbot	`Discordbot`
Gigabot	`Gigabot`

Create a `robots.txt` File

Create a text-only file and save it under the name `robots.txt`. In the file, place sets of instructions for the spiders.

To address a spider, enter `User-agent:` and the spider's name. The following example tells Bing's Bingbot to skip the `/private/` folder:

```
User-agent: Bingbot
Disallow: /private/
```

If you address one spider by name, you will probably need to address multiple spiders by name. Create a `User-agent:` and `Disallow:` set for each spider you want to affect. The following example tells Facebot not to crawl the site at all, by specifying `Disallow:  /`; tells DuckDuckBot to skip the `/test/` folder and the `/dev/` folder; and tells Yahoo! Slurp to skip the `/dev/` folder:

```
User-agent: facebookexternalhit
Disallow: /
User-agent: DuckDuckBot
Disallow: /test/
Disallow: /dev/
User-agent: Slurp
Disallow: /dev/
```

To address all spiders, enter `User-agent:  *`. The following example tells all spiders to skip the `/private/` folder and the `/temp/` folder:

```
User-agent: *
Disallow: /private/
Disallow: /temp/
```

Deploy Your `robots.txt` File

Once you have created your `robots.txt` file, copy it to the root directory of your website. This is the only place that spiders look for the file.

Mark a Web Page Not to Be Indexed

You can mark an individual web page with a `noindex` meta tag to tell spiders not to index the page. To do so, place the following meta tag in the `head` section of the web page:

```
<meta name ="robots" content="noindex">
```

Understanding Accessibility Issues for Websites

To make sure your website can be enjoyed by as wide an audience as possible, you should make it accessible to those with disabilities as well as those without. This means designing and implementing your website to take into account visual, auditory, cognitive, and motor impairments. Doing so means more work, but it increases your website's audience and helps deliver a more diverse and inclusive online community.

This section identifies common accessibility barriers and shows you ways of addressing them.

Dealing with Visual Accessibility Issues

Visitors with visual impairments may experience several accessibility issues when accessing websites.

- **Color contrast.** Visitors with visual impairments such as low vision, color blindness, or diabetic retinopathy may have difficulty distinguishing between colors. To minimize this issue, use high-contrast colors on your web pages, especially for essential content such as text.

- **Font size.** Many people may find small fonts hard to read. To reduce this problem, use font sizes of at least 16 pixels for all text content.

- **Text formatting.** Dense blocks of text can prove impenetrable even for visitors with good vision. To mitigate this problem, structure your text content using headings and subheadings so that visitors can easily navigate through the content. Clearly structured content also helps visitors who have cognitive impairments and people using mobile devices, especially devices with small screens.

Dealing with Auditory Accessibility Issues

Users with hearing impairments may have difficulty accessing and understanding audio content on your website.

- **Audio content without captions.** Users with hearing impairments may rely partly or fully on captions when playing audio content. To avoid problems, provide captions for all audio content.

- **Audio content without transcripts.** Similarly, provide transcripts for textual audio content so that users with hearing impairments can read through the content's text. If a piece of audio content is text-free, state this in writing.

Dealing with Cognitive Accessibility Issues

Users with cognitive impairments may have difficulty with two aspects of websites.

- **Complex language.** Keep language clear and straightforward wherever possible. This will help not only users with cognitive impairments but also users for whom English is not their first language. Should such users choose to use machine translation to better read your web pages, clear language will help produce understandable translations.

- **Complicated navigation.** Make the navigation for your website as straightforward as possible. Depending on the website, this may mean including multiple means of navigating, such as links in a sidebar on the left plus a breadcrumb bar at the top that shows the categories and levels through which the user has navigated to reach the current page. Make sure that the user can quickly return to the website's home page no matter how deeply they drill down into the site.

Dealing with Keyboard Accessibility Issues

Make sure that your website is keyboard accessible so that visitors can navigate it using only a keyboard rather than having to use a pointing device.

The most common problem for keyboard accessibility is when you create a keyboard trap. A *keyboard trap* is an element, such as a modal dialog box or pop-up window, that retains the focus when the visitor has navigated to it and requires the use of a pointing device to move to another part of the page. Using only the keyboard, the visitor remains trapped on the element. To avoid keyboard traps, do not use modal dialog boxes and pop-up windows, and test each page using only a keyboard before deploying it.

Another keyboard accessibility problem is forms that include elements, such as radio buttons and drop-down lists, that require the use of a pointing device. To avoid this problem, test your forms to verify that all the elements they contain are keyboard accessible.

Dealing with Mobile Accessibility Issues

Many visitors to your website will use mobile devices, such as smartphones and tablets, so making sure that your web pages are mobile accessible is vital. Two main issues normally predominate.

- **Small font sizes.** Small font sizes can make reading painful even on large screens, but on tiny screens they can prevent readers from deciphering the words unless they zoom in. To avoid problems, practice responsive design as discussed in Chapter 10, and test your web pages on devices with small screens to make sure they are readable.

- **Complex navigation.** As discussed for cognitive accessibility issues earlier in this section, make your website's navigation as straightforward as possible to allow visitors using mobile devices to navigate the site easily.

Meet Chrome's Live Development Tools

Most browsers include built-in live development tools that enable you to inspect a web page's code, make changes to it, and save the changes to the file. These tools can provide a quicker way to solve problems in your live web pages than working in a code editor, uploading the edited file, and then checking that the problems have gone. This section introduces you to Chrome's live development tools, which are known as DevTools for short.

Normally, you would use live development tools with great care when working on live pages, those publicly accessible on your website. If you use a staging server, work there instead for greater latitude to make mistakes.

Display the Chrome DevTools

Launch Chrome as usual, and then go to the web page on which you want to work. Right-click (A) anywhere on the page to display the contextual menu, and then click **Inspect** (B). From the keyboard, you can simply press Ctrl + Shift + I on Windows or Linux or ⌘ + Shift + I on the Mac.

From the contextual menu, you can also display the source code for the web page by clicking **View page source** (C). On Windows and Linux, you can skip opening the contextual menu and simply press the keyboard shortcut, Ctrl + U.

The Chrome window displays the DevTools pane, as shown in the nearby illustration. By default, Chrome shrinks the current web page to a pane (D) on the left of the window and displays the DevTools pane docked on the right side of the window. You can change the docking position by clicking the DevTools **Menu** button (E, ⋮) and then clicking **Dock to left** (▯), **Dock to bottom** (▭), **Dock to right** (▯), or **Undock to separate window** (▢), as needed. Moving DevTools to a separate window is especially helpful when your computer has multiple monitors connected.

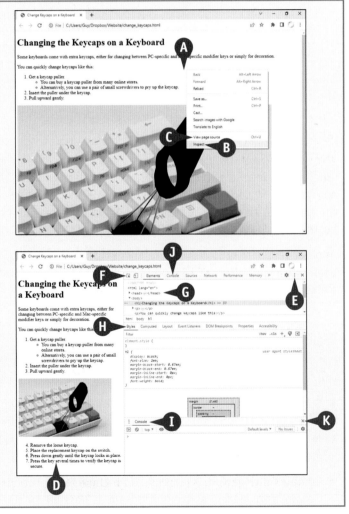

At first, when you display the DevTools, you normally see the following components:

- **Tab bar (F).** You click the tabs on this bar to navigate among the main panes of DevTools.

- **Elements pane (G).** This pane enables you to examine the HTML structure of the web page. The Elements pane displays the Document Object Model tree, the structure of elements in the HTML document. The Document Object Model is referred to as the *DOM tree* for short.

- **Elements pane tab bar (H).** This tab bar enables you to display different sets of information by clicking the Styles tab, the Computed tab, the Layout tab, the Event Listeners tab, the DOM Breakpoints tab, the Properties tab, or the Accessibility tab.

- **Console drawer (I).** The DevTools provide two means of giving console commands: the Console drawer, which appears by default at the bottom of the screen, and the Console pane, which you can display by clicking the Console tab (J) on the tab bar. You can toggle the display of the Console drawer by pressing [Esc]. Alternatively, click the DevTools **Menu** button (E, ⋮) and then click **Hide console drawer** or **Show console drawer**, as needed. To close the Console drawer quickly, click **Close** (K, ✕).

Choose a Theme and Settings for DevTools

DevTools has two themes, the Light theme and the Dark theme. DevTools starts off with the Light theme, but you can switch to the Dark theme if you prefer it. The Dark theme may feel easier on your eyes if you are working in a dimly lit room. You can also set the theme to System Preference to make DevTools adjust the theme to suit your computer's operating system setting.

To choose a theme and configure settings, click **Settings** (⚙) in the upper-right corner of the DevTools pane. The Settings pane appears, showing the Preferences tab at first.

In the Appearance section, click **Theme** (L, ▼), and then click **System preference**, **Light**, or **Dark**, as appropriate.

While you are on the Settings screen, look through the other settings to make yourself aware of what is there. Here are two features you may want to enable immediately:

- **Automatically Reveal Files in Sidebar (M).** When you click an element in the Elements pane, DevTools expands the element's source file in the Source's panel and highlights the element's code.

- **Autocompletion (N).** DevTools suggests completions for code as you type.

When you finish choosing settings, click **Close** (O, ✕) to close the Settings pane and return to DevTools.

Troubleshoot CSS with Chrome DevTools

Chrome's DevTools include features for debugging problems with CSS. For example, you may sometimes find that when you display a web page in a browser, its formatting looks significantly different from what you intended.

One way to identify and resolve such problems is to open the CSS files in question and read through their contents. This can be an effective troubleshooting method, but you may find that using DevTools enables you to sort out the problems more quickly and with less effort.

Open DevTools

When you run into a problem with CSS not delivering the look you want, open DevTools by right-clicking (A) the problematic page and then clicking **Inspect** (B) on the contextual menu. Chrome displays DevTools.

Navigate the Elements Pane and the DOM Tree

By default, DevTools displays the viewport (C) on the left, showing the web page at a smaller size. You can resize the viewport by dragging the border that separates it from the DevTools pane — in this case, the right border (D).

By default, the Elements pane appears foremost in the DevTools area; if the Elements pane is not foremost, click the **Elements** tab (E) to bring the pane to the front.

The Elements pane displays the DOM tree of the active HTML document. You can expand and collapse sections of the DOM tree as needed. Click **Expand** (F, ▶) to expand a section. Click **Collapse** (G, ▼) to collapse a section.

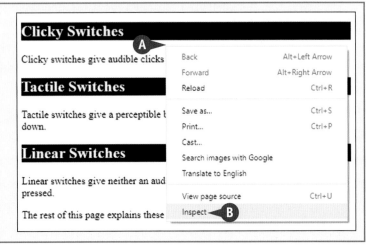

Inspect an Element

To inspect an element, move the pointer over it in the DOM tree. DevTools highlights the corresponding section of the page in the viewport.

The nearby illustration shows the result of holding the pointer over the h1 element (H): DevTools highlights the heading (I) in the viewport and displays a pop-up balloon (J) showing the element type (K) and size (L).

To identify CSS problems with an element, click that element in the DOM tree. The Styles pane shows the formatting applied to the element.

The nearby illustration shows the result of clicking an h2 element (M). DevTools highlights the element (N) in the viewport and displays a pop-up balloon (O). The Styles pane (P) in the right section of the DevTools pane shows the styles that are being applied to the element.

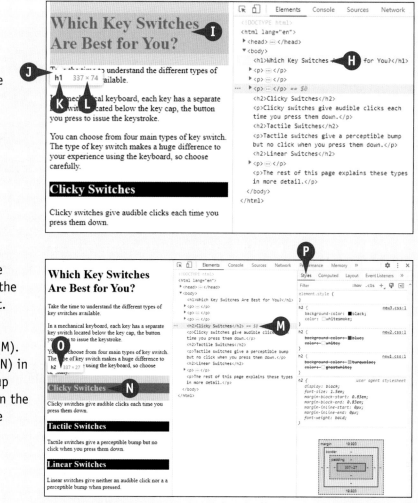

continued ▶

The Styles pane in Chrome DevTools enables you to see exactly what styles the browser is applying to an element you select. By examining the information in the Styles pane, you can quickly identify conflicts between different style sheets the HTML document is using. You can turn off individual properties in the style sheets to fine-tune the style cascade until the document's formatting appears the way you want it to look.

Examine the Styles Applied to an Element

Once you have clicked the element you want to inspect, the Styles pane displays the styles applied to that element. In the nearby illustration, you can see five h2 styles in play.

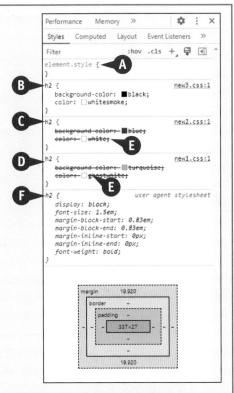

- `element.style` (A). This readout shows inline styles, styles applied directly to the element — in this case, the h2 element. In the example, no inline style is applied, as will often be the case when you apply formatting via internal style sheets or external style sheets. However, the Styles pane still shows the `element.style` readout so that you can verify no inline styles are applied — or apply an Inline style if you so want.

- Three h2 styles, one each in the new3.css file (B), the new2.css file (C), and the new1.css file (D). The HTML document has three external style sheets linked, new1.css, new2.css, and new3.css, applied in that order. As you can see, each of these style sheets defines the h2 style, specifying the `background-color` property and the `color` property. The last of the three style sheets, new3.css, overrides the preceding two style sheets, so the browser uses its settings. The Styles pane lists new3.css first of the three external style sheets because the h2 element uses its styles. The Styles pane displays strikethrough (E) on the properties for the h2 element in new2.css and new1.css to indicate that these properties have been overridden.

- The h2 style for the "user agent stylesheet" (F) — the style sheet the browser is using. The browser's own styles reside at the lowest level of the style cascade and are used to style elements that have not been styled otherwise.

Apply or Adjust an Inline Style

If you want to override the formatting for one particular instance of an element, you can apply an inline style by adding the style information to the `element.style` definition at the top of the Styles pane when the element is selected in the DOM. If an inline style is already there, you can adjust it as needed.

For example, in the nearby illustration, the `element.style` definition now applies yellow color (G):

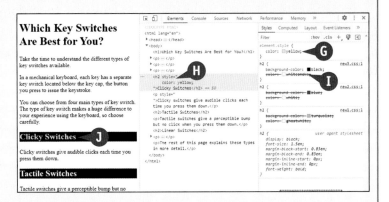

```
element.style {
    color: yellow;
}
```

When you add this information in the Styles pane, DevTools automatically inserts the `style` attribute in the opening `<h2>` tag (H). The `color` property in the new3.css style sheet is overridden and appears in strikethrough (I). And in the viewport, the `h2` element takes on the formatting (J).

Turn Style Properties On or Off

When you need to experiment with the various conflicting properties for an element you have selected in the DOM, go to the Styles pane and move the pointer over the style that you want to change. DevTools displays a check box for each property, enabling you to turn properties on by selecting them (K, ✓) or off by deselecting them (L, ☐).

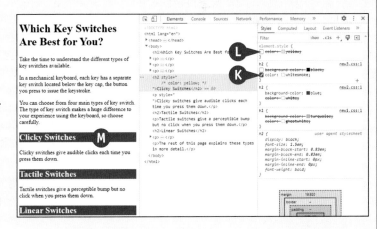

When you deselect a property's check box, the next instance of that property in the cascade becomes active. In the example, deselecting `color: yellow;` in `element.style` makes `color: whitesmoke;` in new3.css active. Similarly, deselecting `background-color: black;` in new3.css makes `background-color: blue;` in new2.css active. The viewport shows the effect of the changes (M).

continued ▶

Chrome DevTools enables you to edit the text of the HTML document in the DOM. This capability can be handy for making changes you identify are needed while you are working on the CSS. You can also edit the HTML of the HTML document, which you may need to do for various reasons, such as fixing problems with the style cascade. You can open a style sheet for editing in the Sources pane in DevTools, and you can delete a style sheet link from the HTML document's head element if necessary.

Edit the Text of the HTML Document

When you need to make a change in the text of the HTML document on which you are using DevTools, right-click the element you want to edit (A) and then click **Edit text** (B) on the contextual menu.

DevTools opens the element for editing. Type your corrections (C), and then click elsewhere to apply them and to switch out of Text Editing Mode. Your changes appear in the DOM and in the viewport.

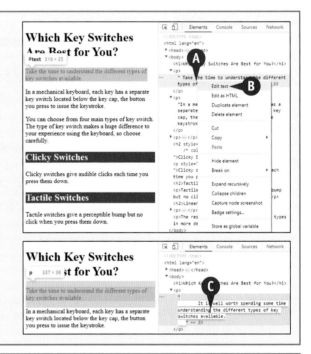

Edit the HTML of the HTML Document

When you want to edit the text of the HTML document you are examining in DevTools, right-click the element you want to edit (D) and then click **Edit as HTML** (E) on the contextual menu.

DevTools opens the HTML for editing. Make your changes, and then click outside the mini-editor to apply the changes and to switch out of HTML Editing Mode. The effect of your changes appears in the viewport.

Open a Style Sheet for Editing

When you need to change one of the style sheet files linked to the HTML document you are working on in DevTools, click the style sheet file's name (F) in the Styles pane. Each name is a link, as the underline beneath it suggests.

DevTools switches from the Elements pane to the Sources pane, shown in the nearby illustration. Here, the Page pane (G) displays the path to the selected CSS file. The right pane (H) shows the contents of the CSS file, which you can edit freely. DevTools provides helpful features such as automatic completion (I).

When you finish working on the CSS file, click **Elements** (J) to display the Elements pane again.

Remove a Style Sheet from the HTML Document

If you need to remove a style sheet altogether from the HTML document, go to the DOM in the Elements pane and expand the `head` section of the document if it is collapsed. Right-click the `link` element (K) for the style sheet, and then click **Delete element** (L) on the contextual menu. DevTools deletes the element, removing the style sheet link.

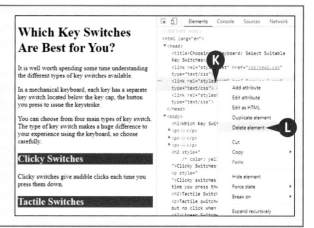

Using a Staging Server

A *staging server* is a preproduction environment you use for testing changes and new pages for your website before taking them live. The staging server contains a replica of the live site, usually running the same software, using the same configuration, and holding the same data.

The staging server provides a safe environment in which you can test your new pages, updates, new features, and performance enhancements without exposing them to your website's visitors or affecting the site's performance. Once you have finished testing your new material and troubleshooting problems and are confident that everything works, you can deploy the changes to the live site.

Grasp the Benefits of a Staging Server

A staging server can offer several benefits.

- **Provides a safe test environment.** The staging server gives you a test environment configured the same way as your actual website but which you can use to test changes to pages or apps without causing problems for website visitors. This environment enables you to identify issues and fix them before you deploy the code to the live website.

- **Acts as a location for collaboration.** You and your colleagues can work together on code on the staging server. The shared workspace can enhance collaboration and may promote faster development than working in separate silos. That is in theory; your experience may vary.

- **Allows streamlined deployment.** Testing the code on the staging server helps you ensure that the code will work correctly when you deploy it to the live website. This testing stage makes deployment more routine and less fraught, which is usually welcome.

Where Is the Staging Server Located?

The staging server can be located either on your company's premises, as part of the network infrastructure, or off the premises in a server farm or in a cloud-based environment. As of this writing, off-premises solutions are more popular than in-house solutions.

Assess Whether You Need a Staging Server

If you run a website of any size or complexity, you will likely benefit from having a staging server, for the reasons explained in the previous subsection. But if you simply have a small website of your own and if the possibility of disruptions to website visitors is a minor worry rather than a major concern, you probably do not need a staging server.

How Do You Set Up a Staging Server?

To set up a staging server, you will normally need to take the following seven steps:

1 Choose where to host the staging server. Some companies and organizations host staging servers on their own networks, but using an off-premises server host is more typical. Assuming you will use a server host, work out what technical specifications the server will need for the testing and development activities you plan, and determine your budget. Then explore which hosting providers might meet your needs, evaluating both providers that offer dedicated servers and those that provide cloud-based servers.

2 Choose your server configuration. After picking your host, choose which of the host's server configurations you want. Most hosts offer a wide range of configurations with endless types of processors, a range of choices of RAM amount, and anything from modest to massive storage space. Specify the operating system you want — usually Windows or Linux. Make sure you can upgrade the configuration easily if your website's staging demands increase.

3 Install the operating system, web server, and web stack. Once you have control of your server, install the operating system, the web server, and the development environment you need.

4 Secure the server. Even if the server is physically parked in a server farm or exists only as a cloud-based virtual machine, you need to secure it. Verify that only the services you need are running, and stop other services. Lock down ports against intrusion, and configure a firewall to help ward off unwanted advances.

5 Configure the server for development and testing. Create an environment for developing and testing your website. Create user accounts for the people who will access the staging server, setting appropriate permissions for each user account. Configure a means of backup so that you will be able to recover the server if a failure occurs. Once the server is up and running, verify a backup and test the recovery system.

6 Document the server. As you work to set up the server, document the configuration so that other administrators will be able to start work on the server quickly and without confusion.

7 Copy your website to the server. Copy your website to the server either directly from a development environment or by using a version-control system. You and your colleagues can then start using the server.

Understanding Front-End Frameworks

When you need to build a website or web app rapidly, you may want to use a front-end framework to speed up and standardize the process. In computer terms, the *front end* is the user interface of an app, while the *back end* is the part of the app that handles data storage and processing.

A *front-end framework* is a predesigned set of HTML, CSS, and JavaScript code and UI components, such as buttons and forms, that enables you to build interfaces more rapidly than manual development does. Various front-end frameworks are available, as explained at the end of this section.

Advantages and Disadvantages of Front-End Frameworks

Front-end frameworks have the following advantages:

- **They enable rapid development.** By using a front-end framework's prebuilt components and templates, you can create a website or a web app much more quickly than by creating everything from scratch.

- **They deliver a consistent look and feel.** The components and templates help you to give your websites and apps a consistent look and feel. You may find this especially helpful when working with other developers on a project.

- **They create cross-browser–compatible code.** Front-end frameworks are built to create code that runs well on different browsers and devices, allowing you to concentrate on development without having to devote serious time to testing and troubleshooting.

- **They have community support.** Many developers participate in developing, improving, and documenting front-end frameworks. So when you use a framework, you can benefit from the community's knowledge and experience.

What goes up must come down, and front-end frameworks have some disadvantages to counterbalance their advantages.

- **They have a steep learning curve.** You'll need to invest some time in choosing the best framework for you, plus time learning how to use the framework.

- **The standardization reduces flexibility.** Using prefabricated components speeds up development, but you are limited to those components unless you write custom code. Depending on what websites and apps you are developing, this limitation may or may not be a problem, but you should bear it in mind.

- **Framework overhead may slow your website's load time.** Using a framework may saddle your website with extra code that slows down its load time. Similarly, a framework may increase an app's file size.

- **Framework updates may require website updates.** When the front-end framework you are using receives updates, you may need to update both your skills with the framework and your code that uses the framework.

Should You Use a Front-End Framework?

Whether you should use a front-end framework for your web development can be a tricky decision.

Generally speaking, you may benefit from using a framework on a project that:

- Is large and complicated
- Will likely need scaling up or extending in the long term
- Requires complex user interaction, much data manipulation, and real-time updates
- Has a short timeline and a tight budget

A framework may also be helpful if you have only limited experience developing front ends. If this is the case, the framework can help you create a workable front end with less effort. However, you should factor in the time that you will need to spend getting up to speed with the front-end framework before you can be productive with it.

Which Are the Leading Front-End Frameworks?

Table 12-2 lists the top 10 front-end frameworks as of April 2023, giving their initial release year, their relative weight in terms of code, and their approximate difficulty. The table also mentions major companies that use the frameworks.

Table 12-2: Top 10 Front-End Frameworks				
Framework	**Released**	**Weight**	**Difficulty**	**Used By**
React	2011	Light	Easy	PayPal, Netflix, Walmart
Angular	2010	Heavy	Hard	BMW, Forbes
JQuery	2006	Light	Easy	LinkedIn, Slack
Vue.js	2015	Light	Easy	GitLab, Xiaomi
Backbone.js	2010	Light	Easy	Airbnb, SoundCloud
Ember.js	2011	Heavy	Hard	LinkedIn, Square
Semantic-UI	2013	Heavy	Easy	Xerox, Zendesk
Svelte	2016	Light	Easy	Spotify, Square
Foundation	2011	Heavy	Hard	eBay, National Geographic
Preact	2015	Light	Easy	Uber, Comcast

Index

A

\<a> tag, 93
absolute links, 93
absolute positioning, 215
accessibility issues, 278–279
Activity Bar (Visual Studio Code), 17
adding
    article elements to web pages, 58–59
    check boxes to forms, 264–265
    columns to tables, 130–131
    command buttons to forms, 268–269
    comments to web pages, 39
    drop-down lists of options to forms, 266–267
    headings and text to web pages, 36–37
    keywords to web pages, 274–275
    media queries, 232–233
    padding for tap targets, 234
    radio buttons to forms, 262–263
    rows to tables, 130–131
    text input controls to forms, 260–261
adjacent sibling selector, 194, 195, 197
adjusting
    inline style, 285
    layout of Visual Studio Code window, 18
    letter spacing, 172–173
    line height, 172–173
    padding and spacing for tables, 136–137
    tap target color, 235
Adobe, 11
Adobe Fonts, 187
Alexa Crawler, 276–277
align attribute, 140
align-content property, 225
aligning rows, cells, and tables, 140–141
align-items property, 225
align-self property, 225
alt attribute, 84, 86
alt text, displaying for images in browsers, 87
anchor element, 92

anchors
    creating links to, 97
    in hyperlinks, 45
animations
    CSS, 248–249
    keyframe, 252–253
Apple Safari
    about, 22–23
    displaying web page source code in, 41
    for viewing web pages, 35
applying
    contextual formatting with pseudo-classes, 192–193
    CSS to pseudo-elements, 200–201
    direct formatting to web pages, 40
    inline style, 285
    linear gradients to elements, 242–243
    radial gradients to elements, 244–245
    relative sizing, 230–231
    styles
        using class selectors, 160–161
        using element selectors, 159
        using ID selectors, 162–163
    text decoration, 180–181
    text shadows, 178
    transitions to HTML elements, 250–251
Arbitrary Rotation command (GIMP), 74
article elements, 52, 58–59
aside element, 52, 60–61
aspect ratio, cropping images to specific, 77
assigning
    IDs to elements in HTML files, 162
    return values for check boxes, 265
audio
    autoplay for, 109
    including in web pages, 108–109
auditory accessibility issues, 278
Auto Save, configuring in Visual Studio Code, 19
autofill, 22
autoplay, for audio, 109